BABY DOCTOR

BABY
DOCTOR

Perri Klass

RANDOM HOUSE

NEW YORK

Portions of this work were originally published, in
slightly different form, in *Balance, The Boston Globe Sunday Magazine,
Discover, Glamour, Massachusetts Medicine,
New Woman, The New York Times Book Review,
The New York Times Magazine,* and *TriQuarterly.*

Library of Congress Cataloging-in-Publication Data
Klass, Perri
Baby doctor / Perri Klass. — 1st ed.
p.   cm.
ISBN 0-679-40957-2
1. Klass, Perri.   2. Women pediatricians—United States—
Biography.   3. Pediatrics—Popular works.   I. Title.
RJ43.K53A3   1992
618.92′00092—dc20
[B]   91-51022

Manufactured in the United States of America
2 4 6 8 7 5 3
First Edition
The text of this book is set in Galliard.

For Maxine Groffsky, the most fabulously glamorous and sophisticated agent any girl from New Jersey ever had, with love and gratitude.

Harriet came to the conclusion that she couldn't—not possibly. She picked up the telephone, got put through to Telegrams, and dictated a brief, snappy message to her long-suffering agent. "Tell Bootle I absolutely refuse introduce love-interest—Vane."

After that she felt better, but the novel was perfectly impossible. Wasn't there anything else she could do?

Dorothy L. Sayers
Have His Carcase

Acknowledgments

In putting this book together, I found myself reliving my residency, rereading the somewhat erratic journal I kept, looking back through old ward sign-out sheets. Fortunately there was no all-night call involved. Although this process brought back the shadow of many stressful moments, it also reminded me of the many people who helped me through those years, who educated me, who supported me, who edited me, who told me to pull up my socks and stop whining.

I went through my residency program with a terrific group of doctors, and I especially appreciated, and continue to appreciate, the friendship of Doctors Barbara Duffy, Diane Rup, and Eileen Costello. As a bumbling intern I had the good fortune to be supervised by stellar senior residents, and I remember with particular gratitude Doctors Ho-Wen Hsu and Lynn Haynie. I had wise teachers and excellent advisers on the medical faculty, and remain deeply grateful for the guidance and inspiration of Doctors Orah Platt, Jane Newberger, Larry Kaplan, Pearl O'Rourke, Grace Caputo, Gerry Hass, and T. Berry Brazelton. The directors of my residency program, Doctors David Nathan and Fred Lovejoy, not only guided my pediatric training, but also showed special consideration in accommodating my career as a writer.

Making it through residency required a lot of family forbearance and assistance, across the generations. Larry Wolff had the worst of it; he was the one who had to live with me. I am afraid that he ended up doing a pediatric residency vicariously, when all he had wanted was to be a history professor, but he accepted the rigors of hospital schedules and hospital conversation with good grace, and helped me edit my hospital stories into the bargain. I am in his debt for much aid and comfort, for domestic joys and literary rigor. Our son, Benjamin Orlando Klass, brightened up my life every single day, and taught me many things that a pediatrician needs to know, both about children and about their parents. He even performed once in a hospital Christmas show, playing the part of a child with an ear infection, and confirming his impression that Mama went to the hospital all the time in order to laugh with friends and sing silly songs. Our daughter, Josephine Charlotte Paulina Wolff, arrived too late to enjoy my residency (though she was along for the ride during the last eight months), but she has contributed tremendously to the compiling of this book, scribbling on the manuscript and attempting, whenever possible, to break the word processor.

My parents, Morton and Sheila Klass, offered encouragement and good cheer, no matter how woebegone my middle-of-the-night phone calls from the hospital. They raised me to be a writer, encouraged me to be a doctor, when the fit took me, and kept secret all along their deep desire to be grandparents. I am also grateful to Larry's parents, Bob and Renee Wolff, for much friendship, support, and warm interest in my writing, and for their loving grandparental attentions to Benjamin and Josephine.

And, speaking of middle-of-the-night phone calls from the hospital, I will never think of my residency without thinking with much affection of Mitch Katz, who was doing his own residency three thousand miles away. When our call schedules coincided, we would talk hospital to hospital, waiting for one beeper or the other to go off and terminate the call. ("So, here we are, I'm the senior in the cardiac intensive care unit and you're the senior in the pediatric intensive care unit." "Frightening, isn't it?" "Very frightening.") It's hard to have such a good friend be so far away, but good to have such a friend, wherever he may be.

My writing about medicine has benefited over the years from the intelligent editorial attentions of Marilyn Minden and

Gil Rogin at *Discover*, Lisa Poniatowski at *Massachusetts Medicine*, Lisa Bane at *Glamour*, Ande Zellman at *The Boston Globe Sunday Magazine*, and Kim Heron and Katherine Bouton at *The New York Times Magazine*.

I remain deeply grateful to William Abrahams for all the encouragement that he has given me as a writer, and I remember with special gratitude his magnificent support and wise advice during the darkest moments of my residency. Kate Medina, my editor at Random House, has helped me with the greatest sensitivity and intelligence in the assembling of this book. Finally, Maxine Groffsky, my agent, has guided my writing career with humor, style, and unerring instincts; this book would certainly not exist without her.

Contents

Introduction

When I graduated from medical school, I was a doctor but not yet a pediatrician. I did have the right to sign MD after my name (and my mother had the right to use it when addressing letters to me). I did not, however, have any experience, any expertise, or any idea what I was doing. Babies are born knowing how to be babies, but to become a pediatrician, you spend three years, first as a pediatric intern and then as a pediatric resident.

This on-the-job training is more than that—it is on-the-baby training. I became a pediatrician because I like taking care of children, because I appreciate their powers of recuperation, even regeneration. Residency meant that for the first time, babies and children were truly handed over to me. For every doctor, there has to be a very first patient. And after that there has to be a first patient with meningitis, a first patient with diabetes, a first patient with congestive heart failure. Reading about each disease in a textbook is not the same; until you have watched through the night with a sick diabetic, you don't know how to take care of diabetic ketoacidosis.

That is the rationale of residency, which compresses as many firsts as possible into a few years, during which you work as many hours as humanly possible and then some. I did my training at a big pediatric hospital—the water fountains were built low to the ground, and the specialists were all pediatricians. Pediatric nephrologists, cardiologists, endocrinologists, gastroenterologists, pediatric surgeons, and pediatric psychiatrists. It was a world of sick children and their families, a hospital with a sing-along or a puppet show or a visiting magician every afternoon and a dietary service which routinely served cupcakes frosted with green icing and decorated to look like frogs.

The patients came from Boston, but also from around the world, families flying in from Saudi Arabia, for example, bringing their babies for complex cardiac surgery. We took care of children with diseases so rare that we never discussed them without some comment like "Seven cases in the literature, and this is number eight." Hereditary tyrosinemia, Treacher Collins syndrome, von Gierke disease. We also, of course, took care of kids with normal everyday pediatric problems, kids with runny noses or sprained ankles in the emergency room, kids with appendicitis and asthma. And we took care of a small select population of adults—grown-ups who had lifelong chronic medical problems and had been cared for in this hospital since they were children. As they aged into their thirties and forties, they kept coming back—adults with cystic fibrosis or sickle-cell disease, complex congenital heart disease or hemophilia. One reason they came back is that it's just much nicer to be hospitalized in a pediatric hospital than in an adult hospital. We draw blood with very tiny needles. We spend a lot of time trying to make the experience less cold, less boring, less scary.

So for three years, I spent most of my time in a children's hospital, learning to take care of the patients. This book was written during that time, and it combines stories of my patients with the story of the struggle to become a pediatrician, to come to terms with the harsh realities of pediatric illness, the devastation of unhappy endings. I find I have also told the story of my own insecurities, of the constant nagging doubts I had about whether I was doing the right thing, whether I was about to hurt or even harm, or kill a patient, whether my patients would survive, and whether I and my family would survive the ordeal of residency.

My son, Benjamin, was born during my second year of medical school, so he was two and a half when I started my residency. He was five and a half when I finished, and probably couldn't remember a time when his mother wasn't away one of every three or four nights. It's hard to be a resident with a small child, but then, it's hard to be a resident with a spouse, a lover, close friends, or even houseplants. Residency leaves you depleted, with not very much to give to the people you love the most. But while it's true that those of us who had young children were sometimes jealous of the way that those without could just go home and go to sleep, it's also true that Benjamin was the brightest spot in my life all through residency. It wasn't easy on him, however, and it wasn't easy on his father, Larry. I was always home later than I meant to be, and more tired than I wanted to be, frequently asleep sitting up.

This book exists because between life at the hospital and with my family, it seemed that all my time was spoken for, and spoken for again. I needed some corner of my life which was all my own, and that corner was writing. I had been writing about my training all through medical school, and it had given me a voice at a time when I would otherwise have had none. As hospital wisdom goes, the medical student is on that part of the totem pole that is buried in the ground. I had found that I could go home and tell in my own words the stories of what I saw and what happened to me, and write out my revenge on people who oppressed me (or, let's face it, surpassed me), write out my anguish about my inadequacies. But most of all, I could describe the astonishing contacts with life and death which make up everyday routine in the hospital. It was a chance to sit down and find my own words, rather than trying constantly for the right medical student answer.

To get through residency, almost everyone juggles, everyone balances. There are very few people for whom medicine is all, the hospital the only imperative. My own particular juggling act involved my family, my job, and writing, but all around me I saw people working hard on other combinations. I wrote the stories in this book to help myself understand what was happening to me. Writing them helped me remember who

I was and why I was doing what I was doing, and that made it easier not only to do my job, but also to come home and act like a normal person, albeit a tired normal person. And ultimately, after three years, a person who was, at last, a pediatrician.

BABY DOCTOR

I

BEGINNING

Daisy said in her gentle way:

"I love to keep house, and mean to have a nice one for Demi when we grow up and live together."

Nan replied with decision:

"Well, I haven't got any brother, and I don't want any house to fuss over. I shall have an office, with lots of bottles and drawers and pestle things in it, and I shall drive round in a horse and chaise and cure sick people. That will be such fun."

"Ugh! How can you bear the bad-smelling stuff and the nasty little powders and castor oil and senna and hive syrup?" cried Daisy, with a shudder.

"I shan't have to take any, so I don't care. Besides, they make people well, and I like to cure folks. . . ."

"Shall you put leeches on people, and cut off legs and pull out teeth?" asked Daisy, quaking at the thought.

"Yes, I shall do everything; I don't care if the people are all smashed up, I shall mend them. My grandpa was a doctor, and I saw him sew a great cut in a man's cheek, and I held the sponge, and wasn't frightened a bit, and grandpa said I was a brave girl."

> Louisa May Alcott
> *Little Men*

I nternship is the most intense, legendary, extreme year of residency, and for most of us, I suspect, the most intense year of our lives. I *think* that I remember it fairly clearly, but the fact is that I know I have forgotten what it really felt like. I remember individual days, particular patients, frustrations and disasters and small triumphs, colleagues and parents, but I have lost much of the true sense of sleep deprivation, pressure, and terror. For months on end I spent every third or fourth night in the hospital; my whole life was divided up into on call, postcall, and swing (those blessed days which are neither on nor post, the days you both begin and end in your own bed). I worried constantly about what I didn't know and what I hadn't done, and I clung tightly to a clipboard heavy with unread articles and past patient histories, topped always with the day's "scut list," a series of boxes to be checked off. I was tired, scared, and resentful; outside the hospital, it seemed to me, the world was going its cheerful way, friends and family were out enjoying the good weather, or safe at home in bed, and there I was, shut up all day, staying up all night, dealing with pain and stress and yet another baby with diarrhea. This kind of weariness and resentment sometimes translated into an arrogant impatience with the outside world: why didn't they all bow down when I came along? Didn't they know I had been in the hospital for thirty-six hours straight saving babies' lives? How dare they make me wait in line at the bank machine, or put me on hold at the parking office? How dare they expect me to remember that we were out of milk and pick some up on the way home? My personality, never exceptionally sweet, did not improve during residency, and I am not sure that anyone's does.

Internship was the year when I never learned the names of my son's teachers at the day-care center, because I was not the one to pick him up or drop him off. It's the year I didn't read the newspaper and slept through the few movies I saw. I meant to keep a journal, but I almost never wrote in it. The articles I did write, the hospital stories and personal essays, were my attempt to keep track of a year that I could not control.

1

....

Starting Small

As a resident, you rotate through different hospital settings. I started off in the strangest and most intensely pediatric place, the newborn intensive care unit. It was a big room full of very sick babies, many of them premature, all of them attached to wires and monitors and tubes. I started learning which tube was which, and at the same time I started learning how to insert them, how to thread a catheter into one of the arteries in the stump of a newborn's umbilical cord, how to get the world's tiniest breathing tube down into the world's tiniest trachea. And while I tried to find my way around the room, the junior residents and the senior residents and the neonatologists were running to the delivery rooms down the hall to bring back newer babies and smaller babies and babies with new and different congenital anomalies.

The hospital specialized in high-risk births, and women in labor were sent there from all over the state if their fetuses were known to have heart defects or strange chromosomal rearrangements or just if they were coming much too soon. I can remember, as a terrified intern, watching two junior residents practice the choreography of a delivery room resuscitation—they were waiting for a woman to deliver premature conjoined (Siamese) twins. A double resuscitation of two babies stuck together somewhere between the hip and the shoulder! One warming table, two oxygen sources; you stand here, I'll intubate mine first while you give yours bag and mask oxygen—of such plans are NICU legends made.

The lights, the monitors, the beeping of alarms, the sudden blast of the telephone which meant another delivery, another baby—a nurse once compared the place to working inside a pinball machine. During my first month there, one of the neonatologists gathered us all together to discuss "stress in the NICU." He didn't mean the babies (though that has also been studied and has led to attempts to reduce light and noise levels); he meant the young doctors. He asked for nominations: what are the sources of stress in the NICU? And we named them: the deliveries, the babies, the parents, the senior doctors, the nurses.

It can be a very hard place to work. Residents joke that NICU stands for Nurse in Charge Unit, and NICU nurses can be terrifying to interns. Because the babies are so small and so sick, and because the nurses spend eight hours or more at their sides, they are both highly professional and deeply attached. Many of them develop truly astonishing technical skills, and it can make an intern feel bumbling, clumsy, and hopelessly out of place. At the particular NICU where I worked, there was a long and famous tradition of nurses hazing interns, showing them up on morning rounds as ignorant, telling them off if they weren't cutting the mustard.

I first got to know one of my fellow interns one day when

I retreated from the NICU to cry in the bathroom after a sharp (and probably well-deserved) telling off by one of the nurses, only to find the bathroom occupied by the other intern—who was already in tears. I asked in a shaky voice how long she would be, and she replied in an equally shaky voice that she'd be as quick as she could—then she opened the bathroom door, and we cried on each other for a while (crying in the bathroom strikes me as something of a residency motif; it probably reflects not only the extreme emotional vulnerability of residency, but also the almost total lack of privacy—there are few private corners inside a pinball machine).

The NICU is on the cutting edge of medical technology and, not coincidentally, of ethical confusion. When I got over my initial terror, when I started to understand what I was doing a little bit better, I began to worry about the rights and wrongs of saving very tiny newborns—as almost everyone does who spends any time around newborn intensive care. I returned to the NICU later on in my training, learned to go to deliveries and resuscitate babies, worried about ethics, worried about what I would want myself if I had a very sick, very premature infant. But at the beginning, I worried more about getting through the night.

FIRST NIGHT ON CALL

My first patient weighed less than three pounds. So there I am, fresh out of medical school, stealing little glances down at that brand-new name tag pinned to my surgical scrubs: MD. Amazing. And I'm in the neonatal intensive care unit and I'm an intern on call, and how about that? In other words, the rest of my team is going home and I'm more or less in charge. I'm here for the night, my first night on call. And I have a new patient to work on, a little preemie who weighs less than three pounds.

A classmate who also just became an intern put it this way: "I remember how in medical school, when I worked in the hospital, I always used to be so glad I wasn't the intern on call. And now I am."

So I bumble around the intensive care unit, which is a complex place set up to make it possible for a large group of highly trained adults to take care of a group of very sick, very small babies. And of course I don't know where anything is. I can't find the pencil sharpener, I can't find the cardiac resuscitation medicines. I can't even fill out the X-ray form correctly, which is no joke when you want them to come take an emergency X ray of a desperately sick baby and they reject your form. I try to get my work done, pausing every few minutes to get a nurse, the ward secretary, or anyone at all, to show me where to find some crucial item.

"Trust the nurses. They know what they're doing; they're the only ones who do," advised a friend who has already completed several years of residency. And it's true. Every July the fresh new interns arrive and last year's interns become the junior residents, and the juniors become the seniors—so everyone is facing new responsibilities, new expectations. Except the nurses, of course, and they occasionally have to use their experience to protect their patients from the onslaught of July. I sit there at night in this unit, surrounded by babies in incubatorlike warming beds, babies on ventilators, and the nurses, who all have many more years of experience than I do, keeping close watch on their patients. And then when something happens to disturb them, they come and ask me what I want to do. Well, I say casually, what do *you* think we should do?

So I take this little three-pound baby and examine him, and I decide that we have to worry about infection because his mother had a fever. I do a spinal tap on the baby—with a lot of help from a senior doctor who was just passing through.

The nurses draw blood for other lab tests and hook up an intravenous line to give the baby fluids, I tell them to start him on a couple of antibiotics, and I sit down and begin writing a note about him for his medical record.

A baby who weighs less than three pounds is really a very small baby—much too small to be out in the world alone. We are worrying about his temperature control, about his organ systems, all the complex machinery that functions so easily, so matter-of-factly, in full-term babies.

I'm profoundly aware of all the things that can go wrong. At any moment, this baby's nurse could come tap me on the shoulder to tell me the baby is in respiratory distress. He's at risk for a disease that affects premature lungs. If he has trouble breathing, we'll have to give him more oxygen—and maybe put a breathing tube down into his airway, connect him up to a ventilator, and breathe for him. Or he might have a bacterial infection; that might be the reason he was born so early. We've started him on antibiotics, but he may be so sick that he'll be in trouble before the antibiotics take effect. Or he may have some rare bug that these antibiotics don't cover. Or he may have something wrong inside. I worry that he might have a heart murmur that I didn't hear when I listened to him. He may have any one of a number of congenital anomalies—I've never examined a baby this small—would I know if something was abnormal? I wait for evidence that his body is beginning to function. Has he peed? Has he pooped? And of course, I thank God for the years of experience that his nurse brings to this night; surely she will notice if something isn't right.

I am responsible for this baby overnight. This is simply too much to take in. There are senior people for me to go to if I have problems, but the basic responsibility is mine. I'm responsible for twelve babies in an intensive care unit. All night I circulate nervously around my room, looking in on the babies, reading the numbers the nurses have recorded on their flow sheets—the babies' heart rates, their respiratory rates, the oxygen content of their blood. Some of the numbers mean something to me, and many do not, but I copy down as many as I can into my notes. The sight of them on the page reassures me; they are the nurses' numbers, so they must be right. Frequently an alarm goes off; all these babies are attached to cardiac monitors. This first night, whenever I hear an alarm, I tense, sure that a baby is dying, that I'll have to go to the rescue. And every time an alarm goes off, a nurse hurries over with an expression of annoyance and either taps the alarm or taps the baby, and everything is fine.

I don't sleep. I continue to circulate. When I discuss these nights on call with another intern, we refer to our pattern of motion as "buzzing off the walls." I'm souped up on adrenaline: I can see this room even if I close my eyes. I feel as if I'm somehow plugged in to every baby—or as if every baby is somehow plugged in to me, just like another monitor.

The nurses ask me questions. Most of them are framed to prompt a specific answer: wouldn't you like to turn down that baby's ventilator rate? don't you think we could start feeds tomorrow? shouldn't we increase this baby's antibiotic dose? I answer, and then I think about my answers and worry for a while, and finally when I have a list of them I go off and check them with a junior resident. But what's really preying on me is the possibility that there are questions I'm not asking, significant pieces of information that are getting by me. Every time a nurse comes up to show me some lab results, I'm ready for disaster. I look at perfectly normal blood chemistry values as if I expect them to jump off the lab slip and bite me in the leg.

I know, of course, on some level, two very important things. First of all, my terror is appropriate. I've just made an enormous leap; I'm carrying much, much more responsibility than I've ever had before, and I'm completely untested. And second, I would be a real danger to my patients if I weren't so frightened; it's the intern who feels too confident who can really do damage, who can end up being known as Mad Dog or the Assassin. Yes, indeed, my very anxiety is a sign of my good judgment—which helps not at all, as I sit in the middle of the room, waiting for the ceiling to fall on me.

My little almost-three-pound baby is holding his own, though he's working hard to breathe. I watch the way he's pulling with his chest muscles to open his lungs as far as he can, and I begin to think we're going to have to put in a breathing tube. I look at his chest X ray: not bad, not good. I ask his nurse, who has been spending the evening watching him, what she thinks, and she agrees; he'll probably have to go on the ventilator. Ventilators can damage a baby's lungs in the long term, but if a little preemie has to work too hard to breathe, he'll eventually get tired, and his respiratory effort may slow down or stop. Besides, he needs to be able to feed and grow.

So I go ask the junior resident, but he has been called to the delivery room, where a baby in trouble is about to be delivered. He comes back fifteen minutes later, bringing me this new baby, who was a little slow to get started (i.e., she didn't breathe at first, she was blue, she didn't move much), but is now doing well. Doing so well in fact that if she starts eating, she can go up to the regular newborn nursery. This new baby is full term, and looks simply enormous to me; I can't imagine that anything could be wrong with such a big fat healthy baby. But I examine her and do some tests, and then wander back to my little preemie, who's working even harder now and getting less oxygen into his blood for all his trouble.

The junior resident agrees with me; this baby is going to need a breathing tube. We start to set up for this procedure, when a nurse comes to tell me that the preemie's father is here to see him. So I go and introduce myself ("I'm your baby's doctor," I say, feeling like a liar). I remember to congratulate him, first of all, on his new son. I try to prepare him, warn him that the baby is going to look very small. Then I lead him to see his baby, and he almost collapses. "It's too small to live, isn't it?" he says.

I tell him the baby is in fact too small to be born, but has a good chance of living, and is doing quite well. I don't go into any more details about the risks of prematurity; I'll do that later, when the parents are together and have had a little more time to get used to the situation. I have to explain about the breathing tube, and then I send him up to tell his wife about the baby. The junior resident puts the breathing tube into the baby's throat. I learn how to thread an intravenous line into the umbilical artery, finding the little stump of the vessel in the recently cut umbilical cord on the baby's belly. This line will allow us to get samples of arterial blood to see how well the baby is oxygenating.

The night goes on, full of minor crises, but, thank God, none of the major ones I keep expecting. I don't relax, though I do progress to the point where I can deal calmly with absolutely normal blood chemistry values. I worry about my almost-three-pound baby. Should I have put him on the ventilator sooner? Should I have let him tough it out on his own a bit longer? He's doing well toward morning, breathing for himself more and more, and we're helping him less and less with the ventilator; this is called weaning.

When I arrived in the intensive care unit, one of the residents told me what she called the two rules to live by: morning always comes, and mother's milk has twenty calories to the ounce. I think about this as morning approaches and I'm wearily calculating the caloric intake of each of my babies. Because the babies are so small, tiny amounts matter, and drug dosages or fluid requirements or caloric intakes all have to be figured out carefully. You dose drugs in milligram per kilogram of body weight; fluids are in cubic centimeters per kilogram; nutrition in kilocalories per kilogram. I stab my finger at the buttons on my calculator, which seem to be getting smaller; my clipboard is covered with notations like kcal/cc multiplied by cc/oz. Morning is coming, the rest of the team will arrive, and we'll make rounds; I'll tell them what has gone on with each baby overnight, and then I'll be off call. I feel a downright physical need to get rid of the load of responsibility. I'm completely terrified, mildly exhilarated, desperately sleep deprived. My feet hurt and I'm starving. I ask myself, what on earth am I doing here? At other moments, with a more immediate need to know, I ask myself, what am I *doing*?

The night is ending; the babies are still alive. Could it be that the nurses only asked me questions I could answer? Could it be that that doctor who helped me do the spinal tap was hanging around on purpose, knowing it was the first night on call for a brand-new intern? Did I have anything to do with getting these babies through this night? Maybe my first patient and I have more in common than I realized: we are both too immature to be out in the world, but with a lot of help, we may just make it.

On morning rounds, my senior resident asked me how the night had gone. Then, out of his own very recent experience, he offered me what he called the four basic rules of internship: if you see a chair, sit in it; if you see a bed, sleep in it; if you see food, eat it; and don't ask any questions.

PHYSICAL FINDINGS

On morning rounds in the newborn nursery, we were going around the room and discussing one baby after another. A nurse was feeding a red-faced little four-pounder while rocking back and forth in a rocking chair. She held him up. "You can round on this baby only if one of you can recognize him," she said.

Well, we couldn't. I mean, usually the babies lie in their

labeled beds, and you go look at one expecting to see that baby and only that baby. But let's face it, newborns look alike. And in a room with twenty or so of them, who can recognize one specific baby? The nurse can, because she has spent hours feeding and changing the babies she takes care of, and that's how you get to know a baby. Ask a doctor about a baby in the newborn intensive care unit, and you'll hear about its medical problems, you'll get numbers and lab results and diagnostic possibilities. Ask a nurse, and you'll also get information about the baby's likes and dislikes, its personality.

Of course, if there had been something distinctly wrong with the baby, we would all have recognized him immediately. If he had been in some way abnormal looking, or so desperately ill that he was hooked up to every possible machine—then we would have spent so much time watching by his bedside that his would have been one of the truly familiar bodies in the room.

What does it mean that you can know a baby almost inside out, know what his blood looks like, know the acidity of his urine, know how many calories he's taken in over the past twenty-four hours, and still not be able to pick him out of a lineup? Well, partly, it means that newborn babies do look somewhat alike. They don't have much hair, so you can't remember "the blond one with the curls." They all tend to scrunch up their faces and cry when you examine them. But the problem is more general than that.

The fact is, you can examine a patient in detail, listen with care to heart and lungs and stomach, feel all pulses, look deep into the eyes, study a lesion with great attention—and never see the person. That applies to a patient of any age. And there are aspects of medical training that point you in the direction of developing this habit.

As a medical student in the hospital, you run around looking eagerly for "physical findings." I mean, there you are, learning the fine art of physical diagnosis, and you need to see examples of the abnormal. You can listen to a hundred normal hearts, but you still need to hear a murmur. You can feel a hundred normal abdomens, but you need to feel an abdomen with a mass in it. You can do a hundred normal rectal exams, but you need to do one where the prostate is enlarged. The problem, of course, is that not all patients are eager to have ten avid medical students line up to listen to that fascinating murmur—let alone to feel that intriguing mass, let even further alone to check out that amazing prostate. So word spreads in the hospital, great physical finding on the guy in room 5, you gotta listen to his murmur. And medical students may wander in and ask permission, and if the guy is nice he gives it, and everyone listens. There's nothing wrong with this; you have to have something shown to you so you can recognize it the next time. But it can lead to a ghoulishly detached way of seeing patients: did you listen to the murmur in room 5, did you feel that mass in room 8, did you look at the rash in room 16?

Also, as a medical student, you can get fixed on physical findings; you're convinced your physical diagnosis skills are inadequate, you'll report that someone has a heart murmur and then no one else will hear one, you'll report that the pulses are normal and it will turn out there are no pulses in the left foot. You often have to decide whether to be honest and describe what you're really seeing or hearing or feeling, or whether just to say whatever you know the senior people have heard or seen or felt. (When a friend of mine was doing gynecology, he was told to feel an internal mass on a patient. He couldn't feel anything, and decided to be honest about it. The senior doctor went back to show him the mass, and found that it had in fact resolved—my friend was right. The senior doctor complimented him on his diagnostic acumen. "Little did he know," my friend said to me, "that I wouldn't have been able to feel the mass even if it had been there. I can never feel masses.")

Anyway, it's perfectly understandable that at the beginning of clinical training you sometimes lose sight of your patients as you search for their pathology. But, unfortunately, you can go on and on with your training and never learn how to make the transition back to seeing your patients as more than the sums of physical findings.

I don't mean we ignore them. We think about them. We discuss their problems. We look at them more closely than ever, peering inside with X rays and CT scans and all sorts of studies. We know more about them than their wives, husbands, mothers, fathers, roommates do. The point is that you can look at a patient without ever *looking* at the patient. You can even talk to a patient, delivering information and reassurance, offering a prerecorded spiel in your best bedside manner, without ever making any real contact.

What can happen then is this: you can begin to see the patient and the disease as interchangeable. You get more sophisticated, and instead of thinking of the abdominal mass in room 26, you begin thinking in terms of the liver cancer in room 26. Your picture has broadened to take in all the details of the patient's illness—but still not the patient.

If you're lucky, this is in part a peculiarity of training; doctors in training are often so stressed, so focused on not making mistakes, so overloaded with patients and with work, that they regard what we call "social issues" as trimmings. Social issues are everything else that make up a human being. You can hope that when you get further along you'll have the luxury of time to learn more about your patients than just their diseases. And there are senior doctors who manage it—there are even doctors in training who manage it. They're the very talented, very remarkable people.

And then there's the other extreme. Most of us muddle along somewhere in the middle, trying to look at all our patients, trying to learn about them properly but sometimes getting lost in the volume of patients, the density of medical facts. But there is also the other extreme, and I get to tell my other-extreme story, don't I?

I worked once with a surgical resident who wasn't at all

interested in knowing anything about his patients. He lived for the operating room, regarded awake patients as a sort of necessary evil. And there was an unfortunate elderly gentleman on our service who needed to have a foot amputated, and because he wasn't mentally intact, his wife had to be called to get permission for the surgery. So this surgical resident went to call her, and he came back into the surgeons' lounge fuming about how people just don't know what's good for them. Apparently the patient's wife had been quite unwilling to give her consent, and had unwisely attempted to argue with the surgeon. So he had put her in her place, all right. He had told her this amputation was life or death for her husband, and after all he had years of medical school and residency training behind him and she had no medical training at all, and did she really want to question his decision? So she said, no, she supposed not, though really this operation came as a complete shock to her. So anyway, the surgeon concluded, he had permission to amputate Mr. O'Hara's foot. There was a pause. Then two other surgeons said in unison: "But Mr. O'Hara doesn't need his foot amputated. It's Mr. Keating who needs his foot amputated."

"Oh, son of a bitch," said the surgeon who had made the call, or words to that effect. He thought it over for a minute. Then he had an idea (after his supervisor had told him no, we could not amputate Mr. O'Hara's foot, too). "I'll call Mrs. O'Hara back," he said, "and tell her we've tried a new wonder drug and saved his foot after all."

Well, the point is you really can reach an extreme where your patients don't exist for you at all except as problems to be solved; a diseased foot on an operating table, an out-of-whack lab result to be corrected. But even before you get there, you can find yourself wondering uneasily whether you would notice if two patients switched beds on you overnight, whether you would recognize your patients if you met them on the street, fully dressed and in control of things. Hospitals do deprive patients of much of their individuality, and of course they can also deprive doctors. As you push yourself to care for your patients, as you worry over the details of their illnesses, if you don't allow yourself time for that other, more basic, contact, you probably damage yourself far more than you do the patient. The patient, after all, is treated by a doctor who doesn't recognize him. But the doctor has become someone who may be incapable of this kind of recognition. One is in danger of being temporarily deprived, the other of being permanently crippled.

ORDERS OF MAGNITUDE

When I came to the newborn intensive care unit to work, the neonatology fellow said to me, by way of orientation, "This is the part of the hospital that even the surgeons are afraid of." What he meant was, we have by definition the smallest, sickest patients in the hospital. We have the patients with the tiniest brains, the fewest cubic centimeters of blood, the thinnest skin. We have the smallest margin for error: a few millimeters in the placement of an endotracheal tube, a few milligrams in a drug dose, a few minutes in the delivery room.

It's all a matter of scale, a question of perspective. If you habitually did procedures on mice, then even a twenty-six-week preemie would look large to you. But if your idea of small is a normal full-term baby, weighing in at eight pounds or so, then a six-hundred-gram baby (about one and a quarter pounds) looks just insanely small.

After a few weeks in the NICU, my perspective had readjusted nicely. One and a half kilograms (about three pounds) seemed to me like a nice solid weight for a baby; a baby that size would probably be off the vent, eating by mouth, easy to care for. When I called consults from other services—cardiologists or neurologists or gastroenterologists—if anyone commented on how small the babies were, I looked at them with surprise and some distrust. Did these people really know what they were doing if they thought fifteen hundred grams was *small*? I had completely forgotten how creepy and frightening it can be to examine a baby that size, to handle its almost weightless extremities, move the baseball-sized head.

After I was fully acclimated to the NICU, one night I admitted a full-term little girl who was having some mysterious respiratory distress. She looked unbelievably healthy and robust to me, with her plump little arms and legs and her vigorous cry. Why, she must have weighed four kilograms (almost nine pounds)—how sick could she be?

Well, she went on to be very sick indeed. She had persistent fetal circulation, and we could not stay on top of her respiratory status. Inside the womb, a fetus gets its oxygen from its mother, not from its lungs. Very little blood circulates through fetal lungs; there's a special hookup that bypasses the lungs and sends the blood around the rest of the fetus. Normally, when a baby is born it makes the changeover to breathing, and blood begins to travel from the heart to the lungs. This baby, because she was so sick, had not made that transition. She was trying to breathe, but most of her blood was circulating around and around her body without ever getting to her lungs to pick up oxygen.

They sent me upstairs to tell her parents what was going on. I had just looked up persistent fetal circulation in a textbook, memorized the key details—now I heard myself explaining it earnestly to a room full of stricken relatives. As instructed, I advised her parents to come downstairs and say good-bye—we weren't sure she'd make it through till morning. She made it through till morning, but two nights later she suddenly crashed, she looked like she was dying—and again, her parents were called. She recovered again, and eventually, a couple of weeks later, she went home. Her parents were absolutely confident that her life had been saved by the religious amulets they had tucked around her mattress.

I would hover over her bed when I was on call, looking down at her plump little body with all the lines and tubes coming out of it, and feel confused, feel bewildered that such a big healthy-looking baby could be so sick.

Anyway, I finished up my stint in the NICU and for the remainder of internship, I took care of a whole range of children. In my primary care clinic I watched babies grow from two weeks to a year of age. I flattered myself that I was in fact developing some sense of perspective on children, on their illnesses and their development. I learned to start an IV on a recalcitrant sixteen-month-old and a recalcitrant sixteen-year-old. And then at the end of the year, I found myself back in the NICU, and was overwhelmed all over again by how tiny the babies were.

I mean, take your one-kilo preemie. That baby is an order of magnitude smaller than your ten-kilo toddler. And that toddler is an order of magnitude apart from your hundred-kilo adolescent. (And your preemie is fighting to breathe and grow, your toddler has an ear infection with a question of sepsis, and your adolescent has new-onset diabetes mellitus.) Maybe this is why people trained to deal with adults find the NICU so disturbing—with adults there are no orders of magnitude (the fifty-kilogram patient versus the five-hundred-kilogram patient?). Adults always belong to the same species (except for the ones who are said by the house officers to be "from Mars"—but that's not an issue of size).

Children, however, constitute more than one species. Preemies breathe differently, eat differently. They look too small to contain all the apparatus of life. But you take care of them, you work among them, and they stop looking quite so unbelievably small. The NICU nurses casually put IVs into them, draw blood from their veins and arteries. You poke their limbs around when you examine them, and the arms and legs stay attached to the bodies. Your perspective has changed; you are acclimated to the NICU. The next time a new parent comes to visit a healthy little thirty-two-week two-kilo baby and tremulously asks whether something that small can live, you are honestly surprised by the question.

Still, sometimes when I come in in the morning after an evening and night out in the real world, I look at my patients, and all I want to say is, my God, they're so small. They're too small to be babies. But not, of course, too small to be patients.

2

Wards

We still call them the wards. Gone are the days when wards meant big open rooms with beds lined up; the modern pediatric ward now offers private and semiprivate rooms, with full facilities for parents to stay overnight. But the wards, the patient floors, are still the heart of residency training. At the hospital where I trained, the hospitalized patients were divided among three wards: infants and toddlers, school-age children, and adolescents.

As an intern, working on the wards, your job is to admit new patients and care for them during their hospital stay. On your on-call day, you wait for calls from the emergency room, for scheduled patients coming in for carefully planned tests. You question the patients (or their parents), read through their old medical records, talk to their regular doctors. You write orders, following a strict hospital format, telling the nurses everything from what diet the child can eat to what medications need to be given. And then you follow your own set of patients, day by day, checking their lab results, planning their tests and their therapies. And of course, at night you take care of everyone else's patients, too.

Your life is ruled by the various modes of communication that keep a modern hospital running, especially by your beeper, which connects you to the emergency room with its constant supply of new admissions, to every nurse who wonders what you meant by your orders, to your own family calling in from home. But there is also the telephone; there is the computer terminal. There are the endless rounds on which you tell the stories of your patients over and over, reading your painstakingly collected data off your scut sheet. Sometimes you get so caught up in collecting and relaying and transcribing and describing your data that you forget for a minute that there are beds with sick children in them and your job is to take care of these children. Then you answer another page and this one sends you in to examine a baby or change an IV, and you remember where you are—on the wards.

And so, by taking care of these children, you are supposed to learn about children and childhood illness. And you do. But the fact is, most children never see the inside of a hospital ward. Most children, despite the usual complement of pediatric ailments, don't need to be hospitalized. The children who are found on pediatric wards are a combination of what we call the "previously healthy"—essentially well children who have been hit by some particularly serious ailment—and the chronically ill. I spent a great deal of my residency taking care of children who are always in and out of the hospital, children whose childhoods are shaped and sometimes twisted by illnesses that sometimes get worse and sometimes get better, but never go away. They were not quite the children I had pictured when I went into pediatrics originally—I had been picturing the generic Dangerously Ill Child, brought into the hospital Near Death, but Heroically Saved by the timely interventions of Modern Medicine. And there are plenty of those children; they have serious infections—meningitis or bad pneumonia— or they have severe diarrhea and come close to dying from dehydration, or they inadvertently poison themselves, or they get bad cases of croup and can't breathe. And they almost all get better; after they get better they go home and, with luck, grow up and live their lives.

But there are also so many children who come back again and again, whose illnesses are part of their everyday lives: babies with complex congenital anomalies, school-age children with severe asthma, adolescents with cystic fibrosis; hemophilia, sickle-cell disease, muscular dystrophy, inflammatory bowel disease, diabetes, immunodeficiency, spina bifida; expreemies with serious problems left over from their early days (NICU graduates, we call them).

Pediatric interns have various terms for these different patients. Common diseases have common nicknames, of course: *wheezer* for asthmatic (rhymes with *seizer*—for kid with epilepsy, giving rise to many bad songs for the Christmas show), *cystic* for patient with cystic fibrosis, *sickler* for patient with sickle-cell disease. And then there are the *campers* and the *soldiers* and the *members*—are you ready for this? Campers are kids with diseases for which there are special summer camps, especially asthma and diabetes. Soldiers are kids with chronic gastrointestinal disease—GI, get it? And members, well—it happens that the abbreviation for mental retardation with cerebral palsy, MRCP, is the same as the acronym for Member of the Royal College of Physicians.

As a resident, you spend a great deal of your time taking care of children with chronic disease. That's how these in-jokes arise; they are the stuff of your job, the raw material of the wards. You learn from all these children, and from their parents. From them and on them, of course. And find yourself, years later, struggling to express your gratitude, but trying not to sound like someone who is accepting an award and wants to thank all the little people—from three pounds on up.

ROUND AND ROUND
· · · · · · · · ·

What it reminds me of most, if you want to know, is being in labor. There's the feeling—like when the contractions are coming strongly every few minutes, and you have to breathe properly and ride each one out—that if you lose your concentration you'll lose your control. And then before you know it you'll be in the middle of another contraction, and then another, and you'll never get back on top. There's the feeling that if only everything would slow down a little, you could have a real rest. There's that slightly bewildered disbelief that you could have gotten yourself into this.

The alarm goes off. Wake up, realize you're on call today. Immediately begin to feel tense. Immediately begin to worry that you aren't going to get any sleep. Immediately begin to wonder what admissions the fates have in store for you. Get dressed, remember to put your sneakers into your shoulder bag, and feel ridiculously pleased when you manage to find yet another pair of clean underpants to take along to the hospital. Say good-bye to the person who's still asleep in your bed. Run out of the house.

Get to the hospital in time to pre-round on all your patients, except for one who is on another floor. Meet your team for work rounds, and listen to the person who is postcall complain about what an awful night he had. Discover that one of the reasons his night was so awful is that the one patient you didn't have time to pre-round on got extremely sick and is now in the intensive care unit. Feel a little silly that you didn't pre-round on this patient even enough to discover this. Find out about the four admissions who came in last night and feel jealous because they're all relatively straightforward. Get to the cafeteria in time for breakfast after rounds. Find that it's waffle day; eat three and feel abdominal discomfort for the rest of the morning.

Round, round, and round some more. Stay awake in rounds, while the postcall intern nods off with his mouth wide open; exchange glances with the attending, smile and shake your head as if *you* would never dream of sleeping during attending rounds. Immediately after rounds are done, buzz around in an absolute whirl of efficiency, restart an IV, write lots of orders, page several consults. Answer a call from the emergency room for your first admission of the day. From then on, lose track of time; don't eat, don't go to the bathroom. Just try to keep up as the day gets away from you.

It's three in the morning. You thought you were actually going to get to bed by two because you had three admissions, all before nine o'clock. None of them was all that sick, and the people in the emergency room did good workups and started the IVs. You even called your mother when the rates changed at eleven and told her that yes, you're calling from the hospital, you're on call, you're taking care of some very sick patients. Your mother was very impressed. You wish you could get rid of the notion that somehow, without benefit of medical school, she knows more medicine than you do. You wish she were here to help you take care of these patients, or maybe just to take care of you.

Anyway, at 11:30 P.M. the emergency room called with the sickest admission of the day, a seven-year-old child with eight volumes of past medical records (positive charts-greater-than-age sign). And at 11:45 P.M., as you were walking into the emergency room, having hurried down there by way of the candy machines, the ward called to tell you that one of the nice, stable patients you thought was peacefully asleep is instead spiking a temperature.

Admit your new patient. Write some orders. Gaze balefully at the most recent discharge summary in volume eight of the past medical records. Trudge back upstairs to do the septic workup, the blood tests, the urine test, the spinal tap to look for a reason for the other child's temperature. Discover that there is an IV which has stopped working waiting for you on another patient. Fail to put the IV in after four tries, decide the baby is avascular—without veins—and find a way to convert all his medicines to oral preparations, so he doesn't need an IV after all. Feeling proud of yourself for this brilliant stroke of medical management, do a very efficient septic workup on the other patient.

At 3:00 A.M., go to bed, then get up immediately because you've suddenly remembered there were some important tests you didn't order on your most recent admission. Order the tests, then get intercepted on your way back to bed by a nurse, who wants you to come look at a child who is breathing quickly. Look at the child, decide to adjust his medications a little. Then go back to look at your sick new admission, who is sleeping peacefully. Decide to do the same.

Sleep from 4:00 to 6:30 A.M., when you get called because another IV has stopped working and the child needs medications immediately. Get this IV in on the first try and go back to bed, but get up at 7:15 to pre-round because you remember that yesterday you didn't know what was going on with your patients. Run into one of your fellow interns on the stairs, ask how her night was. "Okay," she says, "I got four hours of sleep." "Four!" you say enviously; "I only got two and a half, and that was interrupted."

> *Do you learn a lot when you're on call? Well, yes, you learn an enormous amount. Maybe there is no other way to make this transition, this jump into being a real doctor. It is when you are left alone with patients at night that you begin to make decisions, that you begin to think as a doctor. Does every third night on call make any particular sense? Well, probably not; it generates a level of chronic fatigue that can get in the way of learning, or even working efficiently. Internship is probably a necessary stress, but it doesn't have to be as stressful as it sometimes is.*

Convene for work rounds, thinking to yourself, in your tired mind, that you aren't on call today. Feel tremendously relieved about this. Smile patronizingly at the intern who *is* on call, thinking about how she'll be here all night while you get to go home. After rounds, run to the parents' room and take a hot shower and put on your clean underpants.

Go to attending rounds and fall asleep immediately, waking up every few minutes as you start to fall off your chair; pull yourself upright with a surreptitious little jerk, then nod your head with enthusiasm to show how completely you agree with whatever is being said. Dream a vague little dream about your third-grade teacher and how she didn't give you the part you wanted in the Thanksgiving pageant. Wake up more fully as attending rounds are ending, and go off to a teaching conference for interns. Get there early enough to secure a chair against the back wall, and lean your head back in comfort. Sleep, while some very earnest person discusses some very important subjects. After the conference, wash your face and feel somewhat better. See some of your patients, check some lab results, draw some blood. Feel proud of how well you are functioning.

Try to discuss a complex patient with a subspecialist you have just consulted. Find that you cannot remember why this patient is in the hospital at all. Suggest that the subspecialist read your admission note. Explain: "I'm postcall."

Feel that you are becoming noticeably less efficient as the afternoon wears on. Discover in yourself a tendency to sit down in the rocking chairs provided for parents and rock yourself to sleep. Write out a sign-out sheet for the person on call and start to leave the floor. Get rerouted by a nurse who wants you to come look at the junk she's been suctioning out of a patient's airway. Look at it and agree it's awful looking. Decide that it really needs to be gram stained, and that this is just too scutty a piece of scut to sign out. Take it to the lab and gram stain it, and see nothing; wonder whether it's because your eyes aren't focusing well. Get someone else to look at the slide, too, and feel reassured when he doesn't see anything either.

Go home. Enjoy the fresh air; you haven't seen daylight for a while. Play with your own kid. Put up a kettle of water to make tea, then fall asleep on the couch while all the water boils away. Open your mail: a threatening letter from Mastercard. Decide you're too tired (again) to pay bills, and put the letter on your desk, where it will be safe. Talk with your long-suffering partner, and decide you're both too tired and too bummed-out to cook or do laundry. Put the kid in his stroller and go out into the pleasant evening air. Find a store that's still open and buy some socks and some underpants. Eat Chinese food and notice that your two-and-a-half-year-old child is much more efficient with chopsticks than with a knife and fork. Ask: "Have we been eating in Chinese restaurants a lot lately?"

Work hard not to fall asleep over dinner. Make it home, put the kid to bed. Fall asleep in the shower. Wake up before you actually fall down and hurt yourself. Get into bed, then get out again because you forgot to set the alarm. Then get out again because you don't believe you really set it after all. Then fall asleep and sleep and sleep. In the middle of the night, become aware that someone is poking you—hard. "He's awake and he wants a drink of water, and it's your turn—I was here all alone with him last night!" says a voice in your ear. Ask, intelligently, "Does he *really* need that IV put back in?"

> *It isn't even the being on call that I mind most. Being on call can get you down, but it also carries its own exhilaration, its own concentration. What I hate is that postcall feeling, that certain knowledge that one third of my days are simply shot. I can have a sort of nice time when I'm postcall, but it's a vague unreal nice time; I can hardly remember it the next morning. I'm postcall one third of my days and one half of my at-home nights.*

The alarm goes off. Wake up, realize you aren't on call. Relax. This is your good day, your normal day, your day for waking up *and* going to sleep in your own bed. Feel relatively rested and relatively unstressed all day. Manage to be polite to people. Every so often, remember that you'll be on call tomorrow, and feel tense.

Yes, it's like being in labor. Trying to be brave. Telling yourself it only hurts because you're stretching; the pain tells you it's working. Telling yourself you'll look back at this and be glad you did it. Knowing you want to get through it without drugs. Telling yourself it will all be worth it in the end. And then realizing your rest period is ending, here comes another one, get ready to ride it out, and whatever you do, remember to breathe.

PROBLEM LISTS

We call it "picking up a service" and it's what we do when we change over our duties at the end of the month. Coming out of a month in the newborn intensive care unit, say, you may be starting your stint on the infants and toddlers ward, so you pick up the service of one of the interns who is finishing. In other words, that intern signs over to you a list of patients, and you pick them up. Now, when you pick up someone else's service you are coming in in the middle of a lot of stories. Your predecessor admitted all these patients, heard their detailed accounts of who they were and why they were coming to the hospital. Your predecessor has been writing progress notes in their charts, following every detail of their hospital courses. And then you take over and you have to try to keep track of all the threads. It's very hard to get to know these patients as well as you know the ones you admit yourself, so they tend to be a source of anxiety—until they go home.

Therefore, what you want to hear when you're picking up a service is a nice simple straightforward story. Baby came in sick, baby getting better, baby going home soon. I was picking up a service for my first-ever month on the general wards, and the intern who was signing out to me listed a bunch of nice normal kids, came in sick but now getting better. For each of my patients she had prepared a file card for me, name, ID number, one-line synopsis of the problem: two-month-old male came in with diarrhea and dehydration, ready for discharge as soon as drinking well. Like that. And then she told me about Melissa.

With a sinking heart, I saw that Melissa's file card was full of writing. And sure enough, Melissa was a very complicated kid. She had been born with multiple congenital anomalies— any number of birth defects. Not one of her major body systems worked normally; I went down the list with the other intern. Cardiovascular-respiratory: she'd had cardiac surgery for a malformed heart and still took medication to make her reconstructed heart work better; she had a tracheostomy tube in place because her upper airway was obstructed. Fluid/electrolytes/nutrition (these systems are by convention run in alphabetical order): she had a tendency to retain fluids unless she was medicated with diuretics to help her urinate it all out; she had trouble keeping the electrolytes in her blood in proper balance; she tended not to gain any weight. Gastrointestinal: her upper digestive tract didn't work properly and she had had an operation called a Nissen fundoplication in which part of her stomach had been surgically tightened like a drawstring bag to keep stomach contents from refluxing in the wrong direction. In addition, she had a gastrostomy tube—G-tube— implanted directly in her stomach, through which she was fed. And so on through hematology and immunology and infectious diseases and renal . . . When I went and stood next to Melissa's crib, I couldn't even keep track of the various tubes going in and out of her. There was the trach tube in her neck, the G-tube in her belly, the surgically implanted central venous

IV line which was used for IV access in this baby, all of whose regular veins had been damaged and scarred by repeated IVs. There were medication schedules, feeding schedules, physical therapy schedules, lab schedules.

And in the middle of it all was a one-year-old girl, with a crib full of fancy stuffed animals, lying on her back and chewing contemplatively on her thumb.

Most people think of pediatrics as the care of well children who get sick. That is, after all, how most adults encountered their pediatricians when they were children; it is how they encounter their children's pediatricians as well. Children get sick; they have asthma attacks, or they get infections—sore throats and ear infections or pneumonia or meningitis—mild diseases, serious life-threatening diseases. Or they fall out of trees and break their arms, or they burn themselves, or they eat things they shouldn't. So you take them to the pediatrician or maybe to the emergency room. And in fact that is much of pediatrics and much of the joy of pediatrics, watching kids get well again, watching how quickly they bounce back to full vigor.

But from the perspective of the intern, working in a pediatric hospital, there is also a big and relatively unsung pediatric population of children who never have been well and never will be well. They are severely handicapped children; they are children with multiple congenital anomalies, dysmorphic children. Some of them have relatively well-known conditions, Down's syndrome, for example (which can be associated with various medical problems); but many of them, especially in a hospital like mine, a big academic hospital where people are interested in rare diseases, have problems you may not have heard of. Rett's syndrome, for example, or Treacher Collins, Pierre Robin, CHARGE association, or Lennox-Gasteau. These aren't fancy names for common diseases; they're obscure unusual conditions. As an intern you may not be exactly sure what any one of those conditions entails—until you find yourself taking care of a child with "absolutely classic textbook Treacher Collins." Each individual diagnosis is rare, but all together they add up to a large population of children, and children who tend to require an enormous amount of medical care. I do realize, by the way, that I am lumping together a very diverse group of children—but as a group they do present certain basic issues.

These children tend to have long problem lists. It's not uncommon for a child to have problems in both the orthopedic and the ophthalmologic categories, say—and that's just under the letter O. You can't necessarily take anything for granted when you're caring for such a child—you can't just assume normal kidneys, normal metabolism, or normal anything else.

These children also tend to have profoundly knowledgeable parents, parents who are professionals at dealing with the medical system, at sizing up any new doctor, at finding ways to have unusual services funded by insurance companies or by the state. Parents get used to serving as advocates for their children, refusing tests they see as repetitious or unduly painful, making sure their children get any new possibly beneficial therapy. Often these parents know much more about the particular disease in question than many doctors; always they know much more about the particular child in question than any doctor; and they are not necessarily patient with doctors who fail to acknowledge this.

I found out a lot of this in taking care of Melissa, who stayed on my service for the whole month I spent on the infants ward. When I left, I signed her out to the intern who picked up my service. I got to know her pretty well; I could recite her problem list by heart, and, inevitably, I found myself becoming her advocate. I argued the plastic surgeons into coming to look her over in hopes of correcting some of her facial birth defects. I heard myself explaining, earnestly, over and over, to the plastic surgeons, to the doctors who would be taking care of her in the intensive care unit after surgery, to anyone new who came in contact with her, "Listen, there's nothing wrong with her that she can't eventually grow out of, if only we can get her growing. She can outgrow the need for the trach, she can learn to eat with her mouth, her heart is working better than it used to—and all the literature says she ought to be mentally normal!"

I was arguing, of course, that Melissa was precious, that the work invested in her, the time and trouble (including mine) was aiming toward a real and worthwhile goal. "She has a wonderful personality," I would insist, apropos of nothing in particular. "She's an adorable and playful child." Of course, we would all have taken care of her even if she hadn't been adorable and playful. We would have taken care of her even if she hadn't had any prospect of outgrowing her medical problems. We would have taken care of her even if she hadn't had any chance of being mentally normal. And medically, the care would have been the same. But if she hadn't had such a delightful personality, I wouldn't have spent my scarce spare minutes making faces at her, trying to elicit her smile. And I wouldn't have added all those irrelevant details to her problem list when I discussed her with other doctors; I was in my way apologizing for the complexity of the case, assuring them that it was a battle well worth fighting.

Taking care of Melissa, and other children like her, does of course change the way you look at dysmorphic children. You lose the habit of the quick look-and-look-away, the almost-recoil, as you get more accustomed to various dysmorphisms and what they imply. You start thinking more about medical issues. Is there a cleft palate? How bad—enough to interfere with eating, enough to interfere with breathing? Are the ears not formed correctly—how much hearing does the child have? Are the spastic limbs held in tight contractures—and is there more to do with physical therapy?

Traditionally in medical training you learn about the normal by way of the abnormal. You come to understand more about normal metabolism, for example, by observing what happens in a multitude of cases where normal metabolism is blocked. And certainly, caring for children with multiple anomalies makes you appreciate the miracle of normal development, both prenatal and postnatal, for the astoundingly perfect complexity that it is. As you care for a child whose every bodily system requires your supervision, you begin to understand how effortlessly the normal body manages its affairs and how clumsy are even our most sophisticated attempts to duplicate its calculations, its processes, or its checks and balances. "The dumbest kidney is smarter than the smartest resident," we were told at an early lecture, and all the other organs turn out to have the jump on us as well.

The other thing you learn, taking care of a child like Melissa, is how strong the push to grow and develop can be. Even with no part of her body functioning quite properly, if we could give her the calories, through her IV or through her G-tube, she would use them to fuel as much exploration of her surroundings as she could manage. If we could protect her from infection, if we could keep her heart working properly, she would use the relative comfort, the freedom from pain, the oxygen that her heart was pumping through her body, she would use it all to move from playing with her hands to playing with her toes as well. Which, in pediatrics, is the point.

LEARNING FROM PATIENTS

In a sense, it's the resident's nightmare—the patient who knows much more about medicine and disease than the doctor. There you are, the intern, clinging to your hard-won knowledge, your newly acquired and very tenuous confidence that you know what to do in the hospital; and there sits your patient, the pro.

While you are taking the history, your patient quotes you

some test results, and you write them down, nodding earnestly, wondering all the time what in the world that test is for and why in the world it was done on this patient. "He had a negative NBT," says the patient's mother, matter-of-factly, and all sorts of exciting possibilities cross your mind: Nonblood Test, National Baseball Tryouts, Never Before Tested. Another patient says, "So you'll probably need to check my ammonia level, like they usually do," and you agree emphatically, wondering who *they* are and why they usually do *that*.

It's axiomatic that patients have a great deal to teach young doctors; they teach us about their diseases, of course, and about dealing with disease and pain. They teach us, by their reactions to us, how to form alliances, how to take histories, how to explain what we're doing, how to conduct ourselves at the bedside. But it can be disconcerting when, rather than teaching by example or by demonstration, a patient teaches by didactic methods.

So I stand there in the treatment room, and the patient walks in. He's five years old and he has hypogammaglobulinemia—his white blood cells don't make antibodies properly, which means he's vulnerable to infections. Every four weeks he comes into the hospital and gets IV gamma globulin—antibodies which have been separated out of other people's blood—to boost his immune system. He climbs up on the bed and looks at me suspiciously. "Are you any good at starting IVs?" he asks, with the intensity of a five-year-old who has been stuck with a lot of needles.

"Well," I temporize, not wanting to say yes (what about the one I couldn't start for love or money the day before yesterday?), not wanting to say no (how would you feel about someone starting an IV on you if she admitted to being not very good at it?). "Well," I say, smiling in what is meant to be a confident and reassuring manner, "I've certainly started my share of IVs."

The patient does not look convinced. He exchanges a wary

glance with his mother. "Are you an *intern?*" she asks, and I nod, still smiling my idiotically confident smile.

"Okay, you get one try," says the boy, gritting his teeth and holding out his arm to me.

What can I say? This child knows the score too well. He has had as many IVs in his arms as I have started in my entire (three-month) career as a doctor. He is a professional, and as I tape his arm to the arm board and tie the tourniquet, he makes me feel a little like an amateur.

She was an oncology patient, an eight-year-old with a central line in place for chemotherapy. It was a great convenience, since it meant she no longer needed to go through the pain of having an IV started every time she came to clinic; they just hooked her up to the line surgically implanted in one of her big veins. When she wasn't in the clinic getting chemotherapy, the central line was just an inch of plastic tubing coming out of the skin of her chest. Unfortunately, it was also a way that bacteria could enter her body, a breach in the defensive wall of her skin. Central lines can get infected. She had come into the emergency room with fever, and her white blood cell count was all the way down, destroyed by her chemotherapy, leaving her vulnerable to serious infections. I needed to draw some blood from her central line, to find out whether it was infected. I hadn't ever drawn blood from a central line before, and one of the emergency room attendings gave me careful directions. I went into the room, put on gown and gloves and mask, and started to go through the sequence of steps, when the patient's mother interrupted me to tell me I was doing it all wrong. She cared for that central line at home, flushing fluid through it periodically to keep it working, keeping it clean and protected, checking for leaks or breaks. She knew its quirks and its preferences, and she showed me exactly what to do.

I'm not complaining about this brave and superbly competent mother. The only problem is, she was coming to me for help, and I knew less than she did. I asked her, "Do you think your daughter needs to be admitted?" "Oh yes," she said, and she was right.

There are patients who know my very own hospital as well as I do—or better than I do. They arrive for their asthma admissions, their cystic fibrosis pulmonary cleanouts, their inflammatory bowel flare-ups. Their favorite nurses greet them. They settle in, and I sometimes find myself left chewing over all the sentences I have developed to comfort patients who find themselves suddenly sick, suddenly in a strange and menacing place, suddenly facing unfamiliar routines and tests and procedures.

Instead, to these chronic patients, I need a way to say, welcome back, I'm sure you don't want to be here, I'm sure everyone wanted you not to come back, I admire you for your courage in living with your disease, oh, and by the way, I'm the intern who'll be taking care of you this time around, and please don't assume that I know too much.

I'm afraid I rest some of my own identity, my ability to function as a doctor, on the fact that the hospital is my turf. I know its routines, I speak its language. I am the friendly helpful guide for the families, lost and confused in their time of need. I can be honest and soothing when explaining a blood test. But it sometimes rattles me when the nine-year-old, or the nine-year-old's father, says, "So, how many polys were there on that diff?" That is a question my senior resident should be asking me, wanting to know what proportion of the white blood cells were one particular type of cell, a type that increases with bacterial infection. If the father asks me that, it means he probably knows how to interpret the answer—maybe better than I do. It means I can't get away with my usual vague explanations about how we're doing some tests to see whether it looks like he maybe might have some kind of infection. And that all rattles me.

And of course, the reason it rattles me is probably that

my sense of my own identity as a physician is still so tenuous. I am still telling myself on some level—well, you may not know everything you ought to know, but at least you know more than the patients, right? Well, not all the time.

In a certain sense, every patient knows more about the disease than the doctor does. What a patient feels defines the disease. The patient can know more than all the medical profession combined. Suppose the patient, for example, has tetralogy of Fallot with pulmonary atresia—a complex set of congenital heart defects. Now, the official wisdom is that tets-with-atresia never have "spells," episodes of oxygen deprivation in which the blood is shunted the wrong way in the heart and the skin turns blue. It's supposed to be physiologically impossible with that particular cardiac hookup. But if the patient does have spells, then either the patient has been misdiagnosed and has some other problem, or else the official wisdom is wrong—as it often is. One way or another, the burden of fitting the pieces together rests on the doctors. The patient, like the proverbial customer, is always right.

And so, when a patient goes beyond the knowledge that is the raw material of experience, when a patient starts to learn the medicalese descriptions and the detailed test results, it should not seem strange or inappropriate. The disease belongs to the patient, to be possessed and understood on any level that works. And when the disease is chronic, the kind that threatens to take over (or even to end) the patient's life, then a patient may have the time and the inclination to learn everything there is to know.

It is awkward to be judged, awkward to be knocked off the shaky pedestal of my professional identity. But it is much worse than awkward to be the professionally knowledgeable patient, the child with so much experience of the hospital.

Or, as I imagined that five-year-old with hypogamma-globulinemia saying to me, "Well, it may be *your* ego, but it's *my* arm!"

WHEEZERS
· · · · · · · · · ·

I am on call, and I get paged. It is my senior resident calling, and when I answer the page, she says into the phone, "Wheezer in the ER!" and hangs up. And down I go to the emergency room to get my new patient, relieved to have a new admission who is probably fairly straightforward, grimacing a little to have another new admission with the same old diagnosis.

Asthma is the single most common diagnosis for patients admitted to the medical service of the hospital where I work. When I started my internship in July, they were saying that summer was always a particularly hard time for asthmatics; in January they were saying that asthmatics always get worse when it's cold; and they always say that when the weather is changing, asthma gets worse. One way or another, there always seem to be a lot of patients with asthma in the emergency room, and a good many of them get admitted to the hospital.

Asthma is a disease in which the lining of the airways is too reactive—various kinds of stimuli cause the tubes to contract, creating what is called bronchospasm—spasmodic closure of the bronchial tubes. The precipitating stimuli vary from person to person, though there are certain common precipitants: colds, exercise, weather changes, allergic reactions to animals or dust. Asthma is a common disease in both children and adults, but also occasionally a fatal disease; and children do not have very large passages for air to begin with. A child's airway is always worth worrying about. When adults code—suddenly start to die—it is often because of a cardiac arrest; children, if they get into serious trouble, are almost invariably in respiratory danger. Protect the airway, protect the airway, protect the airway; this was drummed into us all during our first weeks as interns. So in asthma, the airways constrict; and the airways are already small, and the degree of compromise can be significant—which translates as an inadequate supply of oxygen.

Of course, in dealing with adult asthma, you also have to worry about underlying lung disease, about a smoking history and about all the other common disorders of adulthood, from high blood pressure to lung cancer. In pediatrics, we tell ourselves, we have to worry about the size of the airway, but not so much about the basic protoplasm we have to work with. Children are healthy until proven otherwise, assumed to have healthy hearts and basically clear lungs. Of course, in adult medicine, probably, doctors think with relief that at least they do not have to deal with itty-bitty little bronchial tubes.

So I get down to the emergency room and there I find a boy, five years old, who is working hard to breathe. Even before I listen to his chest, I can see several things that let me know this is bad asthma. For one thing, he's wearing an oxygen mask, and he makes no attempt to push it away. For another, his nostrils flare outward with every breath he takes, as he attempts to pull in more air. When I pull up his hospital gown, I can see that he's also using the muscles below and between his ribs to pull air in—he's doing what we call retracting—and I can see those muscles pulling in with every breath. On the other hand, his color is okay—he's a little pale, but he isn't blue around the mouth. An IV is running into his arm, and I know he has already been given a big dose of a medication that should make the smooth muscle inside his airways relax and let the airways dilate.

I take a history from his mother—my patient himself is not in any shape to talk much. I ask a basic set of questions: when was the asthma first diagnosed, ever been in the hospital with it before, ever been in the intensive care unit? The mother says her son was diagnosed at the age of three, has been in the hospital twice before, but never in the unit. That relieves me of the necessity to ask whether he's ever needed intubation—that extreme point when an asthmatic can no longer breathe for himself and needs a tube put into his trachea and a ventilator to do the work for him. That's intensive care unit asthma, potentially lethal asthma. I ask about the medicines that Richard is on at home and about his usual precipitants—what sets off his asthma attack. Exercise, his mother says. I ask if anyone in the home smokes, and rather shamefacedly the mother tells me that she and her husband both do, though they try not to in front of the children. I ask about pets in the home and she tells me there are none. I ask about other people in the family with asthma, and she tells me her sister and her mother both have it.

I go through this list of questions, and a bunch of others, as quickly as I can. Asthma tends to be what we call a cookbook admission; you always ask the same set of questions, you write your admission note following a familiar pattern, and you treat the patient by going down a list of set ingredients. In fact, even while I am talking to Richard's mother, I am beginning my note, "Third hospital admission for this 5 yo wm known asthmatic, no ICU admits."

I examine Richard—I look in his ears, look in his throat, listen to his chest carefully—generally check him out. He seems to be feeling a little bit better, and I let him listen to his own belly with my stethoscope, which makes him laugh. I note down my physical findings in the ritualized shorthand of the hospital: WDWN WM in mod RD, −G, +FR . . . (well-developed well-nourished white male in moderate respiratory distress, no grunting, plus flaring and retracting . . .). I speak reassuringly to his mother, promising her we'll get him upstairs into a bed as soon as possible. She looks exhausted herself, having been up all night with her wheezing son, and now having spent the whole morning in the emergency room. I know from the history I have just taken that she has two other children at home—one older and one younger—and I suspect that she is anxious to get home and make sure everything is all right there.

I go and write orders for all the medications this patient will get; he can't go up to the ward until his orders are written. There's nothing terribly unusual or terribly frightening about him; he doesn't seem to be in danger, he hasn't been taking every drug known to medicine on the outside, so it's all pretty routine. I have medications I can give him which will probably help; he'll get IV treatments and also he'll inhale vaporized drugs from nebulizers, and chances are good that in twenty-four hours he'll feel much better and his chest will sound much better. And then, if everything goes according to plan, I'll switch him to the oral equivalents of the medicine he's been getting IV, and soon after that, he'll go home. Simple. Routine.

Well, of course I know that for Richard and his mother this is by no means routine. There are in fact asthmatics who are in and out of the emergency room, in and out of the hospital, so often that they really learn the ropes; but for Richard and his mother, this is a disruption of their lives—scary needles and unfamiliar rooms. And of course I know that actually every story is different, that the details of Richard's asthma, the way it affects his life and his family's life, the way his parents' smoking and their ability to get his medications into him are reflected in his appearance in the emergency room . . . I know there are many details here that cannot be categorized as cookbook. And I try, rushed as I am, to sort some of these things out. I have asked whether Richard's activity is limited by his asthma, and I am dismayed to hear that frequently he cannot run as far or as fast as other children his age because he starts to wheeze. I have blood test results in front of me that suggest his mother is not telling the truth when she says she has been giving him his asthma medications faithfully, three times a day for the past two weeks. The blood test measures the level of medication in his blood from when he came in to the emergency room, and that level was close to zero—he hasn't been getting his medicine. This is hardly a criminal situation; it isn't even a rare one. These medicines taste bad, children don't like to take them; I still remember someone passing around tastes of asthma medicine at a medical school lecture on the disease, telling us to try it and realize what we were asking children to take.

After Richard goes up to the ward, his nurse works on

him. She gives him the aerosol treatments every hour or two, makes sure the medication runs steadily into his IV, and, most important of all, listens to his chest and watches him breathe much more frequently than I possibly can; I am by this time down in the emergency room with another new admission. A few hours later she pages me to tell me that Richard is still very "tight," a reference to the way his chest sounds; he isn't moving air through it at all well. His respiratory rate is elevated, and she's worried about him.

I go up and see him, draw some blood to check whether his drug level is now as high as it can safely be. I send the blood test off stat, ask her to try a different aerosolized preparation, add yet another medication to his regimen. Eventually the drug level comes back, lower than I want it, so I give him more. Still all fairly cookbook, but routine or not, I have to worry about him. He could get tired of working so hard to breathe; he could stop breathing off enough carbon dioxide; the carbon dioxide level in his blood could go up. He could end up sitting for a while with levels of oxygen in his blood that are a little bit lower than he really needs. He could even have a respiratory arrest. The nurse and I hang around his bed, trying to decide which direction he's moving in—is he getting worse and should I think about sending him to the intensive care unit? Should we get a blood gas on him, which will mean sticking a needle into his artery—a painful process—stressing him out and making him cry, which may make his wheezing worse—but it will tell us for sure the oxygen and carbon dioxide content of his blood. The nurse actually gets the syringe ready and the cup of ice that blood gas samples have to go in, and puts them by his bed.

He gets another aerosol treatment, and I listen to his chest again. It's finally sounding a little bit better; I hear air moving all through his lungs. His nostrils aren't flaring as noticeably. I dump out my cup of ice, throw my syringe away. He's going to follow the routine after all. I smile at him reassuringly (since I am reassured). I smile at his mother reassuringly. I tell her that while Richard is in the hospital, it would be good if we could work out a better asthma regimen for him to follow when he goes home, so he doesn't end up getting this bad again. She nods, eager not to repeat this experience. Unfortunately, working out this regimen is going to involve telling her to quit smoking. There may be things we can do to help out, like for instance finding a less disagreeable preparation of medication for Richard to take, but in the end, we're going to be left telling her to stop smoking, have her husband stop smoking, rid her home of dust, rid Richard's bedroom of rugs and curtains and furry toys—all easy for me to say. I'll set her up with an appointment in the allergy clinic; everyone will try to help her get her son's asthma under control. This is a very common childhood disease, and we have well-greased paths to help people through it.

Sometimes, when you are involved with a very complex patient, when you take care of an ill child over a long period of time, you develop some kind of feel for what this disease means to the patient, to the family. You get a look at alternate possibilities—what life might be like without the disease. You get a hint of how the child imagines the state of being healthy, how the parents picture life without illness, and also of the compensations they have worked out to help them through the life that they have. You learn the details of their story, and the story becomes entangled with the medical details of the illness in your mind. You come to know which treatments mean pain or illness as side effects, and which facts are too painful to confront. You learn the particular euphemisms and evasions that particular patient needs to get through the day. With something like asthma, some "routine" disease, none of that tends to happen. You admit the kid, you plug the kid in (as we say), you treat the kid, you make the kid better, you set the kid up for follow-up, you send the kid home. The disease you see most often, the disease that ought to have by rights the most faces, ends up as the disease without a face.

CLEANOUTS
· · · · · · · · ·

This is something like the weirdest high school you ever saw. A small group of adolescent girls has congregated on the bench in the middle of the hospital corridor, and there is a great deal of giggling. One of the nurses has in fact just gone to ask them to keep the noise down, and after she walks away, the giggles break out again, shoulders shaking with an effort to suppress them. And here, down the hall, apparently all unaware of the girls, come two adolescent boys. One is shirtless, his back held absolutely straight, stomach sucked in. The other is wearing a hospital robe, but instead of pajama pants, he wears bright surfing jams. They are very, very cool, these two boys, and they parade past the girls, talking casually to each other. As they pass, someone whistles, and then the giggling rises.

It is hard enough, God knows, to be an adolescent, even if you aren't sick. Chances are you don't like your body; you don't think it looks right; you wonder if people are looking at you and laughing at you. It is pure hell to be an adolescent with a chronic disease. The way things work out, many of the little kids we take care of in the hospital are well children who get some severe acute illness and need a brief period of treatment: a dangerous infection that needs IV antibiotics, a severe case of diarrhea and dehydration (the famous D & D) that needs some IV fluid, a particularly bad case of croup—you have to protect the baby's airway until the virus goes away. But few healthy adolescents get acute diseases of this kind (they do get into car accidents, of course, but that's not really my part of the hospital; I'm talking about the medical ward, not the surgical ward). Instead, the adolescent ward is full of kids with chronic diseases, kids who spend their whole lives checking in and out of the hospital. They have hemophilia, for example, and come in whenever they start to bleed. Or they have sickle-cell disease and come in when they're in crisis, a condition involving agonizing pain and sometimes oxygen deprivation. Or they have cystic fibrosis.

This group in the hospital hallway really could almost pass for a clique from your local high school. The girls wear lots of makeup, and all have on their own clothes, mostly fancy sweatshirts. But each kid is connected to an IV pole on wheels. One guy is wheeling around a portable oxygen tank; a thin plastic tube looped around his head is delivering extra oxygen directly into his nostrils. Everyone is skinny. And, when you look close, there is something funny about their fingers. The ends of all their fingers are enlarged, bulbous around their nails. This is called clubbing, the result of chronic oxygen deprivation. Heavy cigarette smokers get clubbing after years of devoted smoking. And so do people with cystic fibrosis.

Cystic fibrosis is the most common fatal genetic disease affecting whites. It is a condition in which all the secretions of the body's exocrine glands have an abnormal texture, abnormally thick and tenacious. In other words, the mucus is too sticky. And these secretions clog up the glands, and certain organs of the body stop working properly. The pancreas cannot function, and without a pancreas, it is difficult to absorb certain foods. And the lungs, lined with mucus, become subject to recurrent severe bacterial infections; 98 percent of all patients with this disease die from cardiorespiratory causes.

This is a chronic disease. You don't usually die from it right away, and you don't usually diagnose it right away. You diagnose it, say, sometime in the first five years of life, when a child comes in who is failing to gain weight, who has chronic diarrhea, who has too many respiratory infections, or any of a multitude of nonspecific symptoms. You diagnose it by what we call a sweat test, stimulating some sweat glands, collecting the fluid they produce, and measuring the amount of salt in that fluid; patients with cystic fibrosis have higher salt levels. In fact, there is a folk belief that a baby who tastes too salty is unlucky; and I can remember learning in medical school, as a stray fact to remember, that the complaint, my baby tastes salty when I kiss him, may be a harbinger of cystic fibrosis.

It is not so easy to be a resident on the adolescent ward. These patients aren't so very much younger than we are. They have all the reverence for which adolescents are noted. And they're professional patients. In particular, residents tend to get upset about the IVs. Kids with cystic fibrosis come into the hospital fairly regularly, whenever their lungs start getting worse. They get what we call a cleanout, a course of multiple very strong antibiotics, aimed at eradicating the particularly vicious organisms growing in their lungs. They are often not terribly sick, just not very well either. And they know a hell of a lot about IVs; a cleanout means living with an IV for a couple of weeks. When I worked on the ward, the usual IV procedure was as follows.

One of the CF patients would notice that his IV, which had been in for more than a couple of days, was starting to bother him; the site felt tender. He would check to see which of the residents was around, and if it was someone of whose IV skills he approved, he would remove the existing IV and make an appointment with the resident to have it replaced. Then he would specify to the resident, number one, how many tries he planned to allow before he would demand that a senior resident be called (one to three was the usual number), and number two, precisely what vein on what arm was available for the next IV. IVs are painful, and these patients don't like pain any more than anyone else, but still, we used to resent being ordered around like this. We would joke that we were being assigned the particular veins we got because the patients needed to keep their arms free for video games. Still, it was humiliating to fail in your two allotted attempts, humiliating to watch word go out among the patients: get your next IV from someone else.

One of the truisms of adolescent psychology is that adolescents believe themselves to be immortal. Look at the way they drive, goes the wisdom, look at the way they take drugs.

I can never be hurt, I can never be killed. Disconcertingly, this often turns out to be true of adolescents with fatal diseases as well.

CF patients used to die in childhood. Now we replace the pancreatic enzymes to help them digest their food and save them from malnutrition. We treat them aggressively with superhigh-tech antibiotics. And we make sure their chests get banged on daily, teaching their parents to do chest physiotherapy, using percussion to loosen the deadly mucus. And now half of the patients live into their twenties, and many go on into their thirties.

But then they die. And they know each other; they form a particular sort of community, always in and out of the hospital. There is that group in the hall, not overwhelmingly sick, in for their cleanouts, and then there is also one girl who has stayed in her room, who is in the hospital to die. And they all know her, and they know that what is happening to her is what will happen to all of them, sooner or later, and still many of them struggle to believe they are immortal.

The girl who is dying is named Rachel, and she is seventeen. CF varies a lot; some people have severe, rapidly progressive disease and die in early childhood in spite of aggressive treatment. Others are rarely hospitalized, live lives only marginally affected by the disease all through their teens, their twenties. When we admit a CF patient, we go through piles of old charts, count up how many previous admissions, how often cleanouts are required. Rachel has needed cleanouts every couple of months for three years now. She has been on IV antibiotics at home, most recently, in a last-ditch attempt to keep her out of the hospital. But her lungs got worse and worse, and she is now requiring round-the-clock oxygen. I admitted her, I changed her antibiotics, I ordered increased chest physiotherapy. Nothing is helping; she is continuing to deteriorate. A culture of the bacteria in her sputum is showing bugs that are resistant to pretty much every antibiotic in the pharmacy. A patient like Rachel gets so many courses of antibiotics that her bacteria have lots of time to undergo selection for resistance. We are giving her a relatively new antibiotic, but she already has resistant bugs.

Rachel is, to no one's surprise, totally terrified. It terrifies her to be on oxygen all the time, and it terrifies her that when she takes her oxygen off, she immediately feels air hungry. Most of all, it terrifies her that she is not getting better. She has been on this ward so many times before, and always she has gotten better. She keeps waiting for the familiar return of energy, the easier breathing. She asks me every day when I examine her, do I think her lungs sound better. I don't turn the question around; I know she'd tell me if they *felt* better. She would like to be out in the hall, gossiping with her friends, dressed in one of her ensembles of stretch pants and loose silk-screened tee shirt. She tries hard to gossip with me, and I try to lighten her day. She wants details on one of the male residents, whom she considers good-looking; she wants to know whatever I can tell her about him. I tell her he's married and try to remember to tease her daily about her affection for him. All Rachel wants, and desperately, is to go to high school, to have a boyfriend, to graduate, to have a normal life. The lives of her classmates at school seem the most enviable in the world; they breathe easily, they know nothing about IVs, they eat what they like, drink, smoke. . . . They are going to live to grow up, unless they smash themselves up in cars, and Rachel is beginning to realize that she is not going to live to grow up. She is not going to live to graduate, probably.

There is poignancy in this hunger for normal life, and there is also a certain amount of heroism in the way Rachel is going to meet her death. She does not have an enormous canvas to work with; her life has been short and without remarkable incident. Her heroism is in the vivid pink polish she resolutely paints onto her clubbed fingers, trying to make them beautiful, in her keeping her hair clean and curled, in the grins she exchanges with me when Dr. Handsome walks by. Breathing in her supplemental oxygen, lying back on her hospital bed with the world's most up-to-date antibiotics running uselessly into her veins, she is trying to hold on to pieces of the ordinary adolescence she wants. She is creating it from nothing, in highly difficult circumstances.

Out in the hall, the two parading boys have joined the group of girls. Everyone is agreeing to order out for Chinese food tonight, though there is also a strong pizza lobby. When I come out of Rachel's room and walk past the bench, several people look at me uncertainly. They are all accustomed to the rhythm of the CF deaths. If Rachel goes on getting much worse, discussions will start with Rachel and her parents about how aggressive they want us to be and how much they want us to emphasize comfort. It is terrifying and painful to struggle for breath, but the medications which calm you and relieve your pain also suppress your respirations. Rachel will teeter and die somewhere on that balance, between the pain and the medication. The other patients know this, and they also know that some day, some night, Rachel will fall victim to her disease. There will be weeping family and also weeping nurses; there are nurses on this ward who have known her since she was twelve. I imagine, as I walk by the bench, that the other patients are acknowledging Rachel's mortality, even as they continue to deny their own.

Sometimes it's like the strangest boarding school you can imagine. I once had a patient ask me whether I minded if her boyfriend spent the night with her; she had a private room, she explained, and she was on the pill. She was almost at the end of her cleanout, and feeling quite herself again. The thing that reminded me most vividly of high school was not her urge to spend the night with her boyfriend, but rather her need to let the teacher, or rather doctor, know what a cool sophisticate she was. I mean, there was no need to ask me. She could perfectly well have had her boyfriend in her room, and if a nurse had caught him there, he might have been asked to leave. But no, she had to come to me for official permission.

Fatal illnesses demand heroes and heroines. Suffering and

impending death are supposed to generate nobility of character, a deeper understanding of life's secrets, wisdom, serenity. On the adolescent ward, they fight off death with the tiny details of adolescent life. They only want what other people their age want—to be normal, to be liked, to make it through, and someday to look back on those crazy teenage years, when they thought they were immortal.

BEEPING AROUND

The only metaphor I can think of, I'm afraid, probably says more about me than it does about my subject. And I shudder to think what Freud would have made of it all. But there it is: I keep thinking that maybe men have an easier time adjusting to wearing beepers. I mean, what is a beeper but an appendage, worn below the belt, dangling there, that periodically calls attention to itself in the most peremptory way imaginable. You can be doing something else, you can be surrounded by friends or else enjoying a quiet moment alone, and there goes your beeper, startling you, embarrassing you, and demanding to be satisfied. I mean, in the last analysis, the real problem with the beeper is that it is meant to be your tool, and instead you find yourself its slave. So maybe men do find this more natural. But enough of this.

A beeper, to extricate it from all these heavy-duty associations and symbolic constructs, is a small rectangular object attached to a good strong clip. You clip it onto your pocket or your purse or your waistband or whatever, and it keeps you in touch with the hospital page system. There are many varieties of beepers: the kind that just beep, letting you know you have to call some central number to find out who is trying to reach you, and the kind that beep and then light up the number of the person who is paging you. There are beepers with speakers which actually allow a brief message to be transmitted by telephone, thus giving your fun-loving friends the opportunity to beep you while you're in a patient's room and announce, in crackling but clearly audible voices, "Please come to the beer party in the residents' lounge."

When you are a medical student, the beeper is by and large the prerogative (and the badge of office) of the resident —the real doctor. There were a couple of clinical rotations in medical school during which students were given beepers, and I remember regarding mine with a mixture of pride and awe —would it go off and would I know how to cope with whatever summons it brought, whatever question it asked, if it did? Of course, usually when it went off it was the resident wanting to know if I had found those lost X rays yet, or else maybe my mother, calling to find out what I had learned recently in medical school. And when all was said and done, those medical school beepers were transient attachments (and after all, they're hardly going to beep the medical student if something awful happens).

The very first day of internship, I got my beeper. It was handed to me by one of the residents who was finishing his internship year. It had a dinosaur sticker peeling off the front and a dime taped to the back, to be used if one was outside the hospital and needed to answer a page from a pay phone. This beeper and I immediately embarked on a close and complex relationship, from which it is to be hoped both of us will emerge not too much the worse for wear.

It Beeps for Thee: Ten Typical Beeps in an Intern's Day

1. A nurse taking care of one of your patients who is off on a distant floor calls to ask whether you really want all those lab tests you ordered yesterday evening, and do you realize you ordered those same tests two days ago and they were all done then? Thank her very much; it had slipped your mind. Cancel the tests.
2. A doctor out in the community calls to ask about a

patient of hers who is in the hospital under your care. She doesn't want the patient discharged yet, while you were hoping to send her home today.

3. The medical records department calls to say they can't locate a certain patient's chart and wonder if it might be signed out to you. Explain that you have never heard of the patient and don't have any charts signed out to you and wouldn't know where they were if you did.

4. The emergency room calls you to come admit a patient who has a disease you have never heard of along with two other diseases you have heard of. They further inform you that the patient has been in the emergency room for more than five hours, what with one thing and another, and they would appreciate it if you could get right down there and take him away.

5. Your mother calls to ask whether you're having a nice time, and did you ever ask anyone about your great-aunt's new high blood pressure medicine and what side effects it might be having?

6. The urology resident calls to say he heard you were looking for him. Explain that actually you were looking for the *neurology* resident, but thank him for calling.

7. A patient you sent home two weeks ago calls to tell you he's having some pain in his lower back, and he thought you were such a good doctor he'd like to come see you again.

8. A nurse who is taking care of another one of your patients calls to tell you that his blood pressure is steadily rising, and maybe you should do something about it, when you get a chance.

9. A social worker calls to tell you about an emergency meeting which has been scheduled on one of your patients who is ready to go home but has no home to go to.

10. A brand-new nurse calls to read you a lengthy list of perfectly normal lab results which have just come back on a patient.

It's a love–hate relationship, mostly hate. The beeper wakes you up from sleep, pursues you into the bathroom, where you thought to enjoy a thirty-second break from your day. The beeper interrupts conversations and conferences, and unfailingly prevents you from eating an uninterrupted meal. It is the background music of the hospital, the constant punctuation of hospital hours. No one looks up in a conference when a beeper goes off, unless it continues to beep persistently, letting everyone know that the person it is attached to is more soundly asleep than usual.

The beeper is the symbol of the intern's availability. Sure, other doctors carry beepers, but generally they are beeped mostly by their office or their answering service, or else in case of real emergencies. Not us. We get beeped by everyone and anyone. We get beeped for dumb questions and life-and-death alerts. We get beeped all the time, because we are, at the most basic level, running the hospital. We get beeped because when anything goes wrong, it's the intern's fault until proven otherwise. We are all available to everyone, every minute that we are in the hospital.

And of course, there's nothing to help you appreciate useless irritating nonsense pages like one good emergency page. The beeper goes off and you answer the call and the voice at the other end says the patient seems to be having an allergic reaction. Or else the patient is getting bluer by the minute. And as you rush off to what you know is supposed to be the rescue, you wish most of all that the page had turned out to be from the linen department, asking you whether you had lost all the white coats assigned to you at the beginning of the year (of course you haven't lost them; you just haven't had them washed, that's all).

I'M OKAY, YOU'RE A BEEPER—THINGS TO DO WITH YOUR BEEPER

1. Put cute stickers on it, especially if you're a pediatrician. Hearts are always popular, though cute little teddy bears or bunnies go over well too. These stickers will not in any way affect the malicious nature of your beeper, but they will dress it up a little.

2. Tape a dime (or, if you live in New York, a quarter) onto it. Consider it mad money—if you ever get really mad and just walk out and you're halfway across the city when your beeper goes off, you can at least call in from a pay phone.

3. Fasten your ID card and a credit card or two and a couple of dollar bills around it with rubber bands so you don't have to carry a wallet. This will give you a pleasant sense that your beeper is on your side rather than secretly pledged to your worst enemies. It will also make it much more poignant when you eventually lose the beeper.

4. Drop it in your backpack without turning it off before you go to a movie; it will go off during the most tender soft-voiced love scene and will beep loudly and persistently while you search through the bag for it.

5. Forget to turn it on in the morning, or forget to notice that it is warning you about a low battery. Eventually, they will start paging you over the hospital's overhead public address system, and you can briefly taste the delights of fame.

6. Sing to it. In a show put on by my class in medical school, "Night and Day" was felt to be an appropriate song for a doctor-beeper duet. "Night and day, I am the one!"

7. Take it for a swim. Everyone fantasizes about throwing beepers into the toilet, but few have the courage of their fantasies. So just get in the shower with your

clothes on one morning (easy enough to do when you've been up all night) and teach that beeper who is boss.

8. Buy it flowers; it's only doing its best, poor thing. Make little dresses for it out of construction paper and felt scraps. Kiss it passionately. Don't worry that your unusual behavior will get you into trouble; you're an intern and you're expected to be sleep-deprived and a little bit off balance.

9. Beep yourself out of boring meetings or have a friend do it for you. This can save untold hours and nobody ever minds an intern leaving the room to answer a page.

10. Impress nondoctors. Intimidate waiters in fancy restaurants who want you to order wine you can't afford. A simple gesture to the beeper explains all: I'm on call so I can't drink.

Hospitals are not places of exceptional etiquette. No one ever asks when you answer a page, did I get you at a bad moment? is this a convenient time to talk? Somehow the illusion is preserved that we are all sitting comfortably at big desks, telephones and notepads ready if we need them. In fact, we are usually standing in hospital corridors, having interrupted an examination of a patient or a conversation with two other people—or else, inevitably, we are shouting into the one phone in the cafeteria, our food growing cold on a distant table, a line of other paged doctors already forming.

The page operators can get to know you pretty well; they know who tends to call you, recognize the voice of your significant other, tease you about what you say when you answer (do you go for the more formal identification—this is Dr. Schmo returning a page—or do you just say, hi, it's Joe?).

I suppose in the end it is a symbiosis; you complain bitterly about your beeper, but you also know it for the important umbilical cord that it is. It keeps you connected. It keeps you in communication (no, not an umbilical cord either—maybe a telegraph wire). It means you're a real doctor. And it wakes you up at night, just in case you thought that being a real doctor was going to be easy. And maybe someday in a fit of anger or frustration you will throw it dramatically into the sea (or more prosaically into the toilet) or slam it against the wall or bury it in your now-cold macaroni and cheese. But the mood will pass and you will find that it is miraculously undamaged (even by the cafeteria macaroni and cheese, which can take the paint right off a car) and you will clip it back on and feel for it every now and then with a nervous little pat.

Are you there? you will ask it, now and then, until it puts your mind at ease by calling to you with that familiar shrill voice. Again and again and again.

GUILT

I have this very distinct memory from the first month I ever worked in an emergency room. I was a third-year medical student, and I had no idea what kind of doctor I wanted to be. A father and son had come into the emergency room to-gether, and the triage nurse had scribbled "s/pMVA" on their form. A triage nurse is the person who reviews the patients coming into an emergency room and makes the rapid decisions: absolutely urgent (bleeding to death in front of you), reason-ably urgent (in some pain), not so urgent (headache for the last three days). And s/pMVA, for those of you who didn't guess it immediately, means status post motor-vehicle accident. So this father and son had been driving along in their car, and the car in front of them had stopped short, and they had banged into it. The father had been thrown against the steering wheel. The son, who was about ten, had hit his head on the wind-shield. They were both shaken and bruised, but neither was badly hurt. The father was refusing to let any doctors examine him until he had made sure that his son was all right.

The pediatrician examined the boy, checking out his head and then his whole body for any bruises or evidence of injury. He wrote down everything he saw, knowing that his medical notes could well be part of a court case or an insurance settlement. He asked a series of questions about the accident. Finally, gently, he asked the boy, "Were you wearing a safety belt?"

"No," said the boy. And suddenly, the father, who had been reasonably calm, grabbed my arm and began asking me over and over, "Is he going to be all right? You can tell me, is he OK? Is anything wrong with him? Is he going to be all right?" His voice escalated toward hysteria.

It was my first exposure to acute parental guilt. Now that I'm doing a residency in pediatrics, I see parental guilt of one kind or another almost every day. Now that I have a child of my own, I've felt twinges of it myself. Maybe because I do have a child, I recognized it right away when I heard it coming from that father. What he was saying was this: by asking about the seat belt, you're reminding me that it's all my fault that my son is hurt, and I can't stand it.

An issue that you don't have to deal with in pediatrics (or at least not all that much) is the issue of so-called self-inflicted diseases. I'm not talking about suicide attempts here, but about the sequelae of such habits as drinking and smoking. In adult medicine, you spend a lot of time taking care of lung disease and heart disease in long-term smokers, taking care of debilitated people with drinking problems and liver disease. In pediatrics you don't. You may take care of a two-year-old who swallowed the contents of a bottle of aspirin, or a six-year-old who fell out of a tree, but some doctors find these kinds of things easier to cope with. The whole idea of self-inflicted disease as a separate category is largely fallacious; many if not most diseases are the products of the life the patient has lived. If you live in a certain place, eat certain foods, have a certain number and type of sexual contacts, work at a certain job, handle stress in a certain way—then you're at risk for certain diseases. Still, in pediatrics, we have the luxury of viewing most of our patients as innocent victims.

And usually their parents also see them as innocent victims, and that means they look around for the guilty party. Who left that two-year-old unsupervised, who left the aspirin bottle within reach, why didn't it have a child-proof cap? Who let that six-year-old climb the tree, why wasn't anyone standing by to catch her if she fell?

There are times when, as a pediatrician, you can try to alleviate parental guilt. When I worked in the newborn intensive care unit, I often found myself sitting down for meetings with parents of very sick newborns. I would try to explain: this is what's wrong with your baby, this is what we're doing about it, this is what we think will happen next. And always in that first meeting I'd find occasion to say, it isn't your fault that your child is sick. It isn't your fault that your child was born early, not your fault that he developed an infection, not your fault that her heart isn't properly formed. And then, after I'd said this, people would ask me specific questions: my father said the baby was premature because I worked too hard right before he was born. Is that true? Is it because we had sex while I was pregnant? You know, I had a cold a week ago and I took some cough medicine—could that have affected my baby's heart?

Almost everyone had some secret fear, some carefully worked out chain of causation. Almost all the parents were blaming themselves. And an astonishingly large number had had relatives or friends accuse them. So I would say, over and over, as many times as seemed to be necessary, no, it isn't your fault.

But what about when it is? What *about* that unsupervised two-year-old, that bottle of aspirin with the easy-open cap? There are times when my job isn't simply to reassure. There are times when I'm required to worry about child abuse or neglect, to question parents closely about exactly how some accident happened, why it wasn't prevented.

Karen is a pleasant, too-thin woman, a little older than I. She's knitting an elaborate sweater for her three-year-old daughter, yellow with blue and green balloons on it, and she knits while she talks to me, the needles moving at top speed through the complex pattern. She's also crying, and the tears drip steadily down onto the yarn. She's trying to argue me out of doing a blood test on her daughter. "No more needles, please," she keeps saying.

I feel terrible. I didn't go into this business because I enjoy torturing small children. I've no particular desire to drag this little girl into the treatment room, have a nurse lie across her squirming body and pin down her arms while I stick in a needle and try to hit a vein. But the child has a fever, she may be infected with some new organism taking advantage of her debilitated immune system, and the test is conceivably important, and of course I'll worry if I don't do it.

"I wish you could do it to me instead," says Karen. "It's all my fault, I've ruined her whole life, and now it's just one awful pain after another."

What can I say? I am taking care of this three-year-old girl with AIDS. That's what her mother means about having ruined her daughter's life; the mother has the AIDS virus, and the daughter acquired it while in the uterus. Further, this mother had used intravenous drugs, though not for a year before she became pregnant. She had put her life back together, she thought, had her baby—and then this.

"I wish you could just do all the blood tests on me," she says again.

What can I say? After all, I can't make her daughter well. I want to say, stop blaming yourself, it isn't your fault. I've had this argument with her before, and it leads nowhere. I've asked, what does it matter that you used drugs? You didn't do it to make yourself or your daughter sick. I've asked, would it really matter if you had gotten the virus from a blood transfusion for an operation, instead of from a dirty needle? It would be the same virus, the same disease.

Abruptly she gives up the argument. "Well, if you have to do the blood test, then you have to," she says.

The nurse brings the child into the treatment room. The mother insists on coming in too, and stands stoically by her daughter's side while I draw the blood. Her presence makes me self-conscious about the various precautions I have to take because the child's blood is potentially infectious: the nurse and I wear plastic gloves, I put the tubes of blood in special bags, I label them with warning stickers. I feel as if I'm reminding the mother one more time that her daughter's disease is deadly, that we're all afraid of it.

When the blood is drawn, Karen takes her daughter on her lap and hugs her until the child stops crying and begins to examine her new Band-Aid with interest.

I'm sitting out at the nurse's station, trying to get the computer to work and give me some lab results, when Karen appears, crying once again.

"Is she asleep?" I ask.

Karen nods. "Why does there have to be so much pain?" she asks.

"It's a lousy disease," I say, a rather weak line I've heard myself offering about many diseases. It's the technique of the parent who helps her child spank the table on which he has banged his head: bad table, we don't like that table. It's all the table's fault, hate the table. It's a lousy disease, let's hate it together. Don't hate *me*, even if I do torture your child, even if I can't cure her.

"It's a lousy disease, and she didn't do anything to deserve it," Karen says. I push a box of tissues across the desk, and she takes them one at a time, dries her eyes. It doesn't disturb her to be crying in the middle of the hospital hallway. What has happened to her has put her beyond self-consciousness.

"She doesn't deserve this, she doesn't deserve any of it," Karen says. "It's all my fault, and I can't live with that."

I would like to be wise, I would like to be helpful. I would like best, of course, to say, it isn't your fault and, anyway, I'm going to make her all better. Next best would be, it may be your fault, but I'm going to make her all better. But what I'm left with is just, it isn't your fault.

"It isn't your fault," I say.

"She didn't deserve to have this happen to her," Karen says, one more time.

And I can only offer the endlessly sad truth of the hospital: "This hospital is full of children who didn't do anything to deserve what's happened to them. Terrible things are happening to children, and it isn't anyone's fault." I just have to try to take care of her as well as I can, you have to love her as much as you can. But I don't say that. I don't want to equate my medical care, which is doomed to lose its battle, with Karen's job of loving her child.

If your child is hurt or sick, you look for a reason. And you look first and most severely at yourself. And if there's any way to hold yourself responsible, then you do it relentlessly. And sometimes the doctor can make you feel better. And sometimes the doctor makes you feel worse. And sometimes you can't even hear what the doctor is telling you because the accusing voices in your head are just too loud.

3

Growing Pains

The agonies of residency are the stuff of medical folklore. In recent years, they have also at times been front-page news, as the question is raised: does sleep deprivation mean poor medical care? New York has made laws limiting the hours residents can work, and many people believe that such laws will soon be passed everywhere. But a week ago, in 1992, I heard a senior obstetrician assuring two exhausted residents that there is no scientific evidence anywhere that any amount of stress and sleep deprivation affects resident performance. And then he went on to give his version of the speech that so many senior doctors give: when I was a resident, we lived in the hospital, we fought for the complicated cases, we loved our work, we begged for more. And that's the only way to learn medicine. As I said, medical folklore, medical legend. The proverbial days of the giants (a phrase which never fails to make the residents snicker).

So anyway, when I started my residency I was more or less prepared for some of its harsher aspects. I was nervous about being away from my family so much, about how I would function under hospital pressures, how I would cope with the schedule. And, speaking of stress, I guess I had some vague rather mushy idea that there would also be something sad about seeing all those sick children. Since I had every intention of being a deeply sensitive doctor, I probably saw myself helping some generic grieving family, acting as a tower of strength to children in pain, parents in distress.

But there are no generic families. Children are specific, their stories are specific, and their pain is specific. I would not have been able to predict the most strikingly difficult encounters, the lessons hardest to learn. The horror of a day when the world seems to be full of raped children. The repeated awful sense that I am myself in the business of hurting babies, sticking them with needles, making them cry. The tension of judging a parent competent or incompetent. Or the feeling of a baby actually dying under my hands.

Death is a hospital familiar. By the end of internship, we all knew the rituals of death, the bureaucracy of death. Forms to fill in, and if you use the wrong color ink, the morgue won't release the body to the family. Phone calls from the medical examiner. But before I got used to it (and I did get used to it, more or less), there had to be a first death, a night when the ending of a life had its full and proper impact.

After my first stint on the wards, I rotated through some of the other parts of the hospital. Some time in the emergency room, learning to handle the widely varied complaints: the child with a stuffy nose at three in the morning, the child with high fever and rash, the baby who might have stopped breathing for a few seconds earlier in the evening, and the adolescent with chest pain. I went back to the wards, back to the NICU, back to the emergency room. I was taking things in stride which would have terrified me only a month or two before: another sick preemie, another kid in respiratory distress in the emergency room, another chronic patient with multisystem disease. This next section is about those things which jolted that newfound complacency, that ridiculous attempt to prove to myself that I could take anything the hospital cared to hand me.

Sometimes medical training feels almost parasitic. To put it baldly, you are picking up your learning and your experience and your professional qualification out of the suffering of sick people. Yes, you are taking care of them, yes, you are trying to help, but it's also true that for you, this is a learning experience, while for them it's life and death. And so when I look back on my own growing pains, on the unexpected griefs and guilts of my internship year, I am looking back on patients and their parents who were living with pains of a very different order.

RAPE KIT
· · · · · · · · ·

The rape kit is a small plastic box, and it actually says RAPE KIT on it in red letters. We keep a supply of them in the emergency room, and no one looks forward to using them.

In a pediatric emergency room, you see a lot of sniffles. You look in a good many ears. You hear yourself asking, again and again, "Now, when you say diarrhea, how many bowel movements a day do you mean he's having?" A great many parents use the emergency room for every small ailment of childhood, and it can be a long time between true emergencies. And that is probably all for the best, since no one can really live in an atmosphere of one crisis after another, one near death after another, one death after another.

Life in the emergency room has its comic moments, too. At 2 A.M. on one hideously cold rainy night, I walked into a room to be confronted by a perfectly well-appearing boy, about thirteen years old, and his father.

"What seems to be the problem?" I asked in my most professional and-what-brings-you-out-on-a-night-like-this tone.

"There's no problem," said the father, flatly.

"Oh," I said. "Well, good."

"I want *you* to tell *him* there's no problem." He indicated his son. "Go ahead, tell the lady what happened."

The boy wouldn't look at me. He wouldn't talk to me either, at first, but his father insisted, and finally he whispered to the wall, "Something came out of my penis when I was sleeping."

"There!" said the father triumphantly. "Go ahead, tell him it's normal."

Now, sensitive doctor that I am, I did not say to this man, you mean you dragged your son out in the rain and brought him to the emergency room because you couldn't bring yourself to explain to him about wet dreams? Instead, I excused myself, quietly, and went to find one of the senior doctors working in the emergency room, an older man with children of his own. It seemed to me that after what this boy had already been through, he was entitled to get his little your-body-is-changing lecture from a father figure, not a young woman.

Days I worked in the emergency room sometimes seemed to have patterns to them: one asthmatic after another, one small baby with fever after another, one nonsense case after another (a nonsense case is a fifteen-year-old who has had a wart on his thumb for six months or so and has suddenly decided to come to the emergency room at noon on a Wednesday and would like a note for school saying he couldn't come because he was being treated in the emergency room). And then this one horrible day which was one rape after another.

She was thirteen and a young thirteen, and I really did believe her when she told me she wasn't sexually active. I had asked her father to leave the room while I examined her, and I had put the question cheerfully, in the midst of a string of other questions. (Emergency room lore: the adolescent girl who was asked whether she was sexually active and replied, no, she just lies there, her boyfriend is the active one.) I believed her, but she was a thirteen-year-old female with abdominal pain, and it is a truism of emergency room medicine that all females past puberty are pregnant until proven otherwise (this is just a harsh way of saying that people don't always tell the truth or even know the truth about their level of sexual activity, and before you do X rays or give any medications or take someone off to surgery, you have to verify that she isn't pregnant). So when I sent her urine off to be analyzed, I also sent a pregnancy test.

Abdominal pain and vomiting are extremely common complaints. People come into the emergency room all the time with stories of abdominal pain and vomiting. Sometimes they have stomach bugs, and sometimes they have acute appendicitis. Sometimes they're having miscarriages or ectopic pregnancies (pregnancies outside the uterus, usually in the fallopian tubes). Sometimes they hate school so much it makes their stomachs hurt, and sometimes they've taken overdoses. Abdominal pain is always a hard complaint to evaluate, since the treatment for a stomach bug is to rest in bed and drink lots of fluids, and the treatment for an ectopic pregnancy is to go immediately to the operating room and have your belly cut open. And with all the most careful diagnosis in the world, you can't always say what someone has; the surgeons preach that unless 20 percent of the appendectomies you do are unnecessary, you aren't doing enough operations. In other words, if you aren't operating on a certain number of the people without appendicitis, your index of suspicion is too high, and you're bound to miss some of the acute appendix cases—and if you miss those, they can get very sick indeed.

With this particular patient, I wasn't really thinking surgical emergency. She said she had been having a little belly pain, not too severe, for almost a week, and she'd been doing a lot of vomiting. Her father thought she had lost a little weight, and she wasn't interested in food. I thought maybe a stomach bug, but I wasn't sure.

When the urine pregnancy test came back positive, I needed to get her father out of the room again. One of the other doctors in the emergency room took him aside for me and began asking him some questions about his daughter's medical history. I went back into the little examining room and closed the door, faced the thirteen-year-old. Idiotic sentences occurred to me. ("The good news is, you don't have appendicitis.") Finally I said, "You probably aren't going to be happy to hear this, but your test shows that you're pregnant."

She stared at me for a minute, then shook her head. Then she began asking me how she could have gotten pregnant. As I said, she was a young thirteen. I told her what I thought had to have happened, and she considered for a minute, then asked, "I could get pregnant even if I didn't want him to do it?"

"Did someone do it when you didn't want him to?" I asked, and she began to cry, and then she told me a long and miserable story about a much older boy who she didn't know who had given her a ride home from school one day, saying her mother had sent him. This had happened three weeks earlier.

"Did you tell anyone about this?" I asked.

"He said he would come back and get me if I told," she said.

I told her that it was now up to her whether or not her father was told, that I could tell him or she could tell him, or else she could keep it secret for now. She wanted me to tell him, so I brought him into the room and told him, and then she blurted out her story one more time. I was grateful to him for being tough, for not doubting her story, for putting an arm around her and comforting her. He'd been worried about her, he told me, for a couple of weeks; she'd been acting very quiet, very unlike herself. I made a little speech to the two of them about what her options were, about the clinic I was going to refer her to, about gynecologic exams and prenatal care, about adoption, about abortion. Then the girl's father went out to call her mother, and I was left alone with my patient again. Without planning any such speech, I heard myself saying, "One thing, you know, you mustn't think of this as being about sex." She looked at me in confusion, and I knew I was making a mess of it. "This isn't what sex will be for you," I said. "This was an act of violence; someone did this to you out of anger and hatred. This has nothing to do with making love, and you'll find out about that someday when you feel ready for it, when you agree to it. It's something different." She said nothing, and I wondered whether I should have kept my mouth shut.

Later that afternoon when the police brought in the nine-year-old boy, I actually volunteered to be the one to see him. They had called to tell us they were bringing in a kid who had allegedly just been raped, and I wanted a chance to collect evidence, to do something that might help chase down and convict the offender.

He was a nice bright boy, and I sat in our conference room with him, his parents, the social worker, and the police detective, and he told us what had happened; he had been playing with friends in a field and a couple of older guys had come and watched them, and his friends and he got nervous and decided to go home, but one of the guys followed him and made him go behind an empty building and raped him. The detective asked him a long list of questions about what the man looked like and exactly what he did, and the boy answered patiently, looking from his mother to his father, and his parents smiled at him and encouraged him, and then exchanged very different looks when they thought he wouldn't see.

After all this, I took him into the examining room. His

mother came too (his father said he didn't think he could) and a nurse, who would help me and also act as a witness. I did a quick general physical, looked his whole body over for bruises and other marks. Then I opened the rape kit. We examined his anal and genital areas with ultraviolet light because dried semen fluoresces, and we carefully noted all the areas of white glow. Then I rubbed up some of those areas on a gauze and we did an acid phosphatase test, testing the samples with a chemical that turns purple if the substance is indeed semen. It turned purple, and we put the gauze and the acid phosphatase strip into the special plastic evidence bag and sealed it. We looked carefully for pubic hairs or other clues. We documented every small scrape and laceration.

I took swabs from his mouth and his anus to culture for gonorrhea; if a child has a sexually transmitted disease, this is considered good evidence in court that the child has been molested. The boy was very quiet while I did this, holding his mother's hand. I kept up a rather meaningless flow of talk, trying to encourage him and reassure him and continually promising him that I was almost done. When I finally *was* done, we sealed all the little evidence bags into the rape kit and closed it with stickers and I signed the stickers. And then finally we told him he could go home and take a bath, and I went out and wrote a careful description of the physical examination. A few minutes later the boy's father came up and asked whether I had tested his son for AIDS. No, I said, we don't do that routinely. In fact, I knew, there had been no time for this boy to develop antibodies to the virus, even if it had been transmitted, and the test checks for antibodies. On the other hand, AIDS is a sexually transmitted disease, and it made sense to me that it would be useful to document that this boy was originally negative—just in case he was unlucky enough to turn positive later. Besides, the father said his son had already asked him about it, so I figured that I might as well do the test and let it come back negative. I explained all this to the father, then drew the boy's blood. The boy asked if I was testing him because the rapist was homosexual, and I tried to explain that men who rape small boys are not necessarily homosexual, and anyway, that men who are homosexual do not necessarily have AIDS. But what if he used drugs, the boy said, he might have AIDS from that.

I took the tourniquet off his arm, and just then the psychiatrist knocked on the door. While I was putting the blood into tubes and labeling the tubes, I listened to hear how the psychiatrist would approach this situation.

The psychiatrist looked the boy in the eye, and said, "You know, this man was using his penis as a weapon. This had nothing to do with sex or love."

I have no particular wisdom to offer on the subject of men who rape children or even adults. In medicine, especially perhaps in pediatrics, the villain is supposed to be disease, malformation, bad fortune. If I wanted to deal regularly with situations where there really is a villain, I would have gone into some other field. It makes me angry, it makes me upset, and there's nothing I can do about it.

The next case I took that day was a young couple with their first baby, eight days old. They had come to the emergency room because they were very upset; the baby was spitting up a little bit of milk every time she ate. The nurse described the case, and I immediately volunteered to see them.

"No more rape kits today," I said. "I'm in the mood to give burping lessons."

HURTING BABIES

When you say you are in pediatrics, people generally assure you that that must be very rewarding (it is). Then sometimes they tell you that it must also be very hard because you have to see children sick and even dying (this is also true). They rarely appreciate that on a day-to-day basis it is often not the large pain of death and disease that makes pediatrics a little rough on the soul. Instead, it is the frequency with which I have to hurt kids, cause them pain, that can wring me out emotionally. This probably stamps me as trivial and self-centered; children have serious diseases they have to live with, and there I am, feeling bad because I occasionally have to draw a little blood. On the other hand, the realities of residency are found in the details—the little things I actually do all day, one after another. And it really isn't all heroic Young-Doctors-in-White stuff, either.

So picture to yourself this scene: it is the middle of the middle of the night, four in the morning, and the tired intern finally goes to sleep, her notes written, her sick patients inspected one last time. And half an hour later her beeper goes off; a two-year-old's IV has fallen out and the kid needs to get medicine in the IV at a continuous drip. Well, the intern thinks of many things. She curses her fellow intern who started the IV for not having taped it in better—the art of starting an IV in a two-year-old involves a great deal of tape, boards to hold the arm out straight, little plastic "houses" to put over the connections, and still, with all this protective armor, the average toddler can bite, scratch, and jerk the IV out in thirty seconds, maybe forty if you allow for illness and weakness. The intern also allows herself to think evil things about the nurses—why weren't they guarding the IV more carefully? She tries desperately to think of a way to change all the medications this child is receiving to either oral or intramuscular doses—many creative therapies are developed to avoid starting difficult or untimely IVs. But all the while she is putting on her shoes and shrugging her white coat over her rumpled surgical scrubs, grabbing her clipboard, and trudging down the hall and up the stairs to where the two-year-old is waiting.

So this is the scene: it is an enlightened pediatric hospital, so all painful procedures, from blood drawing and IVs to bone marrow biopsies, are done in so-called treatment rooms. The idea is that children should feel safe in their own hospital beds, protected from needles; the treatment room is the bad place. So the intern finds herself in the treatment room, along with a sleepy but highly indignant two-year-old boy, who immediately begins yelling, "All done! All done! Say bye-bye!" as his mother carries him into the treatment room. This is an enlightened pediatric hospital; parents are encouraged to stay with their children around the clock, so here is a sleepy mother in a flannel nightgown. And there is also a nurse, pushing an IV pole from which hangs the setup—the fluid and tubing to be attached to the new IV.

The intern goes through the ritual of getting ready to start an IV. She assembles her IV needles, her alcohol pads for washing down the skin. She makes a flush, a little syringe full of sterile saline solution to inject into the IV after she gets it started. Then carefully, ritually, she tears her tape—three short narrow pieces to anchor the IV to the skin as soon as it is in, three short wide pieces to really pin it down, five long wide pieces to tape the arm to the arm board.

This is how it works: the child is made to lie down on the bed in the treatment room. He is no fool, so he promptly begins howling as loud as he can. The nurse positions herself across the table from the intern, and by dint of lying across the child manages to keep him relatively immobilized. She tucks his knees behind one of her elbows and uses her hands to steady his pudgy little arm. The child's mother stands next to his head and tries to distract him. The child howls. The intern wraps a tourniquet around the pudgy little arm and looks hopefully for a vein. Pudge and more pudge. Two-year-olds frequently have no veins. The intern checks the hand and then moves slowly up the arm. The other arm is already sore from the old IV. The nurse has to lie across that sore arm. The child cries even more heartrendingly. The mother has to take a break for a second and turns away; while her back is turned, the intern leans over the screaming child to whisper to the nurse, "I went into pediatrics because I enjoy torturing small children at all hours of the day and night."

(Don't get me wrong—I think it's great for parents to stay with their children. I think they're entitled to come with the child into the treatment room. But like many residents, I think it's easier to start IVs and draw blood if no parent is watching, and I sometimes find myself blaming the parent, in my own mind, if something takes an extra try or two.)

So the intern tries once, and the needle goes into the cute little hand and does not enter a vein. The child is crying so hard that he barely acknowledges that he has been stuck with a needle; the howls just continue. The intern says, automatically, "Sorry," though unsure whether she is apologizing to the patient who is getting stuck, his mother who is watching him get stuck, or the nurse who is holding him while he gets stuck. She imagines that all three are looking at her with hatred. She takes out another IV needle and goes looking for a better place to try. The room is hot and the intern is sweating; the child is getting redder and redder. She tries a second time, gets the needle into an infinitesimal vein, but as she tries to advance it, it goes right through the other side, and the vein "blows," in hospital parlance.

"Does this really have to be done right now?" asks the mother, and the intern wonders, wistfully, whether it does. It's getting on for 5 A.M.—if she left it for just a few hours someone new could arrive and do it. But she has already convinced herself that the child needs the medication, and anyway he's already suffered through being woken up and dragged into the treatment room—why put him through all that again?

The intern searches for veins in both feet. She goes back to the arm and thinks she sees something in the hand. She is using the smallest possible needle, and she has the arm taped down to an arm board so the kid can't move it. The nurse is beginning to look winded and the mother is on the verge of tears. The child shows no signs of tiring; the howls are as loud as ever. The intern tries a classic gambit, aimed at comforting the mother. "It's actually good that he can put up such a fight; we worry much more about the children who just lie back and let us do these things." The mother does not look unduly comforted by this piece of medical lore. The intern feels she has been in this treatment room forever. She is becoming quite certain that the IV will never go in, that she will stay crouched over this child and the night will tick away into morning. She feels she has forgotten how to start an IV; she cannot remember what it feels like, she cannot believe she has ever successfully done such a thing. She feels horribly guilty, wants to abase herself before all the other people in the room. She also wants to get the IV in, tape it down, go back to sleep for a couple of hours, and as she focuses on the little blue thread she can just see under the plump surface of the child's hand, the crying of the child recedes. The hovering mother is just at the edge of her consciousness. The nurse is an assistant. The child is a goal.

The intern agonizes the needle in, millimeter by millimeter. She gets it exactly above where she thinks the vein should be sitting, and then she nudges it downward at a very shallow angle, trying to ease it into the vein. When a sudden drop of red flashes up into the needle she knows she's in the vein; she then has to advance the tiny little plastic tube, and she does it more gently than you would think any bone-weary person could. The short narrow pieces of tape go on, the flush goes in. The nurse is beginning to smile with relief (her arms and shoulders and back are painfully cramped). The rest of the tape is deployed strategically, the child's arm permanently adhesived to the arm board, the plastic tubing of the IV taped to his arm, to the board, anything to delay his pulling it all off. The IV is covered at the point where it enters the skin with a little clear plastic house, and then all of this is covered with a white cardboard cup, which in its turn is strapped on with quantities of tape. The mother is finally handed the child, who has finally calmed down a little and is probably plotting how he is going to get that cardboard cup off. The mother, who has recovered her good manners, actually manages to thank the intern. The nurse pats her on the shoulder and tells her, good job, go back to sleep. The intern throws the needles in the special needle-disposal box and then trudges back down the stairs to her on-call room. The theme song from Young Doctors in White does not swell up around her. She does not feel particularly cheerful. In her best judgment, the child needed the medicine. The child now has a new IV and will get the medicine. Someone else might have judged that the child could do without till morning. Someone else might have gotten the IV in on the first stick. The intern sighs and says out loud as she gets into bed, "Another day, another dollar."

Believe me, it is not fun to torture small children. It is, of course, not fun to torture adults either, but at least you can explain to them what you're doing and why you need to do it. And at least most adults have great big easily accessible veins. Small children are different. I used to say that I liked pediatrics because the children had such rational responses to everything—tell them it will hurt, and they cry and complain and kick and scream. All well and good and rational, but it doesn't really help you as you stand in the treatment room and watch two nurses pin a four-year-old down, ready for your ministrations. Generally, you aren't saving lives. You're just obtaining specimens of body fluids or starting IVs. You believe in what you're doing, you believe the child will ultimately be better off for what you did. But as you walk into that treatment room, it can be hard to feel all warm and fulfilled and philanthropic. So you find yourself saying to the patient, "There's going to be an owie"—or an ouchie, or a boo-boo, or a pokie, depending on your own dialect. And the child, sensibly, screams. And occasionally you find yourself repeating over and over to the child, as if it were an exceptionally comforting thought, "You know, I don't like owies either! Nobody likes owies!" And somewhere in your tired brain it seems to you that, what with one thing and another, this is a long way from Young Doctors in White.

THE PATIENT HATES YOU

There are people in this world, I know, who make it a principle to like everyone—at the least to give each new person the benefit of the doubt. I was once sent to a summer camp where an enormous sign dominated the dining hall: A STRANGER IS A FRIEND YOU HAVEN'T MET YET.

Well, I hated that summer camp. And though at the time I attributed it to a morbid fear of dodgeball, maybe the reason I hated the camp was that it was operating on what will always for me remain an alien ideology. I don't like everyone. I don't even *try* to like lots of people. When strangers with smiles come up to me on the street, I assume that they are trying to recruit me into unappetizing religions, and I respond accordingly.

And then there are the people everyone likes. The affable, the amiable, the people with winning personalities. Never has anyone ever suggested I belong in that category. I still remember, for example, the first patient who ever took a really strong dislike to me. I was a medical student and he was a grouchy older gentleman who wasn't particularly pleased to have me walk in and introduce myself. He quizzed me for a few minutes to see whether I was properly acquainted with the sixteen-year saga of his ailments, decided I was insufficiently prepared to care for him, announced that he didn't want "any more god-damn interfering lady doctors," and ordered me to get lost.

When I left the room, I was crushed. It had never occurred to me that I would be rejected by a patient. I mean, I was all set to function as a ministering angel, I was practically a doctor, on the side of right and reason, offering relief (or something like that—it does seem a long time ago). And here was a patient who looked at me with nothing but loathing. To make matters worse, I was working under the direction of a resident who refused to be pushed around by a patient, so I had to continue to serve as the person responsible for this patient's care. Further contact with me didn't make him love me better. Every day I went in and asked how he was doing. Every day he told me to get the hell out of his room. After this exchange of pleasantries, I would attempt to examine him, he would generally refuse, and then I would go and write a note in his chart, copying all his lab values off the computer.

After a few days, I hated him. I hated the thought of going into his room. I hated touching his body—I would have wished him dead except that his illness was so severe I knew such a wish had a reasonable chance of coming true, and didn't want to load myself with too much guilt.

That's not quite a fair story, of course. It's a story about a patient who disliked me for no good reason, a patient whom I disliked only because he behaved so badly toward me. And what I really mean to say is that a patient can dislike a doctor, or a doctor a patient, simply because their personalities don't mesh or because of some unfortunate happening that messes up the relationship. That's something that isn't acknowledged in medical training, and it makes a tremendous difference in caring for patients.

The reason that medical training doesn't take into account the doctor's feelings about the patient is that such feelings are supposed to be masked by professionalism. Now, this concept of professionalism is at once necessary and complex. It's true that the doctor sometimes has to function in defiance of normal human emotions. You watch people in pain, even dying, and you take it in some kind of stride. You cause pain, sticking needles into veins (or spines, or chests, or bladders), and it's all in a day's work. You examine noxious bodily fluids without recoiling. And if in any of those situations you acted like a normal human person, not a doctor, you would somehow be violating your professionalism. At least that's the idea. And just as you aren't supposed to be swayed by grief, or by disgust, you aren't supposed to be handicapped by dislike of any particular patient.

But the fact is, it's a lot easier to get up in the middle of the night to go to the bedside of someone toward whom you feel kindly. It's hard to be awakened with the news that a patient has a fever when the patient is someone you find irritating. That's one of the reasons I went into pediatrics—I tend to like most children.

But say I get up in the middle of the night and go in to see this seventeen-year-old girl, and she's sick, and I'm the doctor and I need to take care of her, but she's also a brat and a half, and she whines all the time, and she looks at me with this bored, disgusted expression whenever I talk to her, and —what can I say—I just don't like her. I know she's young and she's very sick and it's very sad, but I just don't like her. I can manage to do my job, and maybe I don't even mind sticking all those needles into her as much as I would mind sticking someone I liked—but there's also no question that I don't pursue her interests with the same enthusiasm I would have if I really liked her. I mean, I take care of her medically, but you don't find me chasing down extra-special physical therapists for her, setting her up with clinic doctors I think are absolutely fantastic, or even spending any extra time in her room chatting and trying to cheer her up.

I can make myself do a reasonably good job with patients I dislike. The interesting thing is that I still find it hard to cope when a patient doesn't like me. I've come a long way since that patient who rejected me when I was a medical student, and I've come to terms with not liking some of my patients, but I still have trouble allowing them the same rights. I still take it personally.

I remember a child I took care of. I liked him immediately, and I felt deeply sorry for him; he was a ten-year-old who had been very sick for a long time. He was a thin child with a beautiful face, bright and gentle. I liked him and I wanted him to like me. I wanted to ease his pain, take good care of him, make him a little bit better, if that could be done. I had all the right impulses. And then one night when he was very sick, I had to start an IV and draw blood from him. And because it was one of those unlucky nights, and because he had been in the hospital too much and all his veins were used and overused, I had to stick him too many times, make too many attempts to get the IV going, too many tries to get the blood.

After that he wouldn't speak to me. He had started out being brave about the IV, holding out his arm and clenching his teeth, and by the end he was screaming, begging, no more, please don't. He hated me for having tried all those times, for having seen him break down like that. He simply wouldn't speak to me; he turned his head away when I came into his room. Whenever a test had to be done, he asked, with deep distrust, "Is *she* going to do it?" pointing at me, and his parents hastened to assure him that no, some other doctor would do it.

I grew to dread seeing him. I knew that my problems with his veins hadn't occurred because I was a bad doctor, but going into his room made me feel like an utter failure. It was particularly depressing because I really did want to help, to make him better. And his was a complex case, so I was spending hours in meetings to decide on treatment, in conferences where he was discussed. In all these situations, I would speak about his case, function as the doctor taking care of him—and I would feel like a fraud. I would wonder if the people listening to me knew that this patient I was discussing wouldn't even acknowledge my existence.

As his hospitalization progressed, I understood intellectually that he was making me a scapegoat, that he was blaming me for all the pain he was undergoing, for the turn for the worse his illness was taking. I could have analyzed it all quite cogently to a psychiatrist if we had called one in to see him—

or to see me. And yet I still felt terrible whenever I had to go in and examine him. I still felt, I guess, that if I were a better doctor my patient would like me.

The "doctor-patient relationship," I suppose, is assumed to go on between two all-purpose figures, devoid of personality, devoid of preferences. The patient is sick, a composite of symptoms, lab values, medical problems, and the doctor is an agent of medical knowledge. Their relationship proceeds smoothly along the path of medical therapy, and they're kept firmly on course by the doctor's professionalism and the patient's appropriate gratitude. It isn't like that over here in the real world, of course, and I suppose it's more interesting, even if frequently disconcerting. I just have to keep reminding myself of that summer camp.

JUDGING

A baby is admitted to the hospital. The reason for the admission was one of the most common everyday diagnoses in pediatrics. D & D, the nurse abbreviated it on the admission sheet: dehydration and diarrhea. Babies, because they are so small, don't have a whole lot of fluid in them. If they lose more than usual, because of diarrhea, and they don't take in extra to balance it, they can very quickly become dehydrated, even over a matter of hours.

And if they get dehydrated, babies start to look sick, uncomfortable, lethargic. And if they get sufficiently dehydrated, they die. Fortunately, if they get fluid, either orally or intravenously, they do just fine. So in developed countries, this is a frequent reason to hospitalize a baby. In the third world, it's a frequent cause of death: over 25 percent of all deaths in children under five, worldwide, are caused by diarrhea.

So this baby is admitted. She is a very little baby, only

*one month old, and her name is Marie. She has had diar-
rhea for a day and a half. The emergency room doctor
estimates that Marie has lost a little more than 10 percent
of her body weight from dehydration; her eyes are slightly
sunken back into her head, the inside of her mouth is tacky
to the touch rather than wet, and the skin on her belly is
a little bit looser and more flaccid than it would be on a
properly hydrated baby. The emergency room doctor sends
off samples of her blood for various tests, puts an intravenous
line into her arm, and starts running in fluid as fast as
he can. Then he calls upstairs to tell me, the intern on call,
to come on down and admit the baby.*

*Marie's mother, Donna, looking frightened, sits by
the baby's bedside and answers my questions as well as she
can. Donna can't remember when she last changed a wet
diaper. She thinks the baby usually takes four ounces of
formula at a feeding; today she's been taking less than half
that much. The mother speaks softly, as if she's afraid her
answers are somehow wrong. She twists her hands together.
As I lean forward to hear her better, I notice how washed
out and exhausted Donna looks—and how young.*

"Do you have anyone at home to help you out?" I ask.

*"I live with my mother—but she wasn't there last
night."*

"How about the baby's father?"

*Donna just shakes her head. I ask one final question.
"How old are you?"*

"I'm seventeen. Well, in two weeks I'll be seventeen."

Should I have started wondering, there and then, whether
Marie's mother was really able to take care of her? Maybe, but
I certainly didn't. I can tell you exactly what was on my mind
as I finished questioning Donna and then examined the baby,
wrote out my orders for the nurses, and then hurried away. I
was thinking through the baby's medical problem, calculating
how much fluid and what kind to give her to replace what she

had lost, and thinking all the time, in the back of my mind, that I had to hurry upstairs again and check on a four-year-old boy with asthma whose breathing seemed to be getting worse. I did scribble on my admission note, under Social History, "baby lives with 16-yr-old mother and maternal GM. Family will need support during hospitalization."

Marie gets better quickly. The liquid flows into her vein all night, and her body recovers from its extreme state of stress and dryness. The nurses watch her closely, monitoring her pulse, which slows down as the volume of blood in her circulation expands back to normal, so her heart no longer has to pump so quickly. They note on the nursing record that three hours after admission, Marie finally does urinate—proof that she finally has enough water in her body to let go of some of it.

I come by and examine Marie. In my note, I record that Marie is now noticeably more alert than she was on admission, that she is awake and comfortable, and her eyes are no longer sunken. She is, however, still having diarrhea—and the nurses record each diaper change.

And they also note something else: Donna went home as soon as her baby was admitted and didn't come back. She doesn't call, she doesn't come in, all through the next day. And when she finally does come back, Marie's nurse doesn't like her looks. She goes and gets another nurse, asks her to come see. Donna is sitting in a rocking chair next to the baby's crib, but she isn't holding her baby. She's staring straight ahead, with a spaced-out look on her face. When the nurses come in to say the baby's doing much better, the mother seems jittery, on edge, and also somehow distant. They aren't sure she's listening, they aren't sure she's understanding. They ask if she'd like to give Marie a bottle, but she says, no, I have to be going. You do it. And then she goes.

The nurses talk it over that evening at change of shift.

*A sixteen-year-old mother. Only came in once, and stayed
only twenty minutes. A grandmother who hasn't come in
at all. Father of baby not on the scene. Mother seemed like
she might have been on drugs. Mother didn't even pick up
the baby. Finally they agree to bring it up on morning
rounds: they're worried about this baby, about whether her
home is a safe place for her to go back to after this hospitalization. They're worried that this baby may be at risk,
that there is a high likelihood of abuse or at least neglect.*

When Marie's primary nurse brought the subject up with
me the next day, I have to admit I felt a little chagrined—I
had interviewed this mother, admitted this baby, and I hadn't
had the sense to be worried. Now, hearing the nurse describe
the home situation back to me, it seemed obvious that we had
at least to ask the question.

I also felt a little irritated. Interns are always swamped
with work, always glad to take care of a few straightforward
patients who can be counted on to respond to therapy properly,
get better, and go home. And now here was one of my straightforward cases, a kid I had described on morning rounds in a
two-minute burst of abbreviations and medical slang ("one-
month-old with D & D times 36 hours, came into the ER 10-
15 percent dry . . ."), and the nurses were trying to complicate
things. They were turning my straightforward D & D into a
social service problem, and social service problems are notoriously messy, difficult to straighten out, time-consuming, full
of ambiguity.

What was the question to be answered? The question was,
should we, the doctors and nurses caring for this baby, file a
petition (in Massachusetts, called a 51A) with the state department of social services, claiming that we thought Marie
was a child at risk? In theory, a 51A is supposed to be seen as
an application for services. When you file, you are notifying
the state that there is a family in need of help. In theory, there
is no stigma. In fact, a 51A is widely perceived as a direct

accusation of child abuse, both in the hospital ("You know, I heard a 51A was filed on this mother once," someone might contribute on morning rounds, and from then on, we all look at the family differently) and in the community at large, especially the poor inner-city community.

If we did decide to file, the result would be that a social worker would immediately be assigned to investigate Marie's home situation, and would have to decide whether our worry was warranted. Anyone who is worried about the welfare of a child can set this process in motion. The investigation itself is of course a difficult thing; how can you look at a home and tell whether a child is likely to be abused or neglected in that home? You have to be very sure you aren't just ruling against poverty, against the stark details of lives without privilege and comfort.

I have filed the occasional 51A. I filed once when a mother seemed to be absolutely nuts and was in the habit of roaming the hospital halls, carrying on loud conversations with God, half dialogues involving much blood and violence. I was quite literally afraid to let her son go home with her. I have filed my share of the 51As we submit on children who have been beaten, babies who have been shaken to the point of brain damage. But I've also been involved with families where the issues were much less clear-cut, and seen how those families can be torn apart by the accusation. I remember a couple whose toddler had been near death after drinking tainted water. There wasn't any suspicion that the child had been deliberately poisoned, but the hospital social workers decided that the accident might have been the result of parental neglect, and filed a 51A. This destroyed the parents' trust in the hospital, left them feeling they had been attacked when they were most vulnerable, and generally made for a bad situation. Generally, I guess, I don't like to file unless I'm absolutely positive there is evidence of abuse or neglect, unless I really feel that there is no alternative.

So I said I wasn't willing to file the petition, based on what we'd seen so far, and the primary nurse agreed. Our plan was that since we would be keeping Marie in the hospital for a couple more days, until her diarrhea resolved and she was no longer in danger of drying out again, we would just keep a close eye on the mother during that time, watch how she dealt with her baby, and come to a decision.

Donna comes to visit her baby once a day. She doesn't stay very long, and she seems reluctant to pick the baby up or feed her. Marie is now chowing down fairly energetically; she can empty a baby bottle in less than ten minutes. Finally, after a nurse almost insists, Donna does take the baby, settles down in the rocking chair, and feeds her. And after she feeds her, she burps her, quite competently, and then rocks her to sleep. To the nurse, checking on her occasionally from the door, Donna looks relaxed for the first time. In fact, she looks so relaxed that the next time the nurse comes in to check, Donna is asleep herself in the rocker. The nurse, bending down to take the baby from her, wonders whether she smells alcohol.

The nurses record everything, carefully. The length of the visits, the behavior of the mother—everything is noted down in deliberately descriptive, nonjudgmental language. "Mother in, sat with baby for ten minutes. Invited to give bath, but said no." Like that. The nurses and the doctors are all what is called mandated reporters: if they suspect child abuse or neglect, they are mandated by law to report it to the state. Other mandated reporters include teachers and social workers—anyone whose profession involves attention to the welfare of children. As mandated reporters, all the people taking care of Marie are immune from any penalty; they cannot be sued for filing the petition, even if it is not substantiated by the state. They have nothing to fear, for themselves.

But the evidence here is ambiguous. And the nurses find themselves reviewing Donna's behavior more carefully than anyone should actually be monitored, worrying over

whether or not she knows what she's doing with her baby.
The fourth day of the hospitalization, Donna shows up with
an expensive new mobile, which she hangs over the baby's
crib. But she doesn't seem to notice that Marie has just
had another episode of diarrhea, and doesn't change her
diaper, until a nurse comes in and suggests it. But then,
she does change the diaper, efficiently and gently. But then,
she doesn't go on holding her baby, just puts her back down
in the crib. And she leaves after only fifteen minutes, and
leaves the side of the crib down, so the baby could fall out
—and when a nurse speaks to her in the hallway, she doesn't
seem to hear—is she high on something?

The truth is, I hated this, and so did most of the nurses,
I think. There we were, keeping track of that mother's every
move, peeking in to see whether she was touching her baby,
whether she was behaving properly. We all like to see ourselves
as allied with the families we care for, helping parents to understand their children's illnesses, helping the children get better, sending everyone home in triumph. We use words like
empowering, enabling, supporting. And then to find ourselves
spying on a mother, looking for evidence to use against her
—it made us all uncomfortable. And yet, of course, we also
saw ourselves first and foremost as the child's advocates. Everyone who works in pediatrics has seen children damaged, neglected, even seriously hurt by their parents. We didn't want
to make a mistake and send Marie out into a home that wasn't
safe.

On Marie's fourth day in the hospital, a meeting is
held. The two nurses who take care of her most regularly
describe their concerns. A hospital social worker is present,
and agrees that the situation is worrisome. It is not, how-
ever, conclusive, and it happens that I have also uncovered
some objective evidence that, in fact, Donna is doing a good
job with her baby. I called up the neighborhood health

center where Marie gets her regular pediatric care, and am now able to report several things. Number one, Donna brought her baby in right on time for the two-week-old appointment. Number two, she called in as soon as the diarrhea started, and got advice about what to do. True, she couldn't follow the advice successfully, which is to say that the baby's loss of fluid got ahead of her ability to replace it, but still, that happens to a lot of people. I find myself dwelling on this point: Marie is not hospitalized for anything which suggests that she was neglected; she is not a baby who was allowed to dehydrate over days and days while her mother did nothing. Her mother called for help, tried to follow directions, and when she couldn't, brought her baby to the emergency room. It could happen to anyone.

Still, says the social worker, young mother, maybe on drugs, doesn't come in much to visit her baby—

I know, I say. But it's also, young mother, doing her best, keeping her doctor's appointment. Do we really want to undermine her?

No one has an answer. No one feels comfortable about this baby's home, about this mother's competence. But no one is sure what the right thing to do would be. We agree to have one more meeting, on hospital day seven; Marie will be ready to go home, and a decision will have to be made.

And by day seven, Marie really is ready to go. In fact, one alarming sign is that Donna hasn't demanded to take her home yet; Marie is obviously well. Her skin has fully recovered its silky baby plumpness, and she lies on her back and gurgles. She's a lovely little baby, with an adorable dimpled fist in her mouth, sucking away. Her hair curls over her forehead, and if anyone gives her a finger, she holds on for dear life.

People who work with babies—nurses and doctors—are all prone to the occasional rescue fantasy. You look down at this delightful child, cute and appealing and full of bright-eyed alertness, and you face the fact that you are sending this child out into a home which is very far from ideal. So when I looked at Marie, who was all better, who was all ready to go home and soak up love and affection, and I thought about what was probably waiting for her, part of me just wanted to say, forget it, I'll take her home myself and do it right.

I mean, she was obviously going out into a bad situation. The social worker had talked to Donna, and gotten a picture of a home which could most kindly be described as chaotic, with a grandmother who was often away, a grandfather who was no longer allowed to visit—there was a restraining order against him because he had been known to beat up his wife and daughter. There was also a changing cast of cousins and nieces and nephews passing through; there was not much money; and there was Donna herself, often spacey, questionably competent with her daughter, and only sixteen.

On the other hand. On the other hand. She *did* come to visit the baby, even if not as often as we would have liked; she *had* brought the baby to the pediatrician, called in when the baby got sick; she *was* the baby's mother. And filing a child-at-risk petition would seem to her an attack on everything she had managed to do, would be a message that she had been judged and found wanting. And we weren't, any of us, doctors or nurses, actually going to take that bright-eyed little baby home and rescue her. If she didn't stay with her mother, the state would put her into foster care—which is not necessarily a wonderful solution either.

That's one of the most unsatisfying things about this whole system of reporting and investigating children at risk. If the department of social services feels that the home is unsafe, they go to court and ask for custody of the child. Then they often place the child in foster care, and then it's really the luck of the draw. Children may move from foster home to foster home, or may bounce back and forth between their parents and foster parents. Even if parents are not really adequate, they love their children and their children love them in return. Taking a child out of its home can destroy that child's world.

And the flip side of the rescue fantasy is this: you take care of these kids in the hospital, you spend days and nights involved with every detail of body function, and even family function, and then you never find out what happens to them. My job was to take care of the kids when they were acutely ill, and every day I met new children with complicated medical problems, complicated social situations. There was no way for me to keep track of them after they left the hospital; it was someone else's job. But instead of rescuing Marie, the reality was that I was going to make whatever interventions I made in her life (clumsily, with all good intentions), and then very likely never see her again.

> *The final meeting is held, to make the decision. As often happens, the group has enlarged; the social worker has called in the hospital lawyer to advise on the issue of custody. The two nurses have asked the head nurse to be present. And I have called in the resident. The case is outlined by me, and I again find myself going to some trouble to indicate that this baby was admitted for a normal common ailment, that there was no mismanagement by the mother involved. The nurses outline their observations, their worries. The social worker expresses her concern—she obviously favors filing a 51A. And she suggests that since it would be filed during a hospitalization, it would really carry much more weight if it was signed by a doctor—that is, by me.*
>
> *I don't want to do it. There hasn't been any neglect, from a medical point of view, I say, yet again. Then I come out with my real anxiety: this baby's best chance, when all is said and done, is probably with her mother. Not in the foster care system, not with some other relative—her best chance is if her mother grows up, learns how to care for her properly, takes control. What we want to do is help her*

mother do that, not undermine it right now, at one month of age. This mother brought her baby to us for help, and it was the appropriate thing to do—do we now turn around and use it against her?

One of the nurses agrees; the other doesn't. I'm worried, she keeps saying, I'm worried what that baby will look like the next time we see her.

Finally, a compromise is hammered out. No petition will be filed; no one is willing to sign it if I refuse to. On the other hand, no one is comfortable just discharging this baby and waving good-bye. With the cooperation of the neighborhood health center, a plan is set up whereby Donna will have to bring Marie in once a week, to be weighed and measured and generally checked out. This will allow the pediatricians to keep very close tabs on the baby's growth and development, and to intervene if it isn't going well. It's the kind of program these health centers often institute themselves to keep tabs on babies when they're worried; since they need to preserve good relations with the communities they serve, they try not to jump too quickly to filing the stigmatizing 51A. If Donna misses an appointment without calling to reschedule, it will be considered a danger sign; if she misses more than one, it will be considered medical neglect, and a 51A will be filed. And all this will be explained to Donna, carefully, before she takes her baby home.

I went over it with Donna, twice. I said, we can see you have a lot on your plate, we can see you're under a lot of stress. I said, I think you've been doing a really good job, I know you got Marie to her first doctor's appointment, you got her in here when she was sick. I know you love her. But it's hard taking care of a baby all alone, especially when you're young yourself. So to help, we're going to ask the neighborhood health center to be very involved. . . . And so I went on and on. And finally told her if she missed an appointment, it would show that she wasn't managing, that the baby wasn't getting all the care she needed, so it was important to keep the appointments. Donna said she understood. I told her what would happen if she missed more than one appointment, and she said she understood. Then she gathered up Marie's possessions, and took her baby home.

I don't know whether she kept her appointments faithfully at the health center, whether she missed one, whether she missed two, whether the baby grew and developed properly. I do know that Marie didn't come back to the hospital where I work. Didn't turn up dead, didn't even come in sick. But there are lots of other hospitals, and there are lots of children who aren't doing very well, but stay out of the hospital. Did I worry that Marie wasn't safe at home? Yes. Did the nurses? Yes. Marie must be four years old by now, and Donna is twenty. Marie should be walking, talking, a little girl by now, and not a baby anymore. And Donna should be a seasoned mother, well accustomed to caring for her daughter in sickness and in health. I hope they're both okay, and I hope that we all did the right thing, both by interfering as much as we did and by holding back, at the end, and trusting to the two of them to get each other through.

CHEST COMPRESSIONS

The good thing about pediatrics is that almost all of your patients get better. The bad thing is that sometimes they die.

When I started my internship, I had never seen a child die. Not up close, anyway. Even in the hospital, children just don't die all that often. My third or fourth night on call, I ended up at a code, an arrest, a hospital emergency. When word comes over the public address system and many beepers go off in unison and everyone starts running, that's a code. By the time I got there, the little girl was already surrounded by seven doctors, so there wasn't much for me to do; I had been called to bring a new electrocardiograph machine, since the one they had was malfunctioning. So I wheeled the machine in, and then I hung around on the sidelines, wondering whether I could be of any help. But the work was all being done by experts; surgeons were putting in the IV lines, an anesthesiologist was preparing to put in a breathing tube, a cardiologist was watching the electrocardiogram. There were other people hanging around, unwilling to leave while the child's fate was still undecided, and it was from them that I got the story.

Six-year-old girl run over by hit-and-run driver. Brought into emergency room. Very badly hurt but seemed stable. They were taking her up to the operating room and she coded in the hallway. The resuscitation effort was heroic. Everything was being done that could possibly help, and we all knew why. A couple of hours ago, this was a healthy six-year-old with a life expectancy of seventy or more years. And therefore the code was prolonged well past the point where anyone believed it was really going to help. But there was finally an end; there was no bringing this little girl back. The machines were turned off, the doctors moved away from the bed, and a couple of nurses came and cleaned up the body, pulled out all the tubes. "Are her parents here yet?" one of them asked. "No, she was found on the road, brought in by ambulance," said one of the surgeons. "Her parents were called, and they're on their way to the hospital."

And there we were, looking at a child's face, at blond hair with a red plastic barrette in it. I had never seen a child die before. Everyone was upset; everyone had to go back to work for the rest of the night. Some people talked for a minute or two about what had happened medically—why had she suddenly coded? Other people talked for a minute or two about what they would have liked to do to the hit-and-run driver. "We could have another code," one of them said. Eventually, the little group of doctors and nurses gathered for the code dispersed; I went back up to my floor and sat in the on-call room, and tried, you might say, to process the experience.

It was 2 A.M. I have various close friends, but none of them, I suspected, really wanted to be awakened at 2 A.M. to hear the details of a child's death. Finally I called a friend in California, where it was only eleven, a doctor friend, so I could go into medical detail. And after all, I thought, thank God I didn't even know the other kind of detail: what her name was, what she liked to play, what she was afraid of, even what she wanted to be when she grew up. Thank God it wasn't me waiting downstairs to meet the parents, I thought, knowing it would be me one of these days.

Nobody can watch a child die, I suppose, and take it calmly. It's unnatural for children to die. When I did adult medicine, many of the deaths were such evident and over-whelmingly merciful releases that it was possible to accept them calmly. Doctors often got frustrated because they felt *they* had lost a battle, that the patient's death reflected some failure of medical skill. But you could feel that medical defeat, and at the same time feel a sense of human acceptance, or something like that. With children, except in the rare cases of chronic merciless disease, it isn't like that. In fact, it's just the opposite: you may feel able to accept the sequence of events from a medical point of view, understanding that the child was too badly hurt to live, but you still feel outraged.

When I started my internship, I had never seen a child die. Obviously, I had also never been the doctor standing by the bed when a child was getting sicker. I worried a lot about what I would do when that happened. During orientation, we got various bits of advice: give the kid oxygen, call for help, try not to faint.

I listened to the scare stories. "I know this guy, in a pe-diatrics program in another hospital. And his very first night, his very first admission was a little boy who suddenly started to bleed out of his mouth and nose while the intern was talking to him."

"Oh, my God! I wouldn't have the faintest idea what to do! What did this guy do?"

"He cranked up the bed so that the boy's feet were higher up than his head, and then he went and sat outside in the corridor and cried." (The feet-higher-than-the-head position encourages blood flow to the brain.)

"Are you kidding?"

"No, that's what he did. And actually, it turned out to be a good thing to do, because he attracted a lot of attention, and some senior residents came and helped the kid out."

"Okay," I said, relieved to have one possible course of action all mapped out. Feet-higher-than-head, cry-in-corridor. I ought to be able to manage that. But I was lucky. There was no emergency my first night, and by the time one happened to me, I had seen enough to know what to do. I gave oxygen; I called for help. I gave some extra fluids. I asked the nurses to get some important medications ready. And then help showed up, and the child, of course, pretended he hadn't been the least bit sick. But I know what to do if they look as if they might be dying. That, however, is different from seeing them die.

Late one night I was in the intensive care unit. A baby was close to dying, and two doctors much senior to me were trying to bring her back. They asked me to give chest compressions while they handled the medications and all the rest of the resuscitation. I put my hands around the baby's chest, my fingertips meeting behind her back, and with my thumbs I pressed down on her chest, counting inside my head, trying for 120 compressions per minute. I had done it on a plastic doll. I had done it on a real adult. But I had never done it on a real baby. The heart monitor showed what I was doing; I could see the cardiac action I was generating with my compressions, and I could see it trail away to nothing when I stopped so that the other doctors could check the pulse. I concentrated on that baby's chest, on the feel of flexible cartilage going down under my fingers, on the waves of electrical activity I was generating on the monitor screen, on the rhythm I was counting. I didn't try to get to know the baby. I saw details, of course; I saw the recently cut umbilical cord of the newborn and the dark fine hair and the tiny perfect toes. "Ten fingers, ten toes," we assure parents in the delivery room, and I wondered whether someone had said that to this girl's parents—before it became apparent that other, more important things were wrong inside.

I continued the chest compressions. Medicines were given, blood samples were sent, results came back from the lab. My thumbs began to ache, and someone else took my place, and then later on I took over again. I knew that I would absolutely know for the future, with or without a cardiac monitor attached, how to compress a baby's chest. And I was the one who was doing the compressions when the code ended, when they called it off, when they gave up. Again, it had gone on well past the point where anyone believed it would work. When a baby is born with a badly malformed heart, when that heart cannot pump enough blood to vital organs, and several body systems fail at once—well, there are sometimes situations where there's nothing anyone can do. Still, I was the one who stopped compressing the chest.

The nurses came to clean the baby up. One of the doctors went off to call the parents. The other went over all the details of the code with me, teaching me the lessons I needed to learn, and also reassuring me, and himself, that everything had been done that could have been done. There wasn't any hit-and-run driver to be angry with. If we could have pulled that baby through, we were both thinking, maybe some of her problems could have been fixed, maybe she could have gone on to grow up. That's worth fighting for, right? So you fight for it. And sometimes you win, sometimes you don't. Sometimes they die.

DYING

You know the joke about the king's close friend, convicted of a terrible crime, who was granted the boon of choosing just how he would die—and asked to die of old age.

It's a bit ghoulish, but most of us who work in hospitals end up with lists, formal or informal, of the ways we would like to die. You can't work that close to death without coming to some accommodation, however uneasy: OK, I have to die eventually, and I'm not looking forward to it—but this kind of death, and not that kind, please.

When I was a medical student, the choice was almost always a quick and catastrophic heart attack. Drop dead in your tracks, out of the hospital. No chance of resuscitation, no half-life in the intensive care unit. Go from being well to being—well, whatever it is that comes after.

When you start to think about death, especially with the extra knowledge you get from the hospital, you realize there are the fantasy deaths, and then there are the reality deaths. True, you may not actively fantasize about dying, but there are comforting images that attach to death and beautify it, even sanctify it. One common fantasy is to die in your own home, peaceful and comfortable, surrounded by the people you love best. Gently, you breathe your last breath. My own sensibility was highly affected by certain series of girls' books—the *Anne of Green Gables* series, for example. In those books, set in rural Canada at the turn of the century, death scenes were fairly common. Women regularly watched at deathbeds, old sailors went out with the morning tide. In *Emily's Quest*, the third in the Emily series (by Lucy Maud Montgomery, also author of the Anne books), the title character goes to the deathbed of the elderly teacher she loves. Her aunt explains to her, " 'He is old and tired. His wife has gone—they will not give him the school another year. His old age would be very lonely. Death is his best friend.' "

And so Emily, who is of course a budding writer, bends over the dying Mr. Carpenter, who has a last message for her but can't quite remember it:

"As Emily bent over him the keen, shaggy-browed eyes opened for the last time. Mr. Carpenter essayed a wink but could not compass it."

" 'I've—thought of it,' he whispered. 'Beware—of—italics.' "

"Was there a little impish chuckle at the end of the words? Aunt Louisa always declared there was. Graceless old Mr. Carpenter had died laughing—saying something about Italians. Of course he was delirious. But Aunt Louisa always felt it had been a very unedifying deathbed. She was thankful that few such had come in her experience."

And there it is, perfectly appropriate for a girls' book. No deep wisdom, carefully adjusted by child development specialists to help young people deal with death, just death of a character, dying in character. Blunt and matter-of-fact, but who wouldn't want to die with an impish chuckle? The point is, in the fantasy, to die in your own home, of old age, and to die in character.

Reality deaths are something else again. Death in the hospital is rarely serene. And virtually no one gets to die in character.

How do people die? Well, there are a variety of ways. You can die gasping for air, choking to death. That isn't generally considered a desirable death. You can suffer a cardiac arrest in the hospital and die in a code, a crowd of doctors and nurses losing the heroic struggle to keep you alive. You can slip quite peacefully from coma into death—but who would choose to go out in a coma in the first place? You can bleed to death, which is generally agreed to be a death not too unpleasant for the patient, but horrible for anyone standing near and watching. And so on. You get the idea. It's a gruesome catalogue, but it's an inevitable list to find yourself making when your work involves witnessing many deaths.

So I admit this patient, and she's dying. She's young, but her lung disease is terrible and irreversible, and she's in a lot of pain. Whenever I go in to see her, she asks me to take the pain away, help her die sooner. Both of us know she won't leave the hospital alive. I watch her struggling for each breath, and I find myself thinking, this is not how I would like to die. So I propose to put the patient on a morphine drip, to infuse her with fairly heavy-duty narcotics, keep her comfortable and relatively happy. The only thing is, morphine may depress her respiratory effort, may bring her closer, however gently, to the moment of her death. At first I find this a little hard to deal with emotionally. (In my head are the endless ethical dilemmas of medicine—would you actually be willing to inject her with poison, and if not, isn't it hypocritical to give her a nonpoison that will probably cause her death?) But I find that I'm willing to give the morphine without resolving the dilemma.

Along comes the doctor who has cared for my patient for years. I tell him I'm going to start a morphine drip, and he gets upset. My patient isn't as badly off as all that, he says. If I'd known her for years I'd see that she often has episodes like this—though never anything nearly this bad. No, says this doctor, no morphine drip. Now, of course it's a lot easier for me to contemplate her death, seeing her as she is today, than it is for someone who has known her well, seen her spiral down from healthy to sick. For that doctor, this morphine drip I propose wouldn't be solely a merciful intervention. It would in all probability mean saying good-bye to someone he has known for a long time.

And there's another thing about morphine. To get my patient really comfortable, I may have to, as we say, gork her out. She may lose her lucidity. Of course, she has her lucidity right now, and she's using it to plead for pain medicines. But still, if you give enough morphine, it's hard for the patient to die in character, and I'm by no means the only one in the world who thinks that's important. Would I in the end prefer the pain and the clearheadedness?

We delay the morphine; she gets another day of lucidity and pain. Then she gets worse, gets morphine, and dies that night.

Another patient I took care of was dying. All different body systems were failing. His brain was destroyed. Heroic measures had been tried again and again. There was nowhere to go. It was just a question of time. And I found myself locked in endless discussions with family and nurses about trying to orchestrate the death. We wanted to give him the best death we properly could. With the nurses I discussed the details of ways he could die; he could bleed to death, which we agreed would be unbearable for his family. He could get an infection—would we chase it, try to identify the bug, try to treat it? We all knew there was no hope of recovery, we all knew the end was near, and we wanted to leave the family with a picture of peace, suffering's end. And the nitty-gritty of that goal was the careful death planning.

I don't particularly like thinking about my own death. Unfortunately, my job pushes those thoughts at me. I find that it isn't uncommon for me to ask myself, what would I want if it were *my* child. And inevitably, what would I want if it were *my* death?

For years, before I ever started medical school, I had a very particular picture of how I was going to die. I find that I'm too superstitious to write down all the details, even now —if I write it down, then it will happen, right? Or else I'll die in some completely alien way, and everyone will know that it wasn't my death of choice, because I went and told the world about my death fantasy. So I'll merely say it's a fantasy that's triggered when I see those little fillers they run in newspapers: BUS PLUNGES OFF EMBANKMENT IN PAKISTAN.

But let's face it—what this superstition about describing my own death really reflects is that I'm still unwilling to face my own death, head-to-head. Somehow, somewhere, I will cease to be—and, despite all my theoretical applications of what I see in the hospital to my own life and death, I just can't process the information.

The interesting side to all this is that I suspect that the very old and the very sick often feel the same way I do. They may know many of the rules of the road, they may know how they'll die—but they aren't ready to come to terms with death, any more than I am. The healthy, watching the sick in the hospital, tend to announce that they hope someone will shoot them before they get as sick as so-and-so. But perspective shifts, and you end up with a critically ill patient who isn't interested in any planning for the possibility of death.

Needless to say, you don't get to choose your death. I think of good deaths and bad deaths in the hospital sense now, and I judge many of my decisions against my what-I-would-want-done-for-me index. There's an unexpected familiarity with death that comes with the job I do, one that still shocks me at times. But you see deaths and you cope with deaths and at times you even orchestrate deaths, and you think a little about how you might face your own. What you might die from. And you know, old age still isn't a bad answer.

4

Home Front

In my group of interns, there were a couple of men with young children. Frequently, one or the other would be trying to get out early, to be there to take a baby to a pediatrician's appointment, to be home in time for playtime, before bedtime. I cannot tell you how much I resented these men, good doctors and devoted fathers. What I resented was how laudable, how delightful, how downright adorable everyone thought it was that they wanted to go home and see their children. How the nurses smiled when one admitted he was late because the baby was just so cute this morning he couldn't tear himself away.

Of course, that's probably not how these men remember it. They probably remember it much as I do, a year when they didn't know much about their children, when their children lived on some uncomfortable periphery. I found I was constantly asking Larry to fill me in on our son's routines, which changed subtly from week to week. Subtlety was lost on me; I was too tired, or too grumpy, or in too much of a hurry.

I was determined, of course, in my pigheaded way, that I would ask for no special favors just because I was a mother with a two-year-old at home. When I wanted to leave early, I would say that I had to go pick up my car from the garage. When I was late, I would blame it on traffic. My child would be seen strictly as an asset, the source of all my real-world knowledge of pediatrics (at a lecture on pet-related injuries and diseases, a doctor asked a group of interns how old we thought a child should be before he was allowed a dog of his own. The other interns, none of whom had children, proposed ages from six to ten years old. I was the only one who held out for sixteen years old or more). There would be no tsk-tsking over me, no sense that I was torn between hospital and home, to the detriment of both.

What nonsense. Of course I was torn. Anyone would be torn; internship doesn't leave you enough time, and enough wakefulness, to be much use to your child. So I made a big deal of working when I was sick, saving my sick days (not that interns have sick days) to use in case Benjamin got sick.

I left the house every morning before Larry and Benjamin woke up. As I went through morning rounds at the hospital, I would imagine them getting up slowly, imagine Larry putting Benjamin into a dry diaper and a pair of overalls with snaps along the crotch, picture them making their way to the day-care center. During the day I would occasionally try to picture Benjamin at day care—but for the first time, I didn't know what the room was like, couldn't picture the kids at play, didn't know the teachers. In the afternoon, Larry would pick him up, and they would go home and wait for me, and I would start calling from the hospital: "I think I'll be done in about half an hour," I would say. "I can't wait to see you." "We can't wait to see *you*," Larry would say politely. Forty-five minutes later, they would in fact still be waiting to see me. I would call again. "Hi, I'm sorry, something came up. But now I really am almost done, I should be out of here in five minutes." And then one more call: "God, I can't believe I'm still here. But all I have to do is finish this one note and I'll be starting home. . . ."

WHINE LIST

I feel a little silly and more than a little stilted saying it, but I know that one of the reasons I went to medical school was that I wanted to help people. It was (and is) a perfectly reasonable ambition, a strong motivation to push you through a demanding and sometimes draining educational process, but it's also the kind of thing you start to feel self-conscious about. When you write your application essay for medical school, you have to try to find a new and original way to say that you want to help people. I used to advise students who were applying to medical school, and I used to have to read their essays, and there it would be, in statements ranging from the pompous and grandiose ("I feel I have a great deal to contribute to humanity and that medicine is the best arena for me to make that contribution . . .") to the high-flown and dramatic ("To cure illness! To ease pain! To help the suffering!"). So you can get to feel, after a while, that there is something a little shallow, a little put-on, about your desire to be of use, to minister to people in pain, and you explain your ambition in less altruistic terms, terms that are somehow more comfortable and less glib for everyday discourse.

Still, like just about everyone who goes into medicine, I wanted to help people. I wanted a career where I would be truly needed, where I would make a difference in people's lives (if this were an application essay, I would have to tell the applicant that the wording was more than a little clichéd). And you know what? I found it. I have a job now where I am truly and profoundly needed, where people depend on me in a way

I never even really imagined. And you know what else? I feel needed as well in my life outside the hospital. And you know what else? There are times when it comes close to driving me crazy.

I am right now an intern in pediatrics. I work about a hundred hours a week taking care of children in the hospital. I have a home of my own as well, and a three-year-old son named Benjamin, who is about the cutest thing that ever walked the earth (in my unbiased opinion as a pediatrician, that is). There are a great many details involved in balancing all this, and, to be perfectly frank, most of them are not of tremendous interest. I am tired of reading articles about how someone, usually a woman (occasionally even me), manages to juggle her child, her job. These details are admittedly the very stuff of life, but they are also just that—details. They are the questions of who will bring the kid to day care or will you have someone live in and what about laundry, and they are minutiae which everyone has to work out; but if you care enough about what you do, then you work them out. In my own case, I know that I am in the middle of a uniquely difficult year, a year that I have to go through if I am going to be a doctor, and I know that this year demands unique and frequent accommodations—from me, of course, but also from Benjamin and from his father (who is the one bringing him to day care and picking him up and spending the evening and the night alone with him every third night when I'm on call, and no one has yet invited *him* to write an article on how *he* balances child and career). In fact, the only appropriate attitude for any intern to have toward significant others—spouse, lover, child—is an attitude of abject apology. What we put our loved ones through is highly unpleasant and completely unfair. What can I say— only that this is not a permanent state of affairs, and that I would also twist my life around to accommodate a necessary training period for someone I loved. In other words, I'll pay you back someday, guys.

No, what I want to talk about (what I want to whine and

complain about, actually) is something slightly different. I want to talk about being needed, about giving help and comfort. I can keep up, if just barely, with my schedule. It's the emotional load that sometimes makes me feel I can't go on another day.

The thing is, people in the hospital are truly needy. Even the ones who aren't desperately ill, the ones who aren't dying, whose children aren't dying—their needs are still not trivial. The parents and patients I deal with all day are vulnerable and terrified, and I feel their need for explanations, for help and comfort and reassurance, as a palpable presence in my life.

Say, for example, that you have a brand-new baby, two weeks old, and you're just getting used to being parents. You're no longer afraid to pick her up, you're even getting to be reasonably efficient with a diaper, and you have accepted that standards of neatness and order around your house are likely to be permanently disrupted. You still wake nervously in the night (when she doesn't wake you first) to put a hand on her back and check whether she's breathing, but you're beginning to believe, once and for all, that she's alive, she's yours, and you aren't going to break her in half.

And then one day she seems a little crankier than usual, and then she feels a little bit warm to you, and you call the pediatrician (expecting her to laugh at your new-parent nervousness) and instead she tells you to bring the baby to her office immediately. And she examines the baby and takes the baby's temperature, and then she tells you that you need to bring the baby to an emergency room. And at the emergency room, no one seems to think your problem is trivial, or not a problem for the emergency room. Instead, they start doing one test after another. They take what seems to be a large quantity of blood out of your baby's arm, and the baby screams herself purple. Then they explain, as gently as they can, that they also need a sample of spinal fluid and a sample of urine, and they take the baby off into another room and when she comes back, a terrifyingly long time later, she has two more round little Band-Aids on her, in two disconcerting places—

one on her spine where they did the spinal tap and one below her belly button where they went in with a needle to do a bladder tap and get some urine.

And then the next thing you know, someone is starting an IV in her foot, and it takes three tries to get it going, and when it's finally in, they wrap her foot in yards and yards of gauze, and then finally you really begin to understand that something may be seriously wrong with your baby, and she's going to spend the night in a hospital crib instead of in her basket at home.

Now, this is what I would truly call traumatic, for you as well as for your baby. You watch your baby suffer pain, you stand back and let them stick needles into her, you begin, naturally, to worry about whether this illness is going to damage her in some very profound way, even whether she is going to survive. She looks so unbelievably tiny, as the doctors and nurses bend over her, so tiny and helpless—you can't help feeling that you have somehow failed her. It was your job to keep her healthy and here she is, frighteningly sick. It is your job to protect her from pain, and here you are, handing her over to the people with the needles.

The doctors try their best to explain what's going on, but you're really in no shape to hear or understand anything. The problem is, they say, that such a little baby is not able to fight off infection very well. They can't find any specific infection in your daughter (they've looked in her ears, say, and in her throat) but some of the blood tests suggest that she does indeed have some kind of infection. And therefore the safest thing to do is to start giving her strong antibiotics. Samples of her blood and her urine and her spinal fluid have been sent to the bacteriology lab, where they will be cultured to see if any bacteria grow. If nothing grows in forty-eight to seventy-two hours, your baby will be able to go home, and you can blame everything on a virus, which will go away by itself and doesn't require antibiotics.

I know that's what the doctor is saying to you, obviously,

because I say that myself to terrified parents in the emergency room. I say it as gently as I can, and I repeat it more than once if that seems necessary. Anyone who works with sick children develops an appreciation for how hard a child's illness is on parents. I should have even an extra level of understanding, since, after all, when my son gets sick I am frightened and guilty and miserable.

But really, I'll tell you what I'm thinking while I'm making my would-be reassuring speech. This is a very routine admission, what we call a rule-out sepsis. We admit the baby, we send the cultures, we start the antibiotics, and we wait for the baby to rule out. Ruling out is what happens when the cultures don't grow and we stop the antibiotics and send the patient home. If the baby should happen to rule in, well, she's already on antibiotics. We start them empirically if we think there's any chance at all of sepsis in a child this age; she can't afford to wait even a day if she really does have a bacterial infection.

A rule-out sepsis tends to be an easy admission from the intern's point of view. Down in the emergency room, they've already done a lot of the work for me, sent the blood and the urine and the spinal fluid, started the IV. I have to keep an eye on the baby and make sure she doesn't get sicker, but mostly I just wait for those cultures to grow out or not grow out. I've had nights on call where I admitted three or four babies all for rule-outs, and the next morning, describing them on rounds, could hardly remember which was which.

So there you are, and depending on your way of dealing with stress, you may be anywhere on the spectrum from tense calm to full-blown craziness. And when I come in to look at your baby and give you news on how all the tests are coming out, you may want a lot from me. That's reasonable, that's appropriate, that's your right. But if I'm taking care of ten or twelve patients, and each family feels that way, then sometimes I start feeling as if I don't have enough to give. As an intern, I'm always most worried about my two or three sickest patients, the ones who aren't stable. When I go in and see those parents,

I probably have a level of concern that they would consider appropriate. I want to know every detail they've observed. I respond to their worry because I'm worried myself. When things pick up and the kids get better, I'm jubilant. But the parents of my less sick kids are also desperately concerned and expect to see me worried or jubilant—but one way or another, involved.

So that's work. Everyone's worried, everyone's needy. Everyone's questions need to be addressed with serious attention; if, as I am finally done for the day and about to leave the hospital, you come up to me in the hall to tell me that your daughter is holding her leg in a funny way, well, I have to come see. There is nothing trivial, there is nothing I can dismiss or shrug off until tomorrow. It would be inhuman, unprofessional, and possibly dangerous for me to plead that I'm tired, I'm late to pick up my own kid, I'm not on call anymore.

And then there's home. I'm not much fun to have around the house this year. No intern is much fun, male or female. I'm gone for long periods of time, and then I reappear and I fall asleep on the couch while my son builds Lego towers on my back. I'm totally unreliable, always arriving after the dinner guests are already there or without the milk I promised to pick up. The smallest request—could you please pick Benjamin up at day care today?—is a major big deal. The night I promised to pick him up, I was all done and signed out of the hospital in good time, but then, sure enough, as I was going down the hall I ran into a group of doctors who wanted to talk about one of my patients (it was only 5 P.M. on a Friday, the perfect time for a long conference) and then when I got away from them, I ran into the mother of one of my other patients who had a few questions she'd forgotten to ask me earlier in the day.

I was polite and friendly to all these people, despite the furious impassioned speech boiling up within me about how I had been in the hospital for thirty-five hours straight, and for just once this year I wanted to pick up my kid and pick him up on time and he was waiting for me and he was only three and he wouldn't know what it meant if I didn't show up.

I know what I sound like, and I know it isn't pretty. Still, I can't get away from the feeling that I am feeling sorry for everyone else in the world, and no one is feeling sorry for me—so I have to do that too. I worry for my patients, I worry for my own kid, and I feel sad when things go wrong for anyone else—and so I manage to feel permanently mournful. That is what sleep deprivation does, too; it makes you into a not particularly appetizing person. I run around with a perpetual refrain of my own grievances pounding in my brain, and I think one reason for that is the pervasive sense in my life that I am meeting other people's needs, all the time, day and night, without relief, and it's just too much. I get a sense sometimes of being nibbled at from all directions.

On the other hand, I'm doing exactly what I wanted to do. Mine is the whine of ambition fulfilled, of privilege and choice. There are certainly things wrong with the way young doctors are trained, with the demands and the schedules we have to put up with. Still, I wanted to do this. And I wanted to have a child. I want more children, and I want to be a pediatrician.

That means, among other things, that I am going to do a lot of nurturing. There will always be parents depending on me, and there will be children to whom I am professionally tied, and there will also be my own children. So the different kinds of succor I provide will mirror each other in interesting ways, as I try to offer help to parents and also to function as a parent myself, as I reassure other people about their children and worry about my own. This seems like a worthwhile kind of life; it is certainly not grounds for self-pity, and I have to recognize most of my current grousing as born of the stress of the moment, the sense that I do not have quite enough time or quite enough vigor to do the things I have to do and do them properly. That doesn't mean they're the wrong things to be doing.

My son asks me what I do at the hospital. I tell him that I take care of children. He asks, working it out in his head according to three-year-old rules, "Do you put Band-Aids on them?" Yes, I tell him. "And does it make them all better?" Well, sometimes, I tell him.

When I come home from the hospital, I tell my son, "I missed you." "I missed you too," he assures me, though his tone is the kindly tone of a child obediently parroting into the phone, "I love you, Grandma." "Do you know what I said to everyone all day at the hospital?" I ask him. With enthusiasm, he answers, "You said, 'I miss my little boy, Benjamin.' " "Right," I tell him.

So this is one of the lessons I am choosing to teach my son, by choosing the kind of life we are leading. I would like him to learn that you can do an important job, a job in which you help people in need. And I would like him to learn that just because you are helping people who need you, you don't stop missing the people you love best of all, and you don't have to be ashamed to admit it, either. And best of all I would like him to learn how to do all this without a lot of whining, how to carry it off with style, but he will have to learn that on his own. I only hope that while he is studying wit, grace, and style, no one will wake me up; I'll be the one asleep on the couch with the Lego brick tower on her back.

. . . AND BEING JUDGED

My son, Benjamin, was two and a half years old, and I supposed he and his father were out having dinner somewhere, and I envied them. Me, I was stuck in the hospital, the intern covering the pediatric cardiology ward, feeling more than a little bit sorry for myself.

I have a very distinct memory of the phone call, of Larry's voice, verging on panic: "Benjamin's been burned, and I'm bringing him to the emergency room! Meet us there!" Click.

I found a cardiology fellow to keep an eye on the ward, and I ran down to the emergency room, warning all the doctors that my son was coming in, trying to make sure everything was all set, ready to treat major burns, ready for a full-scale resuscitation. I had the impression that I was being quite calm and sensible, but finally they made me sit down and drink a cup of cold water. You be the mommy, they said to me patiently, a message we repeat to all doctor parents, you be the mommy, let us be the doctors.

Finally Benjamin arrived, somewhat upset but basically intact, and not obviously in need of resuscitation. He and Larry had indeed been in a restaurant, and Benjamin had been running down the aisle, and some patron had been waving a cigarette around, and the result was that Benjamin had two round cigarette burns, right below his eye. The emergency room doctor checked out his eye, which was fine. His wounds were cleaned and dressed with antibacterial lotion, and then Larry and I sat there in the little examining room as first one doctor, then another, and then finally the most senior of all, took Larry through the story of what had happened.

What restaurant did this happen in?

What was Benjamin doing, exactly, when it happened?

What time did it happen?

Do you smoke, sir?

It took Larry a little longer than it took me to catch on to the subtext, to the question beneath the questions. If I hadn't been so distraught, I would have seen it right away; a cigarette burn is about the most suspicious injury a small child can have. A cigarette burn is one of the absolutely classic stigmata of child abuse. And while everyone was being very polite (after all, there I sat in my hospital scrubs, my stethoscope slung around my neck), everyone also wanted to be very sure that the story behind this injury was going to hold together.

It was right then, at that moment, that I began constructing the account of my family that some hypothetical social worker might write. *Father states he was in restaurant with toddler at nine o'clock at night because mother was at work. Father further states he is fully responsible for this child throughout evening, night, and morning. Mother states she cannot possibly leave work to accompany child home, nor can she rearrange her schedule. Family is clearly under significant stress, with child possibly at risk.* . . . I mean, this is classic stuff, the single parent home alone with the young child, the family trying to struggle through exceptionally stressful times. I could almost hear the kind but firm voice telling me they were going to have to take my child into protective custody.

Fortunately, all the doctors interviewing us found my schedule perfectly understandable; of course I had to work all night, of course I couldn't possibly go home. I am sure it never occurred to them to equate our situation with that of, say, a mother working the night shift in a factory, while her husband, exhausted from his own day shift, took care of the child (*family currently under extreme stress* . . .). Still more fortunately, just as I was about to suggest that someone might call the restaurant and verify the story, Benjamin decided to tell his own version. He was no longer in pain, he was immensely pleased to be the center of attention, and he favored the assemblage with a highly dramatic account of the accident, featuring the "bad dumb man" with the cigarette.

And so he and his father eventually went along home, and I went back up to the cardiology ward and worried about other people's children for the rest of the night.

Thirty years ago, pediatricians didn't worry so much about child abuse. It wasn't a recognized entity, carefully described in the textbooks, with color illustrations to indicate some of the classic lesions. It wasn't a moral or a legal obligation to rule out child abuse whenever an injured child came into an

emergency room. Now we know much more about both physical and sexual abuse, although we are still finding out how
widespread they are; and now there is no such thing as a simple
accident. Bring in your infant with a broken arm, your toddler
who ate the bottle of Tylenol, and at some point you may
begin to feel that you are on trial.

This is especially true, of course, with infants and younger
children who cannot speak for themselves; a ten-year-old who
can explain coherently how she fell out of a tree is likely to be
believed—though everyone has examples of children terrorized
into lying, supporting their parents' stories. The most suspicious wounds include burns, especially cigarette burns and
scalds, marks that suggest some portion of the child has been
lowered into hot liquid. But there are lots of other signs,
ranging from the small retinal hemorrhages at the back of the
eye that suggest a baby has been violently shaken, to the array
of bruises at different stages of healing seen on a child who
has been repeatedly beaten.

There is no laboratory test for child abuse. The most we
can do is a skeletal survey, X rays of all the long bones to see
whether there are any old healing fractures—the radiologic
smoking gun that leads to the initial medical description of
the battered-child syndrome. But for most injuries, the doctor
sits in the emergency room, going over the history of the
accident with the parents and wondering, does this make sense,
do I believe this story? We get anxious about child abuse when
the injury doesn't fit with the history; he rolled off the bed,
says the parent, when the baby is only two months old, too
young to roll, and has a broken leg and big bruises all over
his head. We get anxious about child abuse when something
in the parents' manner seems strange or off-key, when they
took an unconscionably long time to bring the child to medical
attention, when they seem drunk, drugged, or simply unin-
terested.

More disturbingly, we get anxious about child abuse more
readily when the parents are poor. The extreme end of the

spectrum is the doctor parent—me in my scrubs sitting there and reminding the doctors, you are dealing with people who are just like you, your profession, your life-style, your social class—could such people possibly abuse their children? In our hearts, most of us are all too inclined to answer no, though we shouldn't need a tragic and highly publicized court case to remind us that the possibility of child abuse exists at all social levels. However, it has been shown in studies that for any given level of suspicion, the poor are more likely to be reported, more likely to have their children taken away.

Most of us, working in the pediatric emergency rooms, know this. The fear in my mind is always that I will take care of some upper-middle-class child, elect to believe the upper-middle-class parents (who speak my language), send the child home with them—and the child will come back dead. On account of this fear, I push myself into asking more and more questions of these parents, annoying them, sometimes embarrassing myself. But then I still have to decide whether or not to call in Social Service. If I do, the social worker will reinterview the parents, will decide with me whether to file a legal motion, informing the state that a child is at risk. If we do, the Department of Social Services will investigate the family, and decide whether to "substantiate" our motion. It's a somewhat cumbersome process, but it's the only means to hand, the only way I have to protect the child at risk.

There is abuse, and then there is neglect. We usually say them together, abuse-and-neglect. When a toddler comes into the emergency room, having just swallowed all of Daddy's antianxiety medicine, it is very rare for anyone to consider deliberate poisoning. But there is always the question of how the child got Daddy's pills, and why the child wasn't supervised. Many of the poisoning cases are interviewed by the social workers.

The problem is, neglect is a big umbrella. For almost any accident, there is always something you could have done differently. You should have strapped the baby into the stroller more securely. You should have kept the two-year-old away from the two-month-old. You should never have left the room to answer the phone. Some doctors, especially those who have never had children of their own, are inclined to consider certain injuries, say a broken bone in an infant, as de facto evidence of parental neglect. Others of us, perhaps sadder and wiser from the misadventures of our own offspring, believe that accidents can, and do, happen.

So there you are in the emergency room with your darling child, and instead of comforting and supporting you both in this hour of pain, the doctors are making you feel worse and worse, taking you back over the story again and again, almost cross-examining you. And you have finally understood what they're getting at; and you realize that you are being suspected, almost automatically, of child abuse. The natural response is to feel angry and insulted; why can't they just look at you and see how much you love your child, what a good parent you are? How dare they, just now at this awful moment, when you would give anything to be able to bear the pain for your child, how dare they imply that you may be to blame?

Well, bear with us. For decades, pediatricians missed child abuse; the children marched past, bruised or burned, and their parents' stories were accepted. Now we live in fear that someone will get by, that we will believe a story that shouldn't be believed. Be patient with us as we ask you all these questions, and understand that we are bound, ethically, morally, and now even legally, to suspect everyone. It may seem harsh and unfair to you that you are not immediately and obviously cleared, but it would be much more unfair if we gave in to our instincts and promptly cleared all parents who seemed "like us." It would be more than unfair; it would be dangerous. We all know too much now; our own innocence is gone, and we are trying, if you will pardon the turn of phrase, to protect the innocent.

5

The Crazy Person

In my heart, I would like to leave this next part out. I would like to write this book as if internship had been a relatively straightforward rite of passage. I went from never having been a doctor to being a doctor, I took care of patients, I was scared, I made mistakes, I laughed, I cried, I ate too many waffles. That would be enough of a story for anyone, enough emotional turmoil, enough growth and development. But something went wrong in my internship year, something weird and un-expected and different happened to me, and warped the year, and probably warped me a little, too, into the bargain.

In the fall of my internship, I became the target of some-one I still refer to in my own mind as the "crazy person." Someone who knew a little about me, had obviously followed my writing career somewhat obsessively, and had apparently unlimited time and energy to spend persecuting me. It was a

lengthy and even creative campaign, as these things go, I suppose (that is, as opposed to sending me letters saying I hate
you, I hope you die). The aim was to discredit me, first as a
writer and then as a doctor.

Although I survived, both as a writer and as a doctor,
living through this craziness, overlying the craziness of internship, made me crazy. There is a paranoia which is relatively
normal during internship, born of weariness and the feeling
that everyone is always after you to do something or other.
The nurses are out to get you, the attendings are out to get
you, the emergency room, the chief residents—and above all,
the patients, who wait till you lie down and then pull out their
IVs or spike their temperatures. And then, in the midst of this
paranoia, I discovered that someone really *was* out to get me.

Both as a medical student and as an intern, I had written
a fair amount about my medical training, often using material
which came very directly out of my everyday experiences in
lecture halls, laboratories, and above all, in the hospitals. In
fact, I developed a sense of myself as rather uniquely privileged,
as someone who passed almost anonymously between two
separate worlds. I could work in the hospital, and my identity
as a writer did not hang over my shoulder, and then I could
go home and sit down at the typewriter. I imagined that in
the hospital I had a kind of diplomatic immunity; no one would
ever mention anything I had written.

Being pursued by the crazy person destroyed that little
illusion. I was not a double agent. I was not one more anonymous intern, going through that year just like everyone else.
I was being persecuted as a writer because of someone I had
run across in the medical world (since the crazy person obviously came from that side of the street), being persecuted as
a doctor because of someone who hated my writing.

And I felt visible. It was big news in the hospital; one of
the interns was the subject of a hate-mail campaign. There she
goes, I imagined everyone saying as I hurried by, disheveled
in my scrubs, trying to pretend I was just one more intern

going to check out one more wheezer. That's the one. Her. Which is largely, of course, just more of the paranoia of internship.

IN MY OWN WORDS

Last October I got something in my mailbox at the hospital. There was the usual quantity of free (and unrequested) information from drug companies—Finally! A pediatric anti-diarrheal agent which tastes so good kids want to take it!!! There were bulletins from the hospital about saving money, not ordering unnecessary diagnostic tests. There were three or four letters offering to lend me astonishingly large sums of money at apparently amazingly low rates—Dear Young Doctor, we know that now, early in your training, is a time of great hopes and great hardship. And there was also a photocopied article tucked into a plain envelope, no message, no sender's name. The article was from *American Beat* by Bob Greene, the story of Jerzy Kosinski sending out, as an ostensibly new book by an unknown author, one of his own manuscripts, which had already been published to great acclaim. Sure enough, no editor or agent recognized the book, not even the publisher that had originally brought it out, and no one thought it was worth publishing. Mr. Kosinski collected any number of comments, highly comic under the circumstances, and was told among other things that his work read like a weak version of Jerzy Kosinski.

I thought it was a funny article. I had no idea who it was from; I couldn't conjure any memory of hearing such an article discussed, of someone promising to put a copy in my mailbox. Still, it could have happened and then slipped my mind; as an intern, it's easy to get a little bit absentminded.

Several days later, I got a call from my literary agent. My publisher had just received some letters accusing me of plagiarism, she said, sounding very upset. She read me the cover letter, and then the paragraph I was accused of copying, which was indeed almost word-for-word identical to a paragraph of my own in an article about medical ethics which had been published in the Harvard Medical *Alumni Bulletin*. The cover letter opened, "A relative of mine was graduated in '86 along with Perri Klass from the Harvard Medical School." It went on to claim that I made a habit of bragging about how I cheated and plagiarized, and concluded, "I am happy to present you with an example of her plagiarization [sic]." With this was mailed a photocopy of a letter to the editor of the Harvard Medical *Alumni Bulletin*, also unsigned, but typed on paper with a name printed across the top: R. Margaret McKay. Ms. McKay claimed that my article was "a plagiarization [sic] from an obscure nursing magazine that was published in 1980." She continued, "I've enclosed a xerox of a xerox I've saved from it and if I can find a copy of the magazine I'll send it in."

Over the next week or so, I got call after call, from editors I had worked with, from people I knew in the publishing world. Everyone had gotten the mailing. The cover letters were varied, and they were typed on stationery from all the different hospitals where Harvard medical students train. The writer claimed to be a number of different things, a nurse, an interested bystander, and, ultimately, one of my medical school classmates. The little paragraph from the Harvard Medical *Alumni Bulletin* was always enclosed, along with the isolated identical paragraph, set in a different typeface, which was purportedly from the "obscure nursing magazine."

This was all extremely disturbing, because, even though the evidence produced against me was so unconvincing, I found that I was defending myself all the time, striving for a puzzled isn't-this-ridiculous tone of voice. Couldn't everyone see that it was ridiculous for someone to have saved a copy of a paragraph (and a not very interesting paragraph at that) and not a copy of the article? To be unable to identify the magazine or the author? And most of all, to refuse to sign the accusing letter? "Plagiarism is the easiest thing in the world to prove," I found myself saying over and over. "You just produce the original."

I was being a little ingenuous there, of course. I wasn't really thinking about the legalities of plagiarism among professional writers, which I know can be a tangled business; I was thinking more of my brief career teaching expository writing, Harvard's required freshman English course, universally known as Expos. It was my job as an Expos teacher to communicate to my students Harvard's tough-minded policy on plagiarism, and to this end I used to spend a fair amount of class time arguing about what did and didn't constitute illicit borrowing. Many students confessed to a fear of inadvertent plagiarism; if you were writing about some set subject, "Stopping by Woods on a Snowy Evening," say, or "The Ethics of In Vitro Fertilization," mightn't you very well end up using words that someone else had already used? I would argue, as I suppose English teachers have argued for decades, if not centuries, that if you used your own words, writing down your own thoughts and opinions, those words would be unique. And I would claim that in any doubtful circumstance a jury made up of people of goodwill would easily be able to tell the difference between coincidence and copying. That jury would examine the supposed original—the book of literary criticism, the roommate's paper, and draw the necessary conclusions. Now here I was, arguing my case before a growing jury—and there was no real original, no accusing document. When those letters went out, I felt distinctly that I was boxing with the wind, strenuously and even shrilly claiming that I hadn't copied my words from something or other.

And then another and far more damaging accusation appeared, and was mailed out to all the same editors, publishers, and magazines. This one concerned an article I had published in *Discover* magazine, an article about being a medical student late at night in the hospital, feeling sorry for myself and fantasizing about changing places with a patient. The letters claimed that this article had been plagiarized from an article published during World War II in a British nursing journal. I had demanded rhetorically why anyone would save a photocopy of a solitary paragraph; here was a whole article. I had asked why anyone would save an article but not know where it came from; the writer of this letter explained that it came out of a scrapbook kept by his mother, who had been a nurse in England during World War II. Most convincing of all was the purported original article, a photocopy of which was enclosed: "There's a War On, You Know," by Maisie Wilson, Nurse Probationer. It was a photocopy of a closely typeset newspaper column, surrounded with injunctions to observe the blackout. There was an apparent fragment of a date ('44) on the top but no periodical name—but after all, it had supposedly been cut out and pasted in a scrapbook forty years ago. My article began as follows:

> Late at night in the hospital, I've had any number of odd and less-than-noble thoughts. I'm talking about a medical student (me), in the hospital on a thirty-hour shift, prevented from sleeping by the uncontrollable changes in condition of the sick, or sometimes by my own need to stay awake and learn something before morning rounds. I'm talking about those dark hours of the soul when one is reduced to scrounging yet again in one's pocket for enough change to coax yet another candy bar out of the vending machine in the cafeteria for a few seconds of sugar rush.

The article by "Maisie Wilson, Nurse Probationer" began like this:

> Late at night in hospital I have had any number of odd and less-then-noble [sic] thoughts. I am speaking as a probationer nurse in hospital on Night Duty, prevented from sleeping by the unpredictable changes in condition

of the patients, or sometimes by my own need to stay awake and learn something before morning, when Sister no doubt will ask me to demonstrate the assembly of a saline apparatus or get a hypo, syringe and coramine and mime its proper administration. I am speaking of those dark hours of the soul when one is reduced to drinking the tenth cup of tea of the night.

And so it went on. All the changes from my piece were changes to make it clear that the "original" was British, or that it dated from World War II. Oh, my friends could pick holes in it well enough (there was a reference to soccer, for example, and surely the right word would have been *football*). And I could even argue that the whole idea of keeping people up all night and all day to be grilled on teaching rounds was unique to the education of medical students and had nothing at all to do with nurse training—but even to myself, I sounded defensive, nervous, and not entirely convincing as I attempted to argue my case.

Now there were other things going on at the same time. I had received, left for me in the hospital mail room, a carefully gift-wrapped box of excrement, further evidence, if I needed it, that I was the target of someone not quite sane. Further, I knew that a couple of years earlier several residents, both at my hospital and at another, had been the targets of anonymous hate letters and had received similar packages. I happened to know this only because my name had been used as a "return address" on one of the letters, and the detectives investigating the matter had come to talk to me. An analysis was done and the typewriter that had been used to type the letters accusing me turned out to be the same typewriter that had been used to type the hate letters sent two years before.

Incidents at the hospital multiplied. A rather official-looking flier documenting my "plagiarization" appeared; it was mailed to every nursing division in the hospital and was found posted in elevators, in the hospital library. I felt increasingly embattled and also increasingly terrified—who was this loony who hated me so much, and why, and what would happen next?

I can see now that there are a number of interesting aspects to this whole experience (I write of it as though it were securely in the past, but since the perpetrator was never caught, I suppose I have no reason to be sure of that). It is, in retrospect, interesting for what it taught me about my own response to accusation, and also for what it showed about the nature of plagiarism and the writer's proprietary feelings about her own words.

When I first saw the letters, the accusations, what I really wanted was to keep them secret. I felt, I think, a little bit the way the victim of a rape must feel—I didn't want too many people to know what had happened, I didn't want to spread the word any further. Accused of crimes I hadn't committed, did I even feel momentarily guilty? Not exactly, but I did feel that anyone I told would have at least a split second of wondering whether the accusations were true, and I didn't want to face split second after split second. Further, I was looking at the people around me with a jaundiced eye: could one of them actually be doing this? For a week or two, I retreated into myself. I stopped going to lectures and conferences in the hospital, and if a colleague asked how I was, I smiled and said fine.

Looking back, I think one reason that I initially had trouble standing up to this was that although I knew I wasn't a plagiarist, I did feel like a fake much of the time. That feeling was a normal and even necessary part of internship; for the first time in my life, this year, I am functioning as a doctor, making decisions about patients and treatment. There is no way to feel truly ready for this, and there is no way to feel truly competent. Like almost all interns, I am frequently overwhelmed by the magnitude of my responsibility, I keep dismal and compulsive account of what I consider my mistakes, and I have great trouble acknowledging that sometimes there is no right or wrong answer, sometimes there is no way to help. If, instead of accusing me of plagiarism, the letters had accused me of medical incompetence (as some of the letters in the past had accused other doctors), I would have been at least a little bit inclined to bow my head and accept that anonymous judgment. I knew I was actually doing okay, I knew that I was closely watched and my superiors were satisfied, and I knew that many, if not most, other interns felt as insecure as I did. But I still felt a little like a fake doctor—and so it was hard to dismiss letters that accused me of being a fake writer.

At any rate, that is the closest I can come to explaining the unhealthy blend of depression and resignation with which I initially accepted this lunatic campaign against me. It took me a week or two to realize that I could not just hide my head and let the mailings continue unanswered, that too many people were receiving them and were too ready to believe them if I kept quiet. Among the editors who got those letters were people who were shocked, people who were fascinated, and at least a couple of people who were downright titillated.

Plagiarism is the easiest thing in the world to prove, I had said. But plagiarism, it turns out, is a very hard accusation for a writer to disprove. If there is no citation, no original, then plagiarism is not proved—but neither is it disproved. The scrapbook story seemed to me reasonably plausible—or at least credibly peculiar. And really, wasn't it stretching credibility to think that someone out there was willing to go to all the trouble of rewriting and retypesetting my little article? In other words, I sometimes felt it was easier to believe in my plagiarism than in my persecutor's craziness. And also, as I became more paranoid, I believed that some people were gleefully eager to believe me dishonest; I have come in for a certain amount of "superwoman" publicity (she writes! she goes to medical school! she has a baby!) that I can imagine engendering a very natural desire to find feet of clay (so that's her secret—she plagiarizes! she goes to medical school! . . .).

If the letters had accused me of being an incompetent

intern, I suppose in the end I would have had to turn to other people for reassurance. I would have needed to be told, maybe over and over, that I was really okay. But I knew I wasn't a plagiarist. I could remember the genesis of that column I was accused of copying from Maisie Wilson, remember a night in my third year of medical school, when I was doing my two months of surgery. I was exhausted, it was late, and I was caring for a patient not that much older than myself, who had developed a fever. I had drawn her blood for various tests, and as I was finishing, it occurred to me that she was now going to put her head back down on her pillow and close her eyes, while I, who would have given anything for a pillow, had to stay awake and find out the results of the blood tests and then go figure out what they meant. I was exhausted, not particularly interested in surgery, and for a few tired put-upon minutes, I distinctly envied that patient. I remember the feel of the room, the sight of the patient drifting off to sleep, and the way I shook myself and told myself not to be so silly, she was a sick woman and I was healthy, and all my heroic suffering was purely in pursuit of my own career goals. And then, because I had already acquired the habit of making my hospital experiences into columns, I remember that I began playing around in my brain with the first few sentences of that article, that piece on envying the patient. My radar was up; tired as I was, I knew an interesting irony when it hit me in the face.

It was my experience and they were my words, and I felt a sense of absolute ownership. I would not have claimed they were particularly brilliant words, or that the ideas were high on the intellectual Richter scale—but they were *mine*. When I stopped feeling resigned and ashamed for no reason at all, when I started considering the accusation more rationally, I found I was ready to fight duels. I then began to feel that everyone who had anything to do with me professionally should immediately see through all the accusations, throw the letters in the garbage without a second thought. Surely any editor could see that all my words were strictly my own—

didn't they all sound like me, after all? In my own ears, the cadences of my own writing are completely distinct—again, not because of any remarkable genius, but because they reverberate with all the tiny decisions that writing involves, the choices of voice and tone and syntax. And also, of course, in these pieces about medicine, which come so directly out of my daily life, they almost unfailingly evoke for me the events that prompted the writing. If I have disguised a patient as a five-year-old girl in my article, when I reread it, I invariably see the eight-year-old boy who actually had the disease about which I was writing.

And yet, of course, no one else can be expected to read my words in this same way. For any other reader, the words are simply there, on paper, standing alone and without reverberations of the original story, the choices I have made along the way. They are a set of words on paper, and they could conceivably have been copied from another set of words on paper. That was not an impossibility or an unthinkable circumstance in any way—except to me. It was, in fact, a frighteningly plausible scenario, especially with that scrapbook clipping bearing witness, and even people who I think had always trusted me completely felt driven to ask whether I could possibly have read such a thing somewhere and then forgotten I had read it. . . .

The detective-story aspect of the story, the investigation of the campaign of anonymous letters, continued for a couple of months. An industrial security firm investigated, interviewing everyone who seemed to be connected with the letters, fingerprinting and checking postmarks and generally getting nowhere. I tended to do my research in mystery novels. I took a great deal of comfort from *Gaudy Night* by Dorothy L. Sayers, long one of my very favorite novels. In this book, there is a campaign of evil-minded mischief at a women's college at Oxford, and one of the villain's techniques is the anonymous letter. I found reassurance in reading a book in which such letters were treated with disgust and contempt by several strong-minded heroines. I was also referred to novels by P. D. James (*Cover Her Face*, *The Black Tower*, *The Skull Beneath the Skin*) and Agatha Christie. If Dorothy L. Sayers were writing this story, I decided, the perpetrator would indeed be someone who was riled up by my publicity—who hated me or perhaps was jealous of me because of my embarrassing role in those superwoman stories. If P. D. James were writing it, there would probably be a more rational intelligence behind the apparent hatred of the campaign; someone would be out for some sort of perfectly sane material gain. And in an Agatha Christie novel—well, I derived a certain ghoulish pleasure from deciding that in an Agatha Christie novel, I would be more likely to turn out the murderer than the murder victim; one of the anonymous letters would reveal my deepest, darkest secret, and I would end by committing murder to try to keep it quiet, killing the person who had written the letter and the one person who had received it (of course, the writers of the anonymous letters in Agatha Christie did not have apparently unlimited access to photocopy machines).

The letters about me had been sent to just about every editor I knew. They had been sent to every magazine that had ever published my writing, and to a good many that never had. They had been sent to the nurses at the hospital where I work. And of course they could have gone almost anywhere. Some people got them and called me up to ask about them. Other people got them and asked my agent or one of the editors I work with regularly. And still other people, I was sure, just read the letters, absorbed the information that there was some kind of fuss about me, about plagiarism, and filed it away. After the letters had been sent to the people in publishing and to the people in my hospital, the next step was obvious: they were sent to the press.

The press packet was made up of two letters (along with the usual photocopied "originals"). These were to be the last letters, the longest, and also the first to touch on the issue of my medical competence. The first letter purported to be from a nurse at the hospital at which I work (typed—badly, with many misspellings, on the appropriate stationery) while the second, sent as cover letter for the nurse's, was more professionally typed, and on the letterhead of another Harvard teaching hospital. The nurse's letter was to a columnist at the *Boston Globe*. She brought up all the old familiar accusations about my plagiarism, and added some new ones—"her fellow medical students avoided her because anyone's experiments that she had access to tended to go wrong. . . ." Then she went on, "In working with Perri Klass I and other nurses have gotten the distinct impression that this person is so lacking in knowlege [sic] and skills that she presents a danger to the patients. We are currently documenting this to present it to our supervisor."

The letter became more dramatic, advising the columnist that if his baby gets sick and has to go to the emergency room, "And if, on top of that misfortune, you get Perri Klass, you have the right to ask for an other intern. If they give you any grief, ask them to page the hospital lawyer. The hospital lawyers are right helpful in reminding staff members about the patient's rights." Finally, after providing telephone numbers (work and home) for a variety of editors, along with the home and work numbers of a long list of my medical school classmates ("You might want to have a chat with some of her classmates and use your reporter's wiles to confirm what I've written"), the letter ended with the following paragraph: "I am aware what a craven act it is to send in an accusatory letter and not sign it, but if Perri Klass ever found out I had sent this I would be a goner. When I get enough documentation on her to present a case against her I will resign . . . before I do it. p.s. pardon the typing."

The cover letter, addressed to an editor at *Newsweek*, claimed to be "leaking" the nurse's letter to him. The writer (the one with the better typewriter and typing, though still somewhat dubious spelling) claimed to have been a classmate of mine, though admitted to not being an intern at the famous hospital on the letterhead, writing "[I] had access to their stationary [sic] and I'm hoping it will lend some credibility to this letter." The writer even tried to draw a larger moral from the catalogue of my misdeeds, hoping perhaps to interest a magazine that might be interested in drawing the big conclusion: "Maybe there's not so much a story in this as there is in a silent, couldn't-be-bothered group of people who were too busy looking out for themselves."

And then those same warnings were posted in the hospital, fliers with my picture (photocopied from the official hospital mug shot of me, which hung, along with those of all the other interns, at every nursing station, on every bulletin board). Fliers warning parents not to let this doctor care for their children. They were hanging in the women's bathroom, on notice boards here and there, in the elevators.

All through the early part of this unpleasant saga, friends who were residents would listen to the catalogue of my tribulations and uniformly would remark something on the order of "Imagine having that much free time!" And that is true; my unknown admirer appeared to be someone with a great deal of time to put into forging and duplicating documents and assembling mailings (and we residents, in weary defense of our exhausted lives, are eager to believe that having a lot of free time is tantamount to having an empty and a meaningless life—which may be true in the case of my pursuer, but should not actually be taken as a general rule).

The other thing many people said to me, back during the early months of this campaign when I was being accused of plagiarism, was that at least I wasn't being accused of medical incompetence, of malpractice. And I had felt myself that as long as I was not assailed in that particular area, I could at least keep my emotional balance.

And now, perhaps inevitably, my anonymous kook had turned to accusations of medical incompetence. And being accused, however bizarrely and however anonymously, of medical incompetence did of course shake me. I had worked hard to reach a point where I felt confident deciding which children could be sent home from the emergency room and which children needed to be admitted, and when the posters about me were put up, I went through a period of demanding that the senior resident or the attending see each child before that final decision was made. I was shaken, my faith in my own judgment rocky, but I was also imagining the tidal wave of events if I did make a wrong decision, the people who would remember that there had been some question about my medical competence. . . . So really, I had the normal intern's uncertainty about making a mistake coupled with a self-consciousness that I was somehow under a potential cloud.

After that, it stopped. No more mailings to editors, no more gift-wrapped boxes of excrement. I had by this time realized that in fact my best (and only) defense lay in being public, in telling my own side of the story and even in writing my own side of the story. I had begun to talk about it with the people I work with, and had been rewarded with a tremendous amount of support and kindness, all of which made the hospital seem a much friendlier place to me again. I was also sent by the hospital authorities to discuss the case with a psychiatrist who specializes in situations of this kind and knows a great deal about them. He was able to describe back to me many of my own responses to being a target, to warn me against the kind of paranoia I had come close to developing about the people around me. He also advised me against any kind of public response, saying that the person writing the letters hungered above all for reaction, any kind of reaction. If I wrote an article about it, I might set the whole thing off again, he warned, whereas it looked instead as if my persecutor had either snapped back to a period of comparative sanity— or else maybe found a new victim.

I thought a great deal about that warning. I do not want to pretend to any kind of heroism. I am writing about what happened to me for no particularly altruistic reason—this is not a case of a writer's revealing all about some excruciatingly horrible experience in the hope that it will help others. I am writing about this because the person who wrote those letters wanted to take away my voice, wanted to claim that it wasn't really mine, and I am not willing to let that happen. I am writing about it, in part, to lay claim again to all my words.

6

Getting Through

So eventually the crazy person went away. Did they ever find out who was doing it? To this day, five or six years later, I run into people who remember something about that story, who want to know who did it. Naturally, I would like to know too. The hospital did conduct an investigation, and I collected gossip about hospital personnel and about my medical school classmates. People would call me up, say they had heard about my problem, and then nominate their candidates. You know who did some pretty crazy things once? You know who really didn't like you back in medical school? You know who used to say she could write those articles much better than you?

A remarkable number of my coworkers contributed stories about strange things that had happened to them in the hospital, peculiar interactions, people who seemed to bear a grudge for years, even crazy letters and phone calls. And when my article about my anonymous pursuer was published, I got letters from people in other professions who had been the targets of hate-mail campaigns, false allegations, and persecutions of other kinds. Some of their stories made me glad that my own story was no worse; people had been physically threatened, accusations had been made that could not be disproved and that had been believed. . . . What almost all the stories seemed to suggest was that it was very hard to stop this kind of persecution, even if the victim was pretty sure about the perpetrator's identity. The police aren't interested unless violence is threatened. If a crazy person fixes on you, you are vulnerable. A writer is, in a sense, lucky: she has a weapon, she can defend herself.

In any case, the crazy person went away and internship continued. Back to the wards, back to the NICU, back to the emergency room. By the middle of the year, you feel like a pro, not so much at being a doctor as at being an intern. A pro at keeping scut lists, starting IVs, writing fast notes. One of the ironies of residency is that you get very good, very quickly, at all sorts of skills you will never use again. This is true for medical specifics—for example, unless you become a neonatologist, you are not likely to use any of the extremely intricate skills you acquire in months spent taking care of tiny preemies. Yes, you need to know something about newborns, and you need to know some things about the implications of premature birth as a child grows up. But what about all that time you spend getting good at doing procedures on babies who weigh less than a kilogram? Down the tubes, if you'll excuse the pun. You'll leave those babies and those procedures behind in the NICU.

It's also true for those skills of residency; you can become a really good intern—organized and fast and terrifically responsible—and then feel a little lost as you realize that in real life you will go practice medicine and never be an intern again. And yes, it will be good to be organized and fast and responsible, but the specifics, the patterns of work and thought you have so painstakingly and painfully acquired, will not be used. On the other hand, the good news is you won't have to be an intern ever again.

By the end of the year, you're almost comfortable in the job, chafing if your superiors watch you too closely. Whatsamatter, think I never took care of a sick diabetic before? Wanna make something of it? The senior residents, instead of complaining that they had to hold our hands too much, were complaining that we never called for help, no matter how sick the patients got. And when an intern called for help with an IV, the senior could no longer stride confidently into the room, ready to show off. At the end of the year, if the intern can't get the IV in, it's because of the child's veins, not the intern's skill.

My colleagues and I were beginning to look ahead to July, to the appearance of new interns, people who would take over our beepers. There is no symbol of the end of internship which matters, no certificate, no trophy. You know that your internship is over when someone else's begins.

GOOD NIGHT

Internship brings you up against many of the life-and-death issues of the day. You turn off respirators and allow people to die, or else you fight death with all the pharmacology and technology you have. You tell the truth to patients, or you lie to them. You treat the rich and the poor alike, or else you make distinctions. Life and death, pain and relief, honesty and falsehood. And so on. The big ones. But right now I want to talk about the biggest issue of them all, the concern that dominates an intern's life, the subject with which we grapple constantly. I mean, of course, fatigue.

I mean, I'm so tired, you wouldn't believe it. I mean, right now, while I'm writing this, I can barely see farther than how tired I am. I mean, I got to the hospital this morning at 7:15 (ridiculous already; I've never been able to think clearly before noon) and I stayed there until 7 P.M. And this was one of the good days.

Whining, of course, is good for the soul, and I whine a lot this year. I also listen to my fellow interns; we greet each other in the morning after being on call with the question "Did you get sleep?" I find myself in long conversations that are really nothing more than recitations on the subject of sleep and sleepiness.

"When I worked in the emergency room, I would work a twelve-hour shift and then go right home and go to bed and sleep twelve hours, I was so exhausted."

"Last week my girlfriend and I went to this inn in the country, and I slept for sixteen solid hours. That's all I did. When I woke up it was time to go home."

"I didn't get any sleep at all last time I was on call, and then I didn't get home until late the next day, and I fell asleep in the elevator going up to my apartment."

What a fascinating subject, sleep. How could we ever have taken it for granted? Did we think it was in the Declaration of Independence or something—Life, Liberty, and Eight Hours a Night?

The thing is, I never quite catch up for very long. I'm in the hospital overnight, I don't get enough sleep, then I come home the next evening and there are all the pleasant out-of-hospital things to do: play with Benjamin, cook noodles, lie around on the couch and read trashy novels, call a friend and complain about my schedule. And tired as I am, old habits die hard, and I've always been bad at getting to sleep early. My natural schedule is to stay awake till three or four in the morning, then sleep till noon. Those are the settings on my physiological clock; as far as I'm concerned, nothing of any value has ever been accomplished before 11 A.M. Well, certainly not by me. So I come home from the hospital and I stay up too late, till midnight or so. I ask you, did I grow up and graduate from college and all to find myself going to bed before midnight? Is this what grown-ups do?

So I never catch up—I'm always tired. But so is everyone else, the ones who swear they walk straight out of the hospital and go home to bed, the ones who insist they always get up at 5 A.M. anyway. We're all tired.

It has the flavor of a rather tired (no pun intended) comedy routine at times, an air of the familiar exchange:

"This intern was so tired—"

"How tired was she?"

"She was sooo tired—"

He was so tired that when he went to listen to a patient's chest, he fell asleep right there, with his head leaning forward onto the old man's chest, with the stethoscope still in his ears, and the old man felt sorry for him and didn't wake him up. She was so tired that she fell asleep in the shower, leaning against the wall, and didn't wake up until all the hot water was used up and the shower turned ice-cold. He was so tired that he fell asleep at the wheel of his car driving home, and he almost crashed.

One Sunday morning, when I'd been in the hospital overnight, I went out for a fancy brunch with family and friends. I was making cheerful conversation, when I literally fell asleep in mid-sentence. A friend tells me that I actually did say, in a dreamy voice, "I'm just going to take a little time out here." And with no more ado, I fell asleep at the table, lolling back in my seat, my mouth hanging open. Nearby diners heard my snore and turned to look at the catatonic who had so kindly been taken out to brunch by well-meaning friends. The people at my table tried to talk around me, but if you aren't used to it, it's hard to ignore a fully dressed adult sleeping soundly in your midst.

In the hospital, of course, we're used to that. There's a rigid hierarchy that governs much of hospital life, but the lowliest intern is permitted to sleep soundly through a lecture by the loftiest attending. Put twenty interns in a room, turn off the lights to show slides, and between eight and twelve of them immediately slouch down and close their eyes. We can't help it, we're too tired. And everybody understands this; you really don't have to feel too self-conscious when you wake with a jerk and realize that you've been publicly and obviously asleep. Sleep is what sitting interns do.

One night at 4 A.M. or so I was sitting in the hospital writing a note about one of my patients. The nurses had the radio on very softly at the nurses' station. I was writing in a haze of tiredness; I'd been awake much, much too long. My neurons crossed, and instead of writing out the patient's history, I began to transcribe the words of the song. "The patient was in his usual state of good health until two days prior to admission when he developed fever and headache and I wish they all could be California girls." I sat staring down at the paper, trying to figure out what was wrong with it. It made perfect sense to me.

What is it like to be so tired so much of the time? In a word, lousy. You wink in and wink out, responding to pressure by clearing the clouds from your mind and concentrating your attention, then later floating back into an unpleasant haze.

Well, you're probably wondering, how about taking care of patients? How do you take care of sick people if you're so tired? It's a good question. In extreme cases, situations where you aren't expected to sleep at all, you're sometimes sent home the next day at noon. Thus you maintain an adequate level of alertness, knowing there's a finite time period, at the end of which you'll go home and inflict yourself on the healthy, not the sick. But generally, I have to admit, I've been surprised by how well you can concentrate even when you're tired. If someone is sick, you do find a way to snap back to a reasonable state of rational thought. I'm more careful on days when I've had very little sleep; I check over my decisions and calculations more carefully, I ask for more advice. Yes indeed; interns are very touchy on this subject. I want it understood that tired or not, I take excellent care of my patients. And if my own child were sick, would I want someone taking care of him who was as tired as I am right now? Absolutely not. Don't be ridiculous.

It feels bad to be this tired. And it makes you into an awful person. You come out of the hospital, miserable and weary, and there's a slow-moving line at the supermarket, and you feel completely outraged. How dare all these people get in your way, you who have been up all night caring for the sick? Here you are, exhausted and badly in need of a shower, and they're all obstructing you, the ungrateful wretches. They should be parting like the Red Sea to let you through. If you find yourself beginning to make a speech about this public obligation, you are indeed overtired. Forget about the super-market and go home to sleep.

Being sleep deprived also makes me oversensitive. Some-one comes by and offers a tiny little constructive comment about some patient management decision I made, and what do I do? I argue, I apologize, and overapologize, I feel ready to weep. Either I feel, oh my God, how could I ever have made such an unbelievably dumb mistake, or else I feel, why are they persecuting me so, I who live only to help others? Neither of these can be considered a healthy response. And that's my personality for much of this year: a tired personality. Fatigue is all.

I don't mean to whine too much, and I don't really have that much hope that things are going to change. I mean, how realistic is it to hope for an internship that starts every day at noon? So all I can do is whine about how tired I am, and then go fall asleep on the couch. I mean, I'm so tired. I mean, you wouldn't believe it. I mean, I wish they all could be California girls.

HELP IS ON THE WAY
· · · · · · · · ·

One night I was on call, along with a third-year medical student, and I was paged about a patient of mine off on another floor, and the nurse said he was looking worse. The medical student had been following this particular patient, so he ran ahead to see what was going on, while I finished talking to a nurse on a different ward, then hurried up after him. I arrived maybe a full minute after the medical student; he had taken a good look at the sick baby and then turned around to hunt for me. As I charged into the room, I saw distinct relief on the medical student's face, and I have to admit, what I thought was, uh-oh, this baby must really be sick. And what I also thought was, why would anyone be relieved to see *me* at a time like this?

We ran up to the baby's crib and ascertained that he was indeed working very hard to breathe, indeed not moving air very well, indeed looking terrible. We gave him oxygen, and with it we blew bronchodilators into his face, medicines to open his airways. I called for a blood-gas syringe and drew blood from his artery to measure his oxygen level, as well as some other lab values; I asked the nurses to bring the crash cart into the room. All the time I spoke in a calm, though rather high-pitched voice, and I was dimly conscious that on my face was a hideous grin, designed perhaps originally to be reassuring, but petrified into a kind of rictus. It wasn't time to call a code yet, I thought, but it might become time to call one at any minute, and he was a very little baby, and was there anything I was forgetting? And the arterial blood gas results looked good, and the baby responded to bronchodilators and started moving air again and stopped retracting so badly.

Later on that evening, the medical student said to me, as we were discussing those moments around the crib, "I was never so glad to see anyone in my whole life as when I looked down the corridor and saw you right behind me."

This brought back to me, with force, the memory of an earlier night on call, when I had been standing at the bedside of a child who I thought might be about to die, doing everything I could think of, and I had looked up to see a senior resident coming into the room in answer to my page. That had been one of my very first experiences of being alone in a near-code situation, and I had been by no means sure I was doing the right things, or even sure I was right in not having called a code. That child did fine, and no code was necessary, and after the excitement was over, when I was discussing what had happened with that senior resident, I said to her, "I was never so glad to see anyone in my whole life as when you walked into that room."

"But you were handling it fine," she said, bolstering the terrified intern.

"But I was terrified out of my mind," I said, hoping maybe for a little more bolstering.

"And you know what?" she asked. "Two years from now when you're a senior, some intern will be just as glad to see you come into a room, and inside you'll still feel exactly the same way you do now."

When I was a third-year medical student, watching interns, I certainly believed that when I reached their stage I would be far more confident, far less terrified. But the fact is that as the level of responsibility increases, despite your increasing competence and your increasing confidence, you don't necessarily get any less terrified. And yet, somehow, you manage to meet your escalating responsibilities, even the ones you are sure you won't be able to handle. I have noticed that when my fellow interns and I arrive in the morning, if the intern coming off call has a story of something sudden and drastic that happened overnight, we will ask very detailed questions, trying to find out exactly what the intern did, trying to judge whether we would know what to do in those circumstances. What did the nurse say when she paged you? What did you do when you got to the room? How did you know how sick the kid was? What meds did you give? What dose? What would you have done if the kid hadn't responded? How did you know what to do? When did you decide to call for help? And then, always, nervously, how long did it take for help to arrive?

One reason you rise to the occasion is that, as Dr. Spock assures parents in the first line of his manual, you know more than you think you do. When the emergency hits and your adrenaline is surging, half-forgotten pieces of information are suddenly accessible and judgments which would be tentative under calmer circumstances suddenly issue from your mouth with the certainty of orders. Another reason you rise to the occasion is that it's your job to; you aren't a medical student anymore, there to learn; you're a doctor, there to take care of patients. And I suppose that if you're the senior resident, and your job is to take care of interns who are in over their heads, then you do that too. But the third reason you rise to the occasion, I think, is because of a sense that you are *entitled* to do so, entitled to make the decisions, call the shots, handle the situation. It may be scary, but it's home turf and it has to be occupied with assurance.

I mean, look at drawing blood and starting IVs. How come I do them all the time now, without dreading them at all, while as a medical student, I worried over them constantly and often failed into the bargain? It isn't just more experience; the change started at the very beginning of internship. The reason is that these procedures are my job now; I'm not a medical student, worrying that I'll stick an unnecessary needle into some poor kid just because I'm not very experienced (and what would the parents say, anyway, if they knew a medical student was practicing on their child?). I'm supposed to draw blood and start IVs; it's my job, it's what an intern does. And somehow, much more often than not, the IVs go in, the blood comes out. And I'm supposed to handle it when a kid stops breathing too well; that's my job too, that's what an intern does. And somehow, even though you feel totally unprepared, even though it entails extending yourself well beyond what confidence you possess, you do your job. And then when the senior resident comes into the room, you realize that you have never been so glad to see anyone in your whole life.

JUNE
· · · · · · · · ·

Early on in my internship year, when I felt ignorant or unsure of myself in the hospital (something that did not generally occur more than once an hour), I would remind myself that by the end of internship all these insecurities would be gone. By the end of internship, I would be knowledgeable and serene, competent and confident. As internship progressed, I stopped concentrating quite so hard on my own panic, but I think I always kept the reassuring thought in the back of my mind: after all, you're just an intern—how much can you be expected to know?

But all good things must come to an end, and even internship, which once stretched ahead of me as an endless vista of nights on call, winds slowly to a finish. March came, and with it the list of the new interns, the ones who would arrive in July. And if there was going to be a new group of interns, that meant that we, the old interns, would be . . . well, we would be junior residents, that's all. Now, to you that may not seem like a very exciting distinction, but to an intern it seems quite important. It's the difference between being the absolute beginner, the doctor on the very bottom level of the pyramid, and being one of the group of more advanced people. There's a certain tone in which senior people say the word *intern*. "So, the *intern* who was taking care of the patient thought that . . ."

Internship year is one of those rites of passage; back at the beginning I imagined that I would not be at all the same person once I had done my internship. How could I be the same person? I would be someone who knew how to be a doctor. And that was what I went on telling myself whenever I found myself in situations where I didn't know what to do. By the end of internship you'll know, I whispered reassuringly in my own ear. And now, at the end of internship, I find, disconcertingly, that I am in fact still the same person, that I am frequently unsure of myself, and that there is an awful lot I still don't know but think I should. And I have lost that lovely comforting sense that I have the rest of my internship to make up the deficiencies.

So what is it that I know at the end of internship that I didn't know a year ago at the beginning? Well, certainly internship has been highly educational. In addition to the extensive information I have absorbed about the clinical management of a range of diseases, there are a couple of essential, more general areas where I think I've made some progress.

First of all, I'm better at deciding who is sick and who is well. This is one of the most basic questions in medicine, and it is especially complex when you're dealing with babies and small children who can't talk. They can cry because they have colic or they can cry because they're cranky or they can cry because they have acute appendicitis or meningitis or broken bones. So before you even worry about the finer points of diagnosis, you have to decide where to place a given patient on the sick–not sick continuum. At the beginning, you're inclined to assume that anyone brought to the hospital is by definition sick. You look at a happy, playful child sitting in the emergency room drinking a bottle and chewing on corn chips, and the parents tell you the child has a runny nose, and you wonder what blood tests you need to do (so you walk out of the room and ask the senior on duty, who asks you what blood tests were routinely done on *you* as a child when *you* had a runny nose, and you ask anxiously whether we can really be sure this isn't meningitis, and should we maybe do a spinal tap?). By the end of the year you're much more comfortable with these decisions, and you argue forcefully for or against various diagnostic procedures; you make clinical decisions. Lots of important decisions can come down to this question of sick versus not sick; there is no magic formula to tell you, for example, whether a seven-month-old with a three-day history of diarrhea needs to have an IV line started for rehydration. It's a question of sick or not sick, or, in this case, dehydrated or not dehydrated. There's no perfect system for deciding whether a two-year-old with a temperature of 104 needs a spinal tap; it comes down to sick versus not sick. (And of course, even as you take a modest pride in your ability to judge this, you know that at some point you are going to send a not-sick child out of the emergency room without doing a spinal tap, and that child is going to develop meningitis, become a sick child, and come back to the emergency room; and you will wonder whether you could have caught it early on if you'd done the tap, and you'll tap the next six or seven babies you see, sick or not. . . .)

This leads to the next major area where I think I've made a lot of progress over the past year: when to call for help. This is probably the single most essential issue for a doctor at any level. If you call for help every time a problem comes up, then it's hard to see what use you are. On the other hand, if you neglect to call for help when you in fact need it, you are subjecting your patients to all sorts of risks.

Now, calling for help can mean a variety of things. On its most basic level, it means the intern, standing by the bed of a child who has stopped breathing, yelling for help. Well, maybe politely asking the nurse to call a code, please. (The intern then begins to administer oxygen to the patient, and within about a minute and a half an announcement is made over the hospital loudspeaker system and fifteen or twenty doctors and nurses come running into the room and resuscitate everyone in sight, including the intern, if it should be necessary.) On a more mundane level, calling for help can mean an intern asking a senior resident to try to start a difficult IV. But much more often, calling for help means discussing decisions with someone else, or asking the person who is supervising you to come look at a patient who is worrying you, or double-checking something you've ordered done. It means acknowledging your own limitations, admitting it when you're dealing with something you've never seen before, wondering aloud whether your judgment was right.

At the beginning of the year, of course, I called for help every ten minutes. I couldn't write a single order without wondering whether I was inadvertently going to kill off my patient; I couldn't react to any sudden change in a sick child's condition without wondering what a "real doctor" would have done. When I was on call at night, I checked in with the senior resident at regular intervals. Then I began to take some pride in not calling the senior too often, and gradually arrived at a point where I called either for help with IVs, which the senior often can't do either, or else for genuine emergencies.

You start to understand that many of the tiny decisions you agonized over early on in the year are decisions that are not going to do any harm either way. Much of medical management is a matter of style—how aggressive do you want to be? which drugs do you like to use?—and you might as well make the decisions yourself and develop a style of your own. You become more confident of your own ability to answer questions, to impersonate a "real doctor." You sign MD after your name with confidence.

(And then, as the year ends, and you feel a teeny bit smug about how rarely and how appropriately you call for help, you realize that when you become a junior resident there will be situations in which interns, calling for help, will call you. And there you will be in some extreme situation, and instead of making the decision that this is too much for you, you need help and guidance, some nervous intern will be looking to you with hope and supplication. This is extremely anxiety producing.)

The third general area of knowledge is this: I think I understand better at the end of the year that there are in fact situations where there is nothing I can do to help. At the beginning of the year, I could never shake the feeling that no matter how bad the disease, no matter how bad the patient's prognosis, if only some really good doctor were here, maybe there would be something to be done. I remember taking care of an adolescent boy with a horrible case of cystic fibrosis, a boy who had essentially come into the hospital to die. Every evening before he went home, the senior resident on my team would say to me, remember that if they call you to see this boy because he can't breathe, remember there isn't anything you can do. We had discussed it all, with the boy and with his family, we had tried everything that could be tried. The boy's parents essentially knew that he was going to suffocate, they had agreed wholeheartedly that he should not be placed on a mechanical ventilator, since there was no hope of reversing his lung disease—but whenever his breathing got a little worse, they panicked, thinking this was it, this was good-bye, and they asked the nurse to call me. And so there I would stand with them, looking at their son, and I would have nothing to offer, and it took me a long time to accept this. I had to accept that it wasn't my fault, that, as my senior resident kept telling me, I hadn't given him this disease. I know this may sound trivial and egotistical (she stands by the bed of a dying child and she worries about herself!), but in fact it is genuinely impossible to function as a doctor if you are constantly holding yourself responsible for the illness or the suffering of your patients. You have to accept the almost unthinkable idea that these people have these horrible diseases, and you do what you can—but sometimes there is nothing you can do.

So there are some of the fruits of internship. In many ways, internship seems like the last great and formal milestone; there are no more graduations, there are no more obvious required ceremonies and group promotions. From here on in, it's a much more individual course you take. But all doctors have to go through that internship year and come out the other side. It's the final decisive passage from nondoctor to doctor.

It's the baptism by fire, the year in the trenches, or any other bloodstained metaphor you like.

So you have to face the fact that with July, the new interns start their year, and they will look up to you, you with your greater experience, the confidence they assume you have developed. You will suddenly become a resource, a source of help and guidance. And all you can say about that is that it's a good thing all this happens in July, when the interns are new and green and maybe a little easier to convince that you know what you're doing. All interns are not equal; you could never impress a seasoned end-of-year intern. Which makes sense, after all; a seasoned end-of-year intern in June by definition knows just as much as any July junior resident.

II

....

MIDDLE

All true histories contain instruction; though, in some, the treasure may be hard to find, and when found, so trivial in quantity that the dry, shrivelled kernel scarcely compensates for the trouble of cracking the nut. Whether this be the case with my history or not, I am hardly competent to judge; I sometimes think it might prove useful to some, and entertaining to others, but the world may judge for itself: shielded by my own obscurity, and by the lapse of years, and a few fictitious names, I do not fear to venture, and will candidly lay before the public what I would not disclose to the most intimate friend.

Anne Brontë
Agnes Grey

I t's nice not to be an intern anymore. Unfortunately, in my program at least, the schedule doesn't get any better your second year. But at least you're not an intern. At least you know the hospital, know the language, know the rules. And above all, there is a group of new interns running around the place, and they demonstrably know less than you do. And that is how you are supposed to realize how far you've come.

In fact, I spent much of my second year in misery and terror at how far I hadn't come. One theme of the year was a complete crisis of confidence. Oh, sure, I had often lacked confidence as an intern—but as an intern, I was at least secure in the knowledge that I was *supposed* to be insecure. As a second-year resident, I worried that I was somehow stuck in my internship, that I made a reasonably good beginner, but then was unable to take the next few steps. I agonized not just because I doubted my own competence, but because the very fact that I was still doubting myself seemed to me to indicate that I was not moving along the way I was supposed to.

All through my internship, I had kept resolving to write more often in my journal; there are a total of three or four notes from that year of my life. During my junior year, I did start keeping a journal more regularly; most of the entries were actually written in the hospital, on the backs of scut sheets. Rereading that journal is not a particularly pleasant experience. The whole year is nothing but a pile of battered sheets; on one side are compulsive lists of patients and acronym-ridden problem lists (UVL d/c'd, NP airway CPAP, Amp & Gent, PN 12.5), on the other self-indulgent outpourings about Doubts. If I wasn't accusing myself of mistakes, I was justifying myself against some criticism I had either received or imagined, explaining how so-and-so hadn't really understood what was going on, and the attending never really watched me in action, and the person who criticized me was always attacking residents.

One problem may have been that the junior resident year at the hospital at which I trained was notoriously a kind of extended adolescence—and adolescents are, after all, self-conscious, self-critical, and self-absorbed. At most hospitals, junior residents run the ward teams, supervising the interns. In my program, however, there were lots of slots to fill in the two different NICUs we covered and in the regular pediatric intensive care unit (PICU, of course). We spent much of junior year in these units, no longer interns, but not yet really in charge.

There has been, in fact, a general trend in medicine toward increased supervision for doctors in training. When I started my residency, the junior resident would be left alone in the NICU at night, if things were relatively quiet. But then they changed the rules and made the neonatology fellows stay "in-house," so the junior would never be alone. So as a junior, you sometimes felt you were still an intern, always under some-one's direct supervision—the neonatology fellow's, the ICU fellow's, the attending's. And the paradox of medical training, of course, is that while you are deeply grateful for the backup, you also find yourself chafing a little: don't they think I can do it?

Patients, of course, should generally be grateful to know that more experienced people are available. The problem for the resident is that sooner or later you have to do something on your own for the first time, and the urge to do it, to have done it, to have it behind you, can be even stronger than your terror, maybe even stronger than your good sense.

Anyway, we complained a lot about that during our second year, about people always breathing down our necks, about how juniors at other hospitals were running teams, something we wouldn't do till our senior year. That's what adolescents do, after all—complain.

I started out my second year by working on the pediatric oncology ward. I went to the NICU and the PICU. The kids in all these places are very sick, all very far from normal childhood health and happiness. As you learn how to keep them alive, and also how to let them go, when they need to be let go, you find you are learning all the basic lessons of medical school and internship over again.

And therefore, if you're lucky, when your own anxieties and doubts are not too noisy and too much in your way, you can pay attention to your patients, to their bodies and to their stories and to their families, and not only take proper care of them, but also learn what they have to teach you.

1

Oncology

My first month as a junior resident was spent on the oncology ward. Some of the children there had just been diagnosed with malignancies, had come into the hospital for the initiation of chemotherapy, radiation, experimental drug protocols. It was a floor on which devastated families were routine, people who had just heard the very worst news they would ever hear. And most of the children, of course, had been "previously healthy."

Other children were long-time oncology patients, coming back in for problems, most often for what we called F and N, fever and neutropenia. Chemotherapy, in order to fight the insanely dividing malignant cells, kills any cells that are dividing rapidly. The cells which line the stomach are affected, often leading to severe nausea. And the cells of the immune system are wiped out as well, producing neutropenia—a lack of white blood cells—leaving the child relatively undefended against bacterial infection. When a child who is neutropenic gets a fever, serious bacterial infection is presumed. The child is hospitalized and started on big-time intravenous antibiotics—the F and N cocktail, we called it. Most of the time it turns out that there is no serious infection—the blood cultures are negative, the child feels fine, the white blood cell count slowly comes back up.

In addition to the new diagnoses and the routine F and N admissions, we took care of the kids who were not doing well: the ones for whom therapy had failed, the ones who hadn't gone into remission, the ones who had developed serious complications. The ones who were dying. The oncologists used to tell us that by working only with the hospitalized patients we were missing the big picture. All the kids with leukemia, now in remission, coming into clinic and looking great. The overall statistics on childhood malignancies have improved by leaps and bounds over the past couple of decades. Most children with cancer now get better. When you work on an inpatient oncology ward, you see the ones who don't.

Although the statistics now look so much better, the idea of childhood cancer retains its powerful impact. Leukemia. Brain tumor. Bone cancer. These are words to make you shiver, the stuff of parental nightmares. For residents, this ward meant hours in the treatment room, starting IVs to put chemotherapy into the bloodstream, doing spinal taps to infuse it directly into the central nervous system, and learning to do bone marrow biopsies (a brutal procedure in which you jam a big needle down into a child's hip bone to suck out some of the marrow). It meant many children on elaborate experimental chemotherapy protocols, getting drugs we hadn't heard of before we found ourselves ordering them. It meant waiting, every day, for cell counts to come back from the hematology lab, to find out who had how many white blood cells, with parents hovering in the doorway—if you have more than five hundred white cells per cubic millimeter of blood, you're considered no longer neutropenic, and you can come off antibiotics and go home, assuming everything else is okay.

The pediatric oncology ward is a miracles-of-modern-medicine kind of place. Even a beginner, a resident who yesterday knew almost nothing about leukemia and today knows only what she remembers from sleeping through attending rounds, finds herself proudly using the first person plural: nowadays, we can do so much for children with leukemia. Pediatric oncology is often cited as an example of the brilliant successes of modern biomedical research. But the ward is also, of course, a place where children come, when the miracles fail.

MIRRORS
· · · · · · · · ·

At the end of my second year of medical school, I started learning how to do a physical examination. It was out of the classrooms and into the hospitals.

At first, of course, it was a little bit daunting to walk into some stranger's hospital room, ask a long list of personal questions, and then politely ask the stranger to disrobe. But you know, you can get used to anything, and more quickly than you expect to. Within a week or so, I took it for granted that total strangers would willingly let me poke and prod. I was accepting my own authority, accepting a certain detachment that allowed me to keep my distance as I did physical exams on strangers—pressing on their bellies, lighting my way deep into their eyes. I was on my way to being a doctor, I was different. I had rights that no one else had (the inalienable right to the rectal exam). I was outside normal human conventions of behavior and privacy.

And one day I walked into a patient's room and found

myself face-to-face with a man my father's age, who looked rather like my father. In addition, he turned out to be a college professor (like my father) and to have a rather professorial way of speaking (like my father). And I was supposed to do a good, thorough physical exam. All my new authority deserted me. I had a nice little talk with the gentleman, and I put my stethoscope on his back and his chest. I didn't make him take off his pajamas. I didn't do a rectal exam. Hell, I didn't even really look at his eyes properly; I shined the light briefly in their direction. Now, of course it wasn't important for his medical care that he get a full exam from the medical student—he had already been examined and reexamined by all his doctors. I was there for the learning experience, which, I suppose, I got.

It is hard to take care of patients who somehow "match" your life, patients who remind you too clearly that there is no stable barrier between the sick and the healthy. If you are the intern in the emergency room, and your name is Sue and you are twenty-seven years old, and they bring in a twenty-seven-year-old woman named Sue who has just tried to commit suicide—well, you are supposed to take care of her, but every time you present her case ("This is a twenty-seven-year-old female . . .") you may feel a little as if you're dictating your own obituary. You go to stick a great big needle in her, and you flinch a little bit as you clean her skin off with alcohol.

Obviously, you find aspects of yourself in many different patients. When I worked on the adolescent ward, I sometimes knew the right words to say to angry patients, because I had been an angry and uncooperative adolescent myself. The Rebecca of Sunnybrook Farm patients were more difficult for me to understand; anyone who is a good-natured adolescent is obviously no close kin of mine. I took care of a newborn baby whose parents wanted desperately to find a way to keep the baby in bed with them overnight, and I remembered the early months of my own son's life, when he migrated every night from his basket to our bed, and I helped bend hospital rules to set up sleeping arrangements for this family. But none of these things was near the bone.

And then there was my first night on the oncology service. I had a three-and-a-half-year-old son who was articulate and demanding. My first night on the oncology service, I admitted a three-and-a-half-year-old boy.

He had been perfectly healthy until developing some cold symptoms, some fevers, some swollen glands, and then he went to the doctor and they did a blood test; and within a couple of hours his family was sitting in a little room waiting for the results of the bone marrow biopsy—waiting to find out whether he had leukemia.

Now, this boy reminded me strongly of my own son. He was very obviously the same age, he had the same vocabulary, the same mix of dazzling unexpected articulateness with familiar silly baby words—and the same baby words, of course, the ones that get hung on to longest, especially in times of stress, *botty* for *bottle*, for example. He was frenetically active, even when overtired; he was sporadically affectionate, cuddling and hugging; and he was even at the same stage of toilet training. I mean, this boy looked very familiar indeed.

Well, I hoped he didn't have leukemia. I was reminded of something that a senior and seemingly battle-hardened doctor had once said after a similar sort of diagnosis—lovely healthy child suddenly turns out to have life-threatening disease—"This is the kind of case where you really go home and hug your own kids tight at the end of the day." I wanted to go home and hug my own kid. Actually, I wanted to bring my own kid in and have him get a blood test—if not a bone marrow biopsy. I mean, if this healthy three-and-a-half-year-old could turn out to have leukemia, then how could I be sure that other healthy three-and-a-half-year-old was all right?

Well, my patient turned out to have leukemia. I was in the room when his parents were told; I was one of the people who tried to help them take in what was happening to them, to help them see the job in front of them and focus on doing it. I did not say—and neither did anyone else—what we all knew was true: your lives have changed this afternoon, your lives will never be the same, you are crossing a barrier into a world you have probably never thought about, you will learn words in an alien language. In a few weeks you will be talking knowledgeably about cell counts and chemotherapy (which you will nonchalantly call chemo), remission and relapse. It is not just his sickness you have to cope with; it is also the end of your life as a healthy family, a family untouched by serious illness.

I didn't say that, partially because I knew these parents understood this, or were coming to understand and accept it. I thought about it, because I was, of course, imagining it happening to my own family, imagining myself trying to cope. And at the same time, of course, I was looking at it as a doctor, commenting to other doctors that this boy was "lucky" in his diagnosis—meaning that he has the kind of leukemia with the highest cure rate, and meaning that he has a number of favorable prognostic signs. I was thinking about the work involved for me in taking care of him and trying to foresee possible problems that might arise in the middle of the night so I could discuss with more senior doctors ahead of time what I would do. And all the time, more things about my patient kept reminding me of my own son.

And isn't this, after all, your most basic parental terror? The semiroutine trip to the pediatrician, the healthy normal-looking child whom you love more than anything, and then the doctor looks concerned and something is wrong—and your child has a serious disease and doctors are telling you that you're lucky because nowadays they have ways to treat this. Certainly I am not the only one who found this case emotionally difficult. The oncologist who did the bone marrow biopsy told me that he was just plain sick and tired of giving bad news to families. So many of the oncology patients we see are familiar inhabitants of the hospital; their lives and their families' lives changed long ago, and they are now used to the hospital, even in a way used to the disease. To see a new family coming to terms with it reminds us all of how scary the terms are, how terrifying the paraphernalia and procedures of the hospital can be.

But still, it was different because the boy matched my own son. It was just plain different. And I do not want to make it sound as if this difference were somehow profoundly to my credit. It is not a tribute to my sensitivity that I looked at this boy and thought of my own. It may have guided me in offering some kind of help to the parents, but then again, I could have been so totally absorbed in what I would have needed to hear in their place that I completely missed their particular needs. And in general, this added emotional impact when a patient somehow matches my own life does not demonstrate that I am a deeply and commendably sensitive being. It is rather, I am afraid, some version of the universal human mechanism by which we seek to ward off evil, to keep sickness away from ourselves and our children.

Seeing a child with a bad disease, I feel the impulse to find reasons why it would happen to this child but not to mine—what are the differences that satisfy those terms? And here was a child with no such differences. I couldn't point to previous illnesses (oh well, that kid's had pneumonia four times and my kid's never had it . . .) or to any kind of parental neglect (well, if they'd noticed it sooner, the way I would have . . .) or to genetic traits (well, of course, with all those family members who had the same disease . . .). These things do not determine which three-and-a-half-year-old gets leukemia. I am afraid that when I hover over such a patient, part of me is bargaining with the deity—I'll take care of this one perfectly, and you'll leave mine alone.

And last of all, the matching patient, the patient who could be you or someone you love is the patient who undermines the doctor's most basic defense. Listen: we are all mortal, we are all subject to bad diseases, and we are all going to die eventually. Even doctors. Even their beloved children. And that's reasonable in a theoretical sense, but if you work in a hospital, you can't let each patient serve as a concrete reminder of that. Your brain simply cannot compute that kind of realistic evidence of its own vulnerability. So what you do, a little bit, is deny that after all the differences are itemized, ultimately you are more like your patients, all patients, than you are different from them. You think of yourself as the doctor—by definition different. And then the patient comes along who is close enough to a mirror image of you or someone you love, and you can't keep the illusion of differentness intact. As a doctor, you see grim evidence of all the dangers, all the diseases, and once you allow yourself to imagine those dangers encroaching on yourself, or on your child, you find yourself haunted by very specific terrors. Your defenses are breached and you are facing the fact that all patients are, to some extent, mirror images of your vulnerable human self, your vulnerable human child.

DEATHWATCH

A child is dying, will maybe die tonight. She has a disease; and there is no cure, and there is nothing more to do to slow down the progress of the disease. She is dying of cancer, a particularly virulent kind, unfortunately discovered too late, unfortunately unresponsive to treatment. She has been through radiation therapy and chemotherapy and surgery, she has had IVs in her arms and legs, and finally had a special large IV surgically implanted in her chest. She has had her blood drawn on multiple, multiple occasions, and new blood transfused into her too many times to count. She has had samples of her bone marrow sucked out into syringes; she has had a piece of her lungs cut out and studied. At the nursing station is a thick folder containing records of past hospitalizations, and on the front is written, Volume 6 of 6.

In the late afternoon all the other doctors on the team went home for the night. Since I am on call, they gave me sign-out on each patient, careful instructions about what might go wrong, what to do if this patient gets a fever, if that patient starts throwing up. My own patients I know, of course, but I am also responsible for all the other patients, so I clutch my clipboard with the sign-out sheets. The sign-out on the dying child is approximately this:

DNR by family's request (do not resuscitate—no heroic measures, no mechanical ventilation, no cardiopulmonary resuscitation)

No painful procedures, no percutaneous blood draws (when a patient gets a fever, we often draw blood not only out of the central line but also percutaneously, through their skin; not to be attempted in this case)

Push morphine for pain, agitation (if the child is in distress, go in and inject narcotics through her IV)

Now, it would be fair to interpret this sign-out as follows: if this child starts to die, go in there and make her death easy, even if you make it quicker. In other words, give narcotics to take the pain away, even though you know they will also take away the will to breathe. You could even, if you really didn't want to mince words, interpret this sign-out as follows: if this child gets into pain or distress, go in there and help her die. Or even, if you have to say what we almost never say, go in there and kill her.

Now, this is not a big moral dilemma for me, and it isn't what I want to write about. When the senior doctor who supervises me is leaving for the day, he goes over this particular sign-out with me one more time, looks me in the eye, and asks me, "Are you comfortable with that?" "Yes, of course," I say. It's true; I have no doubts at all. The one thing anyone can do for this dying child and her family now is take away the pain, and I will do my best to do that even if it means she stops breathing. That seems only obvious and only humane; it has been fully explained to the parents and it is what they want as well.

No, what I want to write about is the deathwatch itself, the role of the doctor waiting to see if this will be the night the child dies. It's evening and I am checking lab results at the computer. I write down numbers on various pieces of paper; I notice a few numbers which demand action on my part—a baby who needs a blood transfusion, a child with low potassium who needs to get a little more of it in his IV fluid. I do not think constantly about the little girl who is dying, but she is always on my mind. She is the great tension of the evening, the drama which puts everything else into perspective. Deaths are not common on most pediatric wards; most children get better, even children with cancer. Death is by no means an everyday event; I have seen deaths, presided over deaths even, but they are still rare and remarkable.

I complete a couple of the requests marked on the sign-out sheet, checking on one patient's urine output, making sure he is putting out a certain number of cubic centimeters per kilogram per hour (proof that his kidneys are working), checking on another patient who has been having bad headaches, but is now sleeping peacefully. I go into the bathroom, and find the mother of the girl who is dying standing at the sink and crying. "Do you think it will happen tonight?" she asks me. "I don't know," I say. She doesn't say, you won't let her feel any pain will you, but I know she has said that again and again to the various doctors in charge of her daughter's care. I also know that what she feels is in part a wish for all this to be over. I don't know her very well; I don't know anything about her, really. I don't know what kind of life she will go back to when her daughter's misery is finally finished; I don't know how she copes with day after day in the hospital. She is a stranger, but tonight of course our lives are touching intimately, even melodramatically. She dries her eyes on a paper towel and leaves the bathroom.

They call me from another floor to say that one of the patients for whom I am responsible needs a new IV, so I go down and try to put one in. Another child who has had IV after IV after IV; his veins are all used up. I try twice and fail, and then, as I am carefully inspecting each square centimeter of his forearm, my beeper goes off. "Please come up here fast," says the nurse. "I think she's going." I abandon the IV (not without some small sense of relief that I do not have to keep sticking needles into this boy) and run back upstairs, ask the nurse to call one of the other residents to do the IV. I go into the little girl's bedroom. She is twisting and turning on her bed. "I can't breathe," she says, "I can't get any air!" Then she screams, screams for help to her mother, who looks for help toward me. I hold an oxygen mask to her face, but she hits at it wildly and screams again. A nurse hands me a syringe and I begin to push morphine into her IV, all the time saying over and over, "It's going to be okay. I'm going to help you breathe better. You're going to calm down now and feel fine. . . ." All in an artificially calm doctor-in-control voice.

In fact, it works. The narcotic relaxes her, and with the terror gone, she's able to breathe. She lies back on her pillow and her father takes her hand and her mother comes closer to the bed; and I hear one of those little exchanges which are not meant for my ears (after all, I hardly know these people): "I don't want to die now, not right now." "Lie back and sleep, Mommy will stay right here."

Understand, there is nothing people can say in this situation that is not the stuff of bad movies. Understand, it could easily be that the child in the bed was crying, "Daddy, don't leave me," the mother telling her, "Soon you'll be with Jesus," that whatever it was they said, it would read on the page like dialogue which would never be allowed into a respectable story. And understand also that as I stand in this crowded little hospital room, I am once more seized with a sense of shock at what I am doing in these people's lives. This is a climax, a crux, their child is dying; and I am a stranger who is supposed to mediate this death.

I am the doctor, but I cannot cure. My job is in some sense to take responsibility, to preside. The nurses know this family much better than I do; the child is not my patient, so I have spent very little time with them. But the nurses cannot take the responsibility for pushing the morphine. They cannot decide what drugs to give, cannot push past the margin of safety in the name of killing pain. I am the official; for a moment I see myself as the referee.

The girl is comfortable now, and I leave the room. One of the nurses is going down to the soda machine on the third floor and she brings me back a Diet Coke and I sit at the desk and sip it, thinking vague thoughts about the conjunctions of cosmic and ridiculous in the hospital: a dying child, a diet soda. I know that it's reasonable of me to think of the night in terms of work I have to do, in terms of getting a half hour for dinner, getting to sleep if I can—even if a child is dying. Even if a child is dying, it's still my night's work.

A friend who is on call on one of the other wards comes up to visit me and we go into the conference room. I tell her about my patient who is dying and she tells me about what's going on on her ward, and then we make a conscious effort to talk about other things, and we gossip a little about the residents in the program, about one of the new renal fellows who is kind of cute but obviously knows it and is he really as good a doctor as he thinks he is? And then we complain that everyone is working so hard that there isn't really any good gossip.

A nurse sticks her head into the conference room to tell me that the girl is now sleeping peacefully and breathing much more easily. I tell her to increase the rate of the intravenous narcotic infusion just slightly for the rest of the night. My friend says good-bye and goes off to her own ward. I go outside and write a note in a patient's chart. I check on the girl again, but when I open the door to her room, I see her parents holding each other, and I back right out again.

I get called once more, a little after midnight, for a similar sort of episode, anxiety and difficulty breathing. Again I push extra narcotics, but this time the girl is in real pain and it's harder to make her feel better. Her father becomes furious at me and starts to scream that I'm supposed to prevent the pain, what the hell do I think I'm doing? and I basically agree with him; I push even more medication and finally the pain goes away. This time I really think she's going to die; her breathing seems shallower to me and her face looks gray. But in fact, nothing changes, she just goes on sleeping.

I decide to go to sleep myself, reminding the nurses to call me if they have any concerns at all, knowing they will. This is my job, not theirs, to preside. In fact, though I get awakened several times, none have to do with this patient, who sleeps her narcotized sleep steadily on till morning. There is no triumph in having kept her alive, and only a small one in having kept her from feeling any more pain than she felt. With the morning come the other doctors; with the morning, I am no longer in charge. Someone else will preside tonight—if she is still alive in three nights, it will be my turn again. The others look at me questioningly as they arrive, and I tell them, "Still alive," and they nod, and another hospital day has begun.

2

....

Outpatients

Part of residency training is what is called continuity clinic. In order to remind you that most medical care does not actually take place in hospitals, in order to introduce you to patients who have nothing catastrophically wrong with them, in order to give you experience taking care of children over the course of years, you go to clinic once a week. When new babies are born who need pediatricians, when kids come into the emergency room and their parents can't supply the name of a regular pediatrician, those kids get referred to the clinic, divided up among the residents. And every so often you find yourself bonding with a particular family on the wards while the child is hospitalized, and they ask if you will be the child's doctor.

People who bring their children to a residents' clinic for medical care are usually not from the very high end of the socioeconomic spectrum. The visits are cheap, and the residents come and go every couple of years—not exactly the upscale model for pediatric care. For my own children, of course, I wanted a well-established, experienced pediatrician, someone whose style I found sympathetic, someone I could anticipate seeing for years and years. On the other hand, residents' clinics offer access to all the accumulated subspecialty expertise and high technology of a big academic hospital. This is sometimes a good thing, and sometimes not, since expertise and technology are not always applied appropriately.

At a teaching hospital, well child clinics are not the only clinics. There are also clinics for children with every kind of disease: immunology clinics and cystic fibrosis clinics and muscular dystrophy clinics. At these clinics, children with chronic medical problems get the specialized care they need, when they are well and when they are sick—but not sick enough to need hospitalization. The newest chronic disease of childhood is AIDS. I began, during my second year of residency, to get involved in a very small way with the AIDS clinic, to take care of a couple of kids with HIV infection. This was again a longitudinal involvement, a question of seeing the same children again and again over months and years, and watching them as they grew.

Doctors are by definition interested in many things that are disgusting or horrible or tragic. We are interested in processes which cause death and decay, and, yes, we are interested because we want to help; but we are also, often, interested because we are interested. Certainly, if you devote your life to the study of kidney disease in children, you do it in part because you want to see these children do better, live longer. But your brain is probably also tickled by certain aspects of renal functioning, by a desire to understand how the kidney works and what happens when it stops working (I choose this example because I have never ever understood how the kidney works; the dumbest kidney may indeed be smarter than the smartest resident, but it is much much smarter than I am). And so, even while I was shaken by the illnesses of children with AIDS, and moved by their courage and by the fortitude and love of those who cared for them, a little voice inside me whispered that it was fascinating to be living through a twentieth-century epidemic. To be watching the reactions of the government and the public and the medical world. To be working with a disease that was only just being understood, to have the hope of new therapies and new discoveries.

Children with AIDS do not live in the hospital. They are hospitalized when they get sick, but their real lives are at home with their parents, their grandparents, their foster parents. A child who is admitted to the hospital becomes a patient. The hospital is a rigidly organized place; if you aren't a nurse or a doctor or a play therapist or a custodian or a blood bank technician etc., etc., why then, you must be a patient. But children who come into the clinics are not full-time patients. Yes, we call them outpatients, but really they are just children, making time in their days for a stop at the hospital. Even if they have chronic diseases, they are still out there living their lives. The disease has not taken over. They come to the clinic to be checked out, to have their medical issues discussed—and then they go back out into the world, where they belong.

WCC

I spend my time in a children's hospital. I start IVs, draw quantities of blood for obscure tests (serum amino acid levels, assays of unusual metabolites, acronyms I can't even decipher), carry out spinal taps and occasional bone marrow biopsies. Most children never stay overnight in a hospital, never have IVs, let alone bone marrow biopsies.

What I do all day is usually irrelevant to the lives that most children lead.

One afternoon a week, I have clinic. I see children who come in for their shots, their checkups—what we call well child care (WCC in the eternal abbreviations of the hospital, where IUTD means immunizations up-to-date). I see children who have diaper rashes or little fevers. I fill out their school forms or their welfare forms or their summer camp physical forms. It's a long distance away from the children on the wards, hospitalized with serious illnesses, the unbelievably miniature babies in the NICU, the children who need extra oxygen to breathe or supermodern superexpensive antibiotics to fight off infection. On the wards, you live with the constant possibility that a child, already very sick, may suddenly get sicker, may stop breathing, may lose the battle to infection, may start to die. In clinic, you answer questions about bedtime battles or the feeding habits of toddlers. Despite all this, clinic is sometimes more terrifying.

The thing is, the kids on the ward are sick, but everyone knows it. Lots of people are thinking about them, and thinking hard. I may be the resident, but there are other residents on my team, there's a senior resident supervising me and an attending physician supervising us both, there are experienced nurses and there are worried watchful parents. Someone will catch me if I miss something; I may be left feeling silly, but the patient will be fine. If I miss something, let some change of condition get by me, there are plenty of people on the wards who will bring it to my attention. I worry much more about missing something in clinic, where the kids are healthy.

The proud parents bring their one-month-old boy into clinic for his first checkup. They're a little bit exhausted, and they've never had a baby before and there isn't any room in their one-bedroom apartment for all the adorable baby clothes, which are still arriving from the mother's large family in Ohio, plus the hand-me-down cribs and strollers and playpens from the father's older siblings in the Boston suburbs. In one month of parenthood, they have used up six rolls of film. In one month of parenthood, they have neither of them slept for more than three hours at a stretch. And to take little Mark for his first checkup, they have dressed him in his best, and also them-selves—they are both much more formally dressed than I am.

Even though I'm a second-year resident, in the clinic I'm the doctor. There's supervision, of course, there's a senior doc-tor present, but I'm the only one who examines each suppos-edly well child in careful detail. I'm the only one who spends a long time discussing child raising with the family. If Mark has a heart murmur, I'm the one who has to hear it. If he has congenital dislocation of the hip, I'm the one who has to notice it when I wishbone his little legs and press them down. If he has, heaven forbid, one of the comparatively common tumors of childhood—a retinoblastoma in his eye, a Wilms' tumor in his kidney—I have to find it with my ophthalmoscope or with my fingers as I press down on his fat little tummy.

Of course, he probably has none of the above. By far the majority of babies have none of the above. *You* probably had no heart murmur, no hip dislocation, no tumor. But some babies do have all those things, and if Mark, all dressed up in his completely impractical white sailor suit, has anything at all, I have to find it. I mean, we're playing for high stakes here, we're talking about detecting problems early, before heart dis-ease stops the child's growth, before dislocated hips prevent him from walking, before a tumor grows—as I said, high stakes. There is no tiny little part of the physical exam which I have not, during my anxieties as a resident, imagined into a life-or-death issue. That fact does not make it any easier to see into the eyes of an uncooperative one-month-old (is there any other kind?).

Think back now on your visits to the pediatrician. Did she give you the distinct feeling that she was looking for a deadly disease at every turn? When she looked in your eyes, after you were old enough to cooperate, did you sense that she was searching for brain tumors? In clinic, I have to deal with the parents of healthy children; it is not my job to involve them in my anxieties about the pathology I might discover, explore with them every possible disastrous alternative, then finally, with surprised relief, hand them back a perfectly normal baby. Mark's parents, after all, are perfectly capable of coming up with their own anxieties. They never see an article or a TV show about a sick child without a quick tiny flash of terror. When they come into the hospital to bring Mark to see me, and they happen to see someone else's child paralyzed in a wheelchair or bald from chemotherapy, there is no way to escape that flash. My job, with Mark's parents, is to reassure: yes, your child is healthy, your child is perfect, you're doing a good job.

So I show his parents how he fits perfectly onto the growth chart, his height, weight, and head circumference all seventy-fifth percentile. I try hard to examine him cheerfully, whatever my private terrors. I make funny noises to distract him, I coo over his cute little belly while I'm pressing on it. It's fun, actually—but I haven't been doing it long enough yet to get over that sense of terror; *am I missing something important?* Maybe you never get over it.

Mark's parents have a long list of questions for me. Will it really spoil him if they pick him up when he cries? Is he gaining enough weight? Why won't his diaper rash go away, when they've been putting cream on it five times a day? Is it normal that he throws up every day, sometimes more than once? And so on. I didn't learn the answers to these questions in medical school; as a matter of fact, I often find myself thinking back on my own son's infancy, what I asked the pediatrician, what she told me. Before clinic, we have teaching conferences in which we discuss various nitty-gritty issues of child care. After all, it doesn't actually help to know the pathophysiology of various rare gastrointestinal disorders if what you need to do is teach parents how to burp a baby (I have a vision of that particular skill being taught in medical school: position the infant longitudinally across the medial section of your clavicle, then hold the dorsum of your opposite hand cupped and apply repeatedly to the infant, over the thoracic and lumbar spine).

And I have some questions of my own. I need to find out how this family is getting along, I need to satisfy myself that Mark's parents are coping reasonably well with all the additional stress and confusion that having a baby has wrought in their lives. I need to offer help if things are going wrong. Somewhere at the back of my mind, along with retinoblastoma, I have to keep the specters of child abuse, child neglect, the nonmedical tragedies that can overwhelm a child and his family.

This can mean that I have to be a busybody. Maybe you are thinking with indignation that of course no pediatrician ever questioned *your* parents with those ideas in mind, that your present pediatrician never worries about *you* that way. But a good pediatrician does this with subtlety, watching your interaction with your child, asking about volatile issues like toilet training or sleeping through the night, checking to make sure that things don't seem to be going somehow, badly, wrong.

On the wards, I start IVs and order medications to be given, dripped carefully into the veins. In clinic, I give shots. Actually, it took me a long time to get comfortable giving immunizations, though I am not phobic about needles. Still, there is something a little barbaric about jabbing into a child's muscle; at first I would leave the room to get the dose of vaccine and then stand in the medication room for five minutes nerving myself to go back and grab and jab. Now it's become automatic; I go to the freezer and get the little plastic tube of oral polio vaccine, I fill a syringe with .5 cubic centimeter of diphtheria-pertussis-tetanus vaccine, I put on a little needle, I take an alcohol swab, a square of gauze, and a little round Band-Aid, and I go back to my patient. I squeeze the sweet pink polio vaccine into the baby's mouth, wait till it's all swallowed down, then squeeze a handful of chubby thigh in my left hand, swab it with alcohol, dry it with gauze, and jab. Needle out, Band-Aid on, screaming baby picked up by parent and given bottle.

It isn't quite that simple, of course. I mean, actually, it is quite that simple, but before I give the DPT shot, I have to go over the side effects with the parents. I explain that there are some fairly common reactions—local pain in the thigh, low-grade fever, crankiness. You may have a somewhat difficult night, I warn. Then I move on to the rare side effects of the pertussis vaccine (pertussis is whooping cough, a disease which can be fatal in infants). Very rare, very unlikely, very controversial—some people believe they're related to the vaccine, and others don't. Still, they're listed on the consent form the parents have to sign: seizures and permanent serious neurologic damage. Hastily I add that the danger from the diseases against which I am vaccinating is felt to be much greater than the danger from the vaccine. All very well, I imagine the parents thinking, but the disease is a faint possibility some time in the future, and she has the vaccine right there in her hand. I ask the parents to sign the consent slip, acknowledging that I have informed them of the dangers of immunization.

I have had some very lengthy discussions with parents, but so far everyone has signed and allowed me to go ahead with the immunization. But I sometimes have a tiny twinge myself as I grab and swab and jab—what if this is that one very rare child who is going to have a real reaction?

I get phone calls from the parents in my clinic. The baby has a cold, the baby has a rash, the baby won't eat. A kid in his day-care center has chicken pox. I got a call once from Texas; a baby had been taken to visit her aunt and had suddenly become constipated (not that I'm implying anything about the aunt). I got a call early in internship about a baby with a temperature of 108 (it was 100.8, it finally turned out; the nervous father wasn't too good at decimals). With any call, I have to decide whether anything serious is going on—does the child need to be seen by a doctor? For the first couple of months of internship, I have to admit that much too frequently when anyone called, I would say, well, maybe someone should look at that; bring the child to the emergency room. So I apologize to all those parents who brought their children out at night, to the overworked residents in the emergency room. I was afraid that I couldn't judge things properly, that I would miss something.

I had one clinic patient who inadvertently taught me a great deal about primary care pediatrics and the perils of teaching hospitals. Albert came to my clinic as a newborn, and a very healthy one. He did have some colic, and his mother and I talked about that, about the crying every evening, and what caused it (no one exactly knows) and what she could do to help (lay him on his stomach and rub his back, put him in his car seat and go for a drive, walk the floor with him, wait for him to outgrow it). A week after his first visit, his mother called me to say she thought he had a fever, so I had her bring him into the emergency room. Because he was still so young —only five weeks—his fever was considered grounds for a rule-out sepsis workup, and an admission for intravenous antibiotics. I visited him on the ward; after a little IV fluid, he looked great, and I told his mother I was almost sure he would rule out and go home in a couple of days.

That evening Albert had a particularly cranky time of it, and one of the nurses taking care of him began to wonder whether he was an unusually irritable baby. Now, "irritable" in pediatrics is a loaded word; used about a child with a fever, it can suggest meningitis, used about a baby without a fever, it may imply neurologic abnormality. If you just mean the baby seems a little grouchy, but essentially normal, you say *cranky* or *fussy*—*irritable* is a word you use if you think something might be wrong. If you describe a baby in the emergency room as irritable, you mean you're planning to do a spinal tap; if you say it about a baby on the ward, people start wondering whether you need advice from a neurologist.

So the nurse's concern was passed on in morning rounds, and the intern who had been on call agreed, and later that day Albert was examined thoroughly by not one but three neurologists. He was by this time completely without fever, and his blood, urine, and spinal fluid cultures were all negative. But he was undeniably cranky—and as the afternoon wore on, and new people kept arriving to examine him, he got even crankier.

The neurologists' verdict was that Albert's neurologic exam was "borderline normal." They advised, however, that just to be safe, a CT scan should be done of his head. They were concerned that he seemed unusually irritable, unusually jittery (another loaded term), and also that his body seemed slightly stiff. Albert's mother had been getting more and more anxious as her baby generated more and more interest, and as the gang of neurologists was leaving, she demanded to know from them just exactly what they were worried about. They tried to tell her that they had made no diagnosis, but she insisted: what's the worst thing this could be? And one of the doctors mentioned cerebral palsy.

Albert's mother thought that this meant the doctors were telling her that her son was going to be mentally retarded and wheelchair bound (cerebral palsy does not actually imply either of those). She was, understandably, devastated. And when I heard the story, I was horrified to think that I had examined this baby and missed his neurologic problems. I went up to the ward and examined him again, and to my chagrin, he still seemed healthy to me.

We arranged for the CT scan to be done in a month or so. Albert ruled out—no bacterial growth from any of his cultures—and went home. I kept in touch with his mother with regular phone calls, since I was now so worried about this child, and she reported that he was eating well and sleeping better. And when he was about six weeks old, his colic went away, just like it was supposed to. His mother was almost starting to believe that he was a normal baby. Then one day she noticed he had a bad diaper rash, and brought him into the clinic. It wasn't my day, so he was seen by the walk-in doc, the resident who sees patients who come to the clinic without appointments. The walk-in doc was an extremely bright resident, with a very large fund of knowledge. He took a careful history from Albert's mother, getting all the details of the neurologists' concern, the impending CT scan. Then he did a very careful exam, noting some patches on the baby's back that were paler in color than the rest of the skin. Then he put neurologic abnormalities together with skin findings, and told the mother that he was making a provisional diagnosis of a disease called incontinentia pigmenti, a genetic disorder that often leads to mental retardation. He would refer the baby to dermatology clinic, he told her, where they would do a skin biopsy and find out for sure.

When this resident paged me to tell me about his visit with my patient, I was once again overcome with a sense of inadequacy. It would be less than accurate to say that I felt I should have made the diagnosis of incontinentia pigmenti, since to my best recollection, I had never heard of the syndrome. I called Albert's mother, who was completely frantic, and assured her that we would get to the bottom of Albert's problems no matter how many specialists, how many diagnostic tests it might take.

Albert came into the dermatology clinic. I joined him there. The dermatologist pointed out to me, with amusement in his voice, that incontinentia pigmenti occurs almost exclusively in girls. In addition, he said, Albert's skin findings were not at all typical. Why had I gotten the mother all worked up like this? Lots of people have irregularities of skin coloring, he pointed out.

The CT scan was normal. At my request, Albert was examined again, by another pediatric neurologist. His exam was felt to be absolutely and completely unremarkable, and the neurologist kindly spent some time showing the baby's mother how her son could do everything that a child his age ought to be able to do. Fix and follow. Reach and grasp. Hold up his head. Turn his head to sounds. And, over the next six months, as Albert grew and thrived and continued to develop exactly on schedule, if not a little ahead, his mother finally came to believe that her son was perfectly healthy. And in my clinic, we came to refer to this story as The Time Perri Did a CT Scan for Colic.

Now that I am comparatively more comfortable with the routine problems, with the phone calls about colds, with the diaper rashes and the ear infections, my clinic still has curves to throw me. I have been asked:

to approve a macrobiotic regime for a two-year-old

to help a mother find some friends with babies the same age as hers

to establish a child's paternity

to tell a six-year-old what will happen to him if he doesn't listen to his teacher.

The patients who were newborns when I started my internship are a year and a half old now, walking, starting to talk. When I see them for their fifteen-month checkups (measles-mumps-rubella immunization), I can't help feeling a small proprietary pride. I've examined, I've advised, I've immunized, and here they are. I know I don't get much credit; I have a small child of my own, after all, and I know who I think gets the credit for his growth and development, and it isn't his pediatrician. Still, it's satisfying to watch children grow up, it's fun to make a contribution. And if something should go wrong, I'll catch it now, won't I? I start to believe a little bit more; I have felt so many normal baby tummies that surely an abnormal one would set off an alarm. I can tell a well-baby phone call from a sick-baby phone call. And if I can tell when they're sick, then I ought to be able to take a deep breath, all those other times, and pronounce them well.

AN OLD VIRUS: CHICKEN POX
· · · · · · · · ·

You bring your sick child to the clinic. The receptionist takes one look and hustles you away from the other waiting patients. You are put into a special precaution room, off at the far end of the clinic, separated from the corridor by double doors festooned with warning signs. The nurse warns you, under no circumstances to let the child leave the room. There will be a wait, she tells you, because the one doctor who is available right now won't see your child.

Name the dread disease: chicken pox, of course. There are other, more serious infections, of course (bacterial meningitis, AIDS, trichinosis, cholera, leprosy), but chicken pox spreads wildly, far more easily than any of those others. One kid with chicken pox sitting in a waiting room can infect every other vulnerable kid in the room. One infected kid on a hospital ward can put the whole ward at risk. One hospital worker who was exposed to chicken pox and then came to work can close down an intensive care unit. Chicken pox is the scourge of the pediatric ward; there is no other infection that so regularly provokes a panic.

Remember chicken pox? I had chicken pox when I was six. I had mumps too, though I missed out on measles and rubella (German measles) thanks to immunization. Now we immunize against measles, mumps, and rubella routinely, at the age of fifteen months. We immunize against diphtheria and whooping cough. Chicken pox is just about the only "routine" childhood illness left, the only major infectious disease that we still expect all children to get, sometime in the first decade of life. In a way, chicken pox may be the child's introduction to illness. Sure, there are colds and ear infections, twenty-four-hour bugs and upset stomachs, but chicken pox is a Disease with a capital D, a distinct entity with clear signs and symptoms. It has a classic rash, poetically described in the medical textbooks as "dewdrop on a rose petal." You stay home from school, you try not to scratch, and your parents tell you, don't worry, it's only chicken pox. Everybody gets it, and everybody gets better.

If everybody gets it and everybody gets better, why are we so paranoid about chicken pox in the hospital? Well, certain patients don't do so well with chicken pox. We worry most about the immunocompromised children, the children receiving chemotherapy, for example. Those kids are susceptible to a far more serious form of chicken pox, with a mortality rate of 20 percent. Newborn babies are also vulnerable—and so are unborn babies. A pregnant woman who has never had chicken pox is at risk; if she gets varicella early in the pregnancy, the virus may cause severe malformations in the fetus, and if she gets it late, the baby may be born infected with a serious form of the disease.

So we worry about those vulnerable children. And we worry about ourselves, about doctors and nurses who may be carriers. Almost everyone gets chicken pox as a child, and most people who don't remember having it probably did have a mild case at one time or another, without realizing it. But every now and then someone dodges the odds and makes it through to adulthood without getting infected. You can verify that, nowadays, by checking an antibody titer to see if there has ever been exposure to the virus, causing the body to manufacture antibodies in self-defense. And if there are no antibodies, then you have an adult who is a setup, a setup to contract the virus and to spread it everywhere; for chicken pox, as every elementary school teacher knows, is infectious *before* those telltale spots break out and continues to be infectious until they have all crusted over.

Older pediatricians sometimes speak reminiscently of chicken pox parties; once upon a time, they say, parents would gather their children together to expose them to the disease; on the same principle, my mother sent my younger brother in to play with me when I got chicken pox. Might as well have it and get it over with. That still makes sense to me. Nowadays, at my son's day-care center, we quarantine infected children as quickly as possible, and the result is of course that we parents go on, year after year, waiting for our children to get it and get it over with. There's no prize for evading the disease as a child; you only grow up to be a vulnerable adult. Pregnant women have one more infection to worry about, and all adults, additionally, are more likely to have severe cases of chicken pox, if they do get it, and are more vulnerable to the complications, which range from pneumonia to hepatitis.

Chicken pox is caused by the varicella zoster virus, a member of the herpesvirus group. Like other members of this group (herpes simplex 1 and 2, and Epstein-Barr virus, which causes mononucleosis), the varicella virus causes first an acute illness, chicken pox, goes on to infect certain target cells in the body, and then settles down for a long latent period. The initial incubation period—the time between exposure to chicken pox and the appearance of the first spots—is about two weeks, though it can be as long as three. That's how long the quarantine would last for any vulnerable hospital worker; that's the period of time to keep in mind when you are trying to calculate whether your four-year-old is indeed due to break out in spots on the second day of the family trip to the Carribean. And right before those spots appear, before anyone knows for sure, the chicken pox victim is already spreading disease left and right.

After the initial episode of chicken pox, the virus settles down for the long haul. In many people, it never flares up again; in others, especially the immunocompromised and the elderly, it may cause a painful skin eruption called zoster (shingles). Because the latent virus lives in nerve cells along the spinal cord, zoster lesions are distributed strictly in those patches of the body surface which are served by those specific parts of the spinal cord. These skin segments, or dermatomes, are very distinct, and it is usually easy to distinguish this clinical picture from the more generalized sprinkling of chicken pox.

Because of the low mortality of chicken pox in children,

a vaccine was not originally seen as a high priority; measles, for example, is much more likely to cause serious complications and death—and still does in many nonimmunized children in the third world. With varicella, there was always the fear that if a vaccine conferred only temporary immunity, there would be a rash (no pun intended) of adults getting more seriously ill as the vaccine wore off. An effective vaccine is now close to release, and will be an obvious boon to children with AIDS and other immune deficiencies, as well as to pregnant women and health care workers who have never had chicken pox. In fact, there will be those who will argue for incorporating it into the regular schedule of childhood immunizations, wiping out this disease, at least in the developed world, as we have wiped out the other childhood diseases. It would be hard to feel regret at the passing of even a comparatively benign illness, since chicken pox, after all, causes plenty of itching and plenty of discomfort every year, causes parents to miss work, children to miss school, and occasionally gets loose on a hospital ward and causes something more serious. Still, perhaps a moment of nostalgia would be in order for that feeling of being a sick child, for the enforced week at home, for the special attention, even for the white gloves some of us had to wear so we wouldn't scratch.

So you brought your child, covered with dewdrops on rose petals, to the clinic, and you got shut up in the special isolation room, and eventually the child was examined by a doctor who had had chicken pox herself as a child and therefore had nothing to fear (the doctor outside who had never had chicken pox won't go near her when she comes out of your room). And she tells you to give the kid plenty of liquids, treat the fever with acetaminophen (giving aspirin to a child with chicken pox is very dangerous; it can lead to an often fatal swelling of the brain called Reye's syndrome). She talks about ways to reduce the itching—baking soda baths, white gloves, or antihistamines.

For those at special risk—the immunocompromised, the

newborn—there are treatments available. There is a special preparation of immunoglobulin containing antibodies to varicella virus—VZIG, it's called, for varicella-zoster immune globulin, and it's given to any high-risk patient who has been exposed to the virus. And there's an antiviral drug, Acyclovir, which is used to treat infection. We use it for leukemia patients with zoster, cystic fibrosis patients with chicken pox—anyone who is especially vulnerable. It works, but it doesn't always work well enough.

Chicken pox is not a heroic disease; it is not the stuff of great literature or operatic death scenes. Even the name is sort of funny. But it is a disease with many overtones, a disease that spreads so easily and rapidly that it cannot be contained (if AIDS were spread like chicken pox, everyone would be dead or dying), a disease that is a fairly gentle introduction to illness for normal children; a disease that can devastate patients with impaired defenses, running amok in their bodies; a disease we chase, imperfectly, with the newest antiviral technologies; a disease we still accept as one of the slings and arrows of childhood, but which we might soon have the technology to eradicate altogether from our children's lives. If that should happen, the rash of chicken pox, which is now instantly recognized by the emergency room receptionist, will become a piece of clinical esoterica. The doctors of today are never very good at diagnosing yesterday's diseases. After all, bring your child to the clinic with *measles*, and you'll cause a furor, as the diagnosis is made with the aid of illustrated textbooks, as every doctor in the place comes rushing in to look at this rare, exotic childhood disease.

A NEW VIRUS: AIDS

There is one question, says the social worker, that comes up with every mother. "The question is always 'Who is going to

die first?' And then comes, 'I wish my child would die first.' "
The social worker is Anita Septimus, pediatric AIDS coordi-
nator at Albert Einstein Hospital in the Bronx, and she is
talking about the mothers of the children born infected with
HIV; by definition these women are infected themselves, and
so they must worry about their own health, about the health
of their young children, and also, inevitably, about who will
outlive whom. Who will care for an ailing child after the mother's death? "I've seen so many mothers who struggle to stay
alive until the kid dies—then it doesn't take much for the
disease to overcome them," Septimus says.

The AIDS epidemic is changing. The rate of seroconver-
sion among gay men in San Francisco has dropped remarkably,
with the widespread acceptance of safe sex practices. The na-
tion's blood supply is now almost completely safe; there will
be very few new cases of AIDS related to transfusions or to
the blood products used to treat hemophilia. The disease has
devastated the American gay community, and will continue to
do so for years to come, as more men who already carry the
virus sicken and die. But increasingly, AIDS is becoming a
disease of poverty, of the inner city, a disease of intravenous
drug users and their sex partners. And as more women are
infected with the virus, pediatric cases of AIDS are becoming
increasingly common.

Almost all children with AIDS acquire the infection congenitally; infected mothers pass the virus to their offspring
sometime during pregnancy or around the time of birth—the
details of transmission are not yet well understood. Not all
children born to infected mothers actually contract the virus;
estimates vary between 30 and 70 percent, depending on the
study, and 30 percent is the figure most often cited in this
country.

The first case of congenitally acquired AIDS was described
in the medical literature in 1981. In 1989, the Centers for
Disease Control in Atlanta reported about fifteen hundred
cases in children under thirteen, about twelve hundred of which

had been congenitally acquired (the others were due to blood products). These numbers do not represent all the children infected with HIV, but only those comparatively few who had been diagnosed as having AIDS; to fit the case definition, a child must not only be seropositive (i.e., have a positive blood test revealing antibodies to HIV), but also must have had specific infections and syndromes that show the virus has severely damaged the immune system. So far, more than eight hundred of those children have died. But it is the shape of the future epidemic that looms as a truly threatening shadow; the unknown numbers of children who are carrying the virus, though they have not been diagnosed with the disease, and the ever larger numbers of seropositive women who will give birth in the coming years. These women are disproportionately black and Hispanic—of those twelve hundred cases of congenital AIDS, only about two hundred occurred in whites, with more than seven hundred in blacks and about three hundred in Hispanics. Epidemiologic studies of pregnant women have yielded seropositivity rates as high as 5 to 8 percent in such high-risk areas as Newark and the Bronx, suggesting that in these places, the pediatric AIDS epidemic may soon overwhelm all existing medical and social service resources. The gay male victims of the epidemic's first wave faced prejudice, hostility, and malignant "righteousness," but they were not absolutely barred by social class from access to funding, to political action, to media attention. The epidemic is now moving into a segment of society with no voice at all, and most voiceless of all, of course, are the children.

Pediatric AIDS is not the same disease as adult AIDS; there are different signs and symptoms, different infections, different questions to be asked and answered. And pediatric AIDS is also unique among the illnesses that afflict children. There are many other diseases that regularly kill off young patients, even in the developed world, even in this age of low infant mortality, this age in which every child is expected to live to adulthood. Certain childhood cancers have high mortality rates, for example; some cardiac defects are not usually correctable; and there are inherited conditions, such as muscular dystrophy and cystic fibrosis, that are inexorably fatal. But pediatric AIDS is the only disease that kills off the whole family; if the child is infected, then the mother is infected, and usually the father too. The magnitude of the tragedy is unparalleled—as are the social problems of caring for sick children whose parents are also sick, or dying, or dead.

Like adults, many children with AIDS remain asymptomatic for years. No one knows the life expectancy of a child born infected with HIV, though doctors working with these children have noticed that they tend to fall into two groups. There are those who "present," as the medical jargon puts it —meaning those who come to medical attention—before the age of two; these children are usually quite sick, and many die within a year of diagnosis. And then there are the children who are not diagnosed until later, who may not be sick at all until they are five or six years old. Some of these children are now eight or nine, and perhaps with aggressive medical treatment, they may have years to go. One unanswered question is whether there are children born infected with the virus who do not ever develop the disease.

Adult AIDS is marked by opportunistic infections, infections not seen in immunologically normal adults. Pediatric AIDS patients, on the other hand, get some opportunistic infections, but also get the same bacterial diseases that other children get; they just get more of them more frequently. One immunologic theory to explain this difference is that adults, before their immune systems are attacked by the virus, have already built an immunologic "memory" of antibodies to common bacteria, and are thus able to fight them off. Children, infected from birth with the immunosuppressive HIV, never get to build this "library," and are struck down by every common childhood bug. One opportunistic infection that *is* commonly seen in children with AIDS, as well as in adults, is pneumocystis carinii pneumonia (PCP); the picture is complicated in children by another mysterious lung disease, lymphocytic interstitial pneumonitis, or LIP, which seems to be an abnormal immune response of the lung. Both of these syndromes cause progressive difficulty in breathing, oxygen lack, chest X-ray changes. PCP can be treated; LIP, essentially, cannot. Another hallmark of pediatric AIDS is what pediatricians call failure to thrive; AIDS has now jumped to a place near the top of the long list of diagnoses to be considered when a child is unable to gain weight and grow normally.

So nowadays in a pediatric hospital, doctors think about AIDS when a child has too many infections, when a child is not growing, when a child has an unusual pneumonia. And after we think about AIDS, we then have to broach the subject with the parents, who may or may not have ever considered the possibility, not only that their child may have the virus, but also that they may be infected themselves.

Tyesha is three and a half, but she only weighs twenty-two pounds, an average weight for a fifteen-month-old. However, she is proportionately small, not emaciated; as she sits contentedly in her mother's lap, she seems lively and alert. The Newark clinic is obviously familiar territory for her, and she is dressed up for a visit, her hair braided into at least eight braids, each fastened with a different-colored barrette. Because she is the size of a one-year-old, but has the coordination and fine motor control of a three-year-old, Tyesha gives an impression of precocity, of a slightly unreal miniaturized maturity.

Tyesha's mother thinks she knows how she acquired the HIV infection. "A guy I was going with a long time ago, I found out he was doing drugs and I cut him off." At the time, she had not heard much about HIV; later on, when she knew more about it, she was glad she had stopped seeing this man. She didn't know she was carrying the virus until her daughter was diagnosed, and she is still in good health, she says, with no symptoms of HIV infection.

As an infant, Tyesha was one of those babies who was

always sick, always at the doctor's, frequently in the hospital. Bad colds, asthma, diarrhea, feeding problems, seizures with fever—none of them illnesses that automatically suggest the diagnosis of AIDS. Still, the combination of frequent infections with chronic difficulty in gaining weight is highly suggestive nowadays, and Tyesha was ultimately diagnosed at the age of one and a half.

"I didn't believe them," says her mother. "I was shocked. Then I was scared. Now I'm living day by day. When she wouldn't eat, I wouldn't eat. Now she's doing a lot better, she's real active, she runs and plays."

Tyesha gets intravenous gamma globulin every month—that's why she's here at the clinic. She also takes prophylactic Bactrim, an antibiotic that wards off infections, including pneumocystis. She's been hospitalized several times, for mysterious fevers or for diarrhea and dehydration, and she has had to be nourished intravenously—but now, according to her mother and her doctors, she is eating better, gaining weight, and making progress developmentally, walking and talking.

"When she was in the hospital, I had to stay up there all the time; when I left, she would holler, 'Doctor, nurse, go get my mommy!'" Tyesha, hearing her mother imitate her words, smiles, almost laughs, though she continues to regard me, a stranger, with suspicion. The door opens and the clinic nutritionist comes in, carrying a tray of little paper cups. They are trying out some new mixtures of dietary supplements, mixing them with different fruit drinks to make them palatable for the children. Tyesha accepts a cup of "Kool-Aid," holding it carefully in both hands, and her mother takes one as well. After the nutritionist leaves, the mother takes one sip and makes a face; Tyesha, however, drains her own cup and then takes her mother's.

I am touring the AIDS clinic at the Children's Hospital of New Jersey with Dr. James Oleske. Pediatric AIDS is an inner-city disease, and hospitals located in the inner cities, where the seropositive women live, where they raise their children and bring them for help, have had to deal with the epidemic. There is excellent care available at this hospital in Newark, at Einstein in the Bronx, at Boston City Hospital. On the day I visit Newark, there are thirty children due to come in and receive their monthly gamma globulin treatments, meant to boost their immune systems and help them fight off bacterial infections. The intravenous infusion takes hours, during which time the children are seen by a variety of specialists, by a neurologist, a nutritionist—anyone who might be able to help with their specific problems. Dr. Oleske is teased by the residents as he walks through the hospital, because of a recent TV movie that depicted his involvement with this disease. Various comments pass back and forth about whether the actor who portrayed him was too good-looking for the part, about whether he really had his heart attack as dramatically as the film suggested. Relaxed and informal, he persistently apologizes for being a little distracted; a child died last night and he and his group spent the whole night in the hospital; when we pass through the pediatric intensive care unit, he stops to read a notice on the bulletin board and to write down the time of the funeral.

In the clinic, a playroom is full of children with their IV gamma globulin infusions under way. They are playing with blocks and puzzles, and generating an impressive amount of noise. Every so often one is summoned out for an interview or an exam; new arrivals show up and get their IVs in a special treatment room down the hall (rule one in pediatrics is to confine painful procedures to certain rooms so the children feel safe in the playroom); other children finish and go home.

The tour takes us on through the inpatient pediatric wards, where Dr. Oleske knows every AIDS patient. He stops to talk to mothers, offers a running commentary as we move from room to room, a commentary that reflects both the medical and the social problems of caring for these children: she comes in when her weight drops too low and we give her IV nutrition . . . that little guy is encephalopathic, always crying for his mother . . . he lives with his grandmother, who has trouble taking care of him but he loves her and to be taken away would hurt him more . . . this is a boarder baby; she needs high-tech care at home and it's hard to get foster placement with all that. . . .

The only people who know Tyesha's diagnosis are her mother, her ten-year-old brother, and her grandmother. "My son's teacher was asking me why was he depressed. I knew he was feeling sad, but I didn't know it was affecting him in school. He's smart—they want to send him to a special school because he's gifted. See, I think he was missing us, when his sister was in the hospital and he was staying with his grandmother. We're real close."

Her current boyfriend, Tyesha's father, on the other hand, has been a problem; he has been abusive to both mother and children, and she has had to take out a restraining order against him. "When Tyesha was in the ICU he tried to make me come home. He scares me sometimes, when his mood changes come, and I don't like him around her." She pauses, looks confused. "But he loves her."

Tyesha has now finished both cups of fruit drink, and has begun to squirm a little in her mother's lap. Finally she settles into a new position, kneeling on her mother's knees, leaning over her mother's shoulders to tap the empty paper cups on the wall behind. I ask, somewhat hesitantly, about the future. Her mother answers by referring to Tyesha's most recent hospitalization, which ended only a couple of weeks ago. "When she got sick, that really scared me. But that time will come. How will I deal with that?" She turns the child around on her lap, shows me the full cheeks, the plump arms. "Her appetite is very good right now." Silence for a few seconds, then she says very softly, "It scares me if I get sick and can't take care of her. I wouldn't want them to take her from me."

Then she begins to talk about spending time with her

children, about going to the park, about what a close family they are, as if she can reassure us both that everything is normal, everything is going to be fine. Tyesha is now watching her mother's face, perhaps aware that she is being discussed. She is looking for an opportunity to put a paper cup to her mother's lips and offer her an imaginary drink. Her mother pretends to drink, then hands back the cup, and the little girl puts a cup over each of her own ears. "At one time," says Tyesha's mother, "I wanted to go back to school—really to do something with myself. Now I'm just going to spend a lot of time with my kids. I'm happy when we go to the park. Lately I've been taking a lot of pictures. I don't know why. I love pictures, but it seems like I'm taking a lot more now."

The problem with writing about sick children is that it is virtually impossible to escape sentimentality. Take a picture of a child, any child, and the odds are reasonably good that the picture will be cute; that's how thousands of parents generate millions of adorable pictures. Write in the caption, this child is dying of AIDS (or cancer or whatever), and you immediately have a tug at the heartstrings. Articles about pediatric AIDS, TV movies, magazine cover stories, all tend inexorably toward such phrases as "innocent victims." They are appealing, they are adorable, and they are dying. With adult AIDS victims there is a profound tendency to attach blame, to identify the risk factor and point the finger. One way people deal with a frightening epidemic is to label its victims and thereby gain some distance: *you* use drugs, *you* have multiple sex partners, it's your fault. And with children, of course, no one, however self-righteous, however eager to blame the victim, can claim that dubious high moral ground. Children, whatever their diseases, remain quintessentially innocent, and of course, adorable.

But does this translate into anything useful? These children, and their families, represent an enormous need. To take care of them properly requires not just sympathy, hugs, and tears, but money and extensive medical and social services. Dr. Arye Rubinstein, director of the Comprehensive AIDS Family Care Center at Einstein, ticks off on his fingers the cost of caring for his patients. Since 1984 his center has worked to provide care for families, using core teams made up of a physician, a nurse, and a social worker. For something in the neighborhood of a hundred and sixty thousand dollars, he says, he can fund a single core team for a year, and a single core team can deal with thirty-five to forty families. Then he does the other arithmetic problem that everyone working in this field does over and over: "Twenty-one thousand six hundred deliveries a year in the Bronx; if four percent are positive, we are going to have eight hundred families!" And the funding, he says, is simply not there.

The labels on the filing cabinets in Dr. Rubinstein's small cement-block office serve as a reminder of the burgeoning of this epidemic. Three drawers of vertical files are labeled, as befits a pediatric immunologist, Immune Deficiencies A–G, G–N, and N–Z. But then there are equally large drawers labeled Pediatric AIDS A–H, and so on, reflecting the proliferation of information about this one particular immunodeficiency, which has a tendency to take over the lives of anyone who starts to take care of these patients.

Anita Septimus, who works in this same program, is a vivid emphatic woman, who talks extremely rapidly, with only occasional overtones of her native French; she has been in this country for twenty-one years. She describes her initial recruitment into the field of pediatric AIDS; it was 1984 and she had, she says, very little knowledge of the disease. She began to develop the social service supports that the children and their families needed, and at first she felt overwhelmed, wondering, "Who is going to take these kids?" She almost quit after three months, when four patients died in rapid succession. But now, "Don't feel sorry for me, I'm doing what I want to do. I have the choice to not do this work—as long as I'm doing it, I want to do it with my heart."

The Bronx, Newark, Miami—these are the front lines. Of those fifteen hundred pediatric AIDS cases, almost five hundred were in New York, two hundred in New Jersey, one hundred in Florida. San Francisco, a city that has been hit hard by the adult AIDS epidemic, has seen very few pediatric cases. However, as the city with the most complete support services for AIDS patients, the city where AIDS awareness is higher than anywhere else, San Francisco is trying hard to prepare for the next wave of the epidemic. "We're looking carefully at what's been done in Newark, New York, Florida, trying to develop programs in anticipation," says Dr. Diane Wara, professor of pediatrics at the University of California, San Francisco, and director of the Division of Pediatric Immunology. "We're just beginning, we have some time."

Dr. Wara stresses the unique nature of San Francisco, a city where, she says, AIDS education has been so pervasive that even the underprivileged have a good deal of information, where the special mix of communities and cultures has given the epidemic a somewhat different face.

"Working with an evolving epidemic is incredibly challenging," says Dr. Wara. "It combines science and sociology —although it's very sad, it's the greatest challenge I've ever faced. We're doing what you read about in the olden times, when doctors worked in communities, especially challenging in a large city with a diverse population." As one special San Francisco story, she offers an eight-year-old patient of hers who is brought in every month for his gamma globulin by a different adult, usually a gay man, from a community center where the family has found help and friendship.

Rest Stop is located about four blocks from Castro Street, the center of gay San Francisco. There are panhandlers on the street outside Rest Stop, but the center itself is quite homey, with a tank of fish and a profusion of plants and comfortable furniture. The kitchen is stocked with a variety of herbal teas, and the bulletin board is crowded with notices: PWA [person with AIDS] in good health seeks apartment . . . HIV positive serum needed for clinical trial . . .

There are announcements for any number of alternative healing methods, massages, "centering," meditation. Paul Steindal, the co-director of Rest Stop, defines it as "a drop-in and support center for people living with HIV concerns." There are support groups, education groups, classes in nutrition, creative writing, "attitudinal healing."

Most of the people sitting around the bright living room are gay men, a couple of them obviously sick, disturbingly thin, one blind. Larry Benko is a large man with a full beard, conscientiously leaving the building every so often to smoke a cigarette. He has a certain fluency when he talks about his son's illness, which I recognize; the medical vocabulary acquired by the parent of a chronically ill child. Going to medical school the hard way, I have heard it called.

"Joey was diagnosed October 20, 1987. He was in the hospital for six weeks with CMV, which made him anemic, so he had eight red cell transfusions. Prednisone kept his red blood cell level up, and now he's been on gamma globulin and pentamidine treatments for a year. Then his T-cell count dropped to nine, and he started on AZT, and his T-cell count increased. He hasn't been back in the hospital since."

Joey is now eight and a half years old. He acquired HIV from a transfusion he received as a newborn; one reason his parents are willing to have his name used, I suspect, is that they can see their son's illness as a tragedy, a horrible medical accident, that does not reflect on them in any way. Still, after people in their San Francisco housing project found out what was wrong with Joey, the other children were forbidden to play with him, and the Benkos' windows were broken.

Paul Steindal says, gesturing around the room, "Joseph's family come out of a fundamentalist Christian background. We are probably persons they would never associate with."

The family has little money. Both parents are from out of state; when Joey's mother speaks, you can hear the Texas in her voice. Now they are regulars at Rest Stop, and when Linda Benko arrives with her two sons, she picks up Steindal's chain of thought, talking about how Joey's AIDS has brought her into contact with people she never expected to know. "I had assumed gay people were a different species of human being, but they have car payments and fears and dreams just like anyone else." Larry Benko also feels that his family has found a welcome here that was denied them elsewhere. "The heterosexual community wants to give him twenty dollars so he'll go away." He remembers Joey's hearing other children saying that "anyone who has AIDS is a goddamn faggot" and later coming to his father to ask, "How do I become gay?"

Meanwhile, Joey and his older brother are ransacking the shelf of board games in one corner of the room, finally settling on Monopoly. Joey wears high-tops and corduroy pants with a hole at the knee, and on being introduced to me, he pulls up his shirt to show me that his tee shirt is green for St. Patrick's Day. Pressed by his mother to tell me something about himself, he finally volunteers that he wants to be a cop, then corrects himself, "an undercover police officer." His brother, dealing out the Monopoly money, contributes, "I just want to be a simple corporate raider."

Linda again questions her son, asking him what he would say if he could say anything for other people to read. "I don't know nothing to say," Joey tells her, and settles down to his game.

"Well, I do," says Linda Benko. "It surprises me that in a country with public education so many young people are so ignorant as to think you can get AIDS from a swimming pool. I've bathed Joey, slept with him, changed his diapers and I don't have it. That should show how contagious AIDS is."

In fact, the data from the foster parents taking care of HIV-positive children and from the seronegative siblings of these children all support the proposition that this virus is not communicated by casual contact, even daily, constant, casual contact. There has been only one case to date of someone who is thought to have contracted the virus from caring for a child at home, and that case involved an unusual amount of direct contact between the caretaker and the child's blood. Otherwise, all the kissing and hugging and drooling and normal mealtime mess involved in raising a baby do not seem to add up to any risk, either for adults or for other children. The current recommendation to caretakers is to wear plastic gloves for diaper changing, and to take precautions if there is any bleeding.

This does not, of course, prevent a certain amount of hysteria over the question of whether HIV-positive children should be allowed to go to school. Over the past few years, there have been a number of celebrated cases, most involving older children, several with hemophilia. The younger seropositive children—the congenital cases—are just reaching school age now, and most are quietly starting school. In the Bronx, says Dr. Rubinstein, they are "entering anonymously, following CDC guidelines, city and state regulations." In San Francisco, before the problem had actually arisen, a medical group was formed to define criteria for admitting seropositive children to the public schools. Joey Benko's parents speak highly of Dr. Wara, who when Joey's diagnosis became known, "educated the school."

Paul Steindal returns over and over to the question of what children can teach adults, how much having Joey around has meant to the other people who come to Rest Stop, many of whom are estranged from their families. "Part of healing is just being around children," he says. A child is instinctively able to understand the idea, "I am living with AIDS, I am not dying with AIDS." Mr. Benko agrees, recalling the playroom at the San Francisco hospital where Joey was treated: "All the children with no hair, big scars, deformities—all they want is the stinking IV out of their arms so they can go home and play again. They didn't look at themselves as dying. They were living for what they had."

"If I were to die from AIDS tomorrow," says Larry Benko, "if I had it, I would have no regrets. I've had a good long life, done things—some I'm not proud of." He pauses, thinking about his son. "All I pray for is time," he says.

Joey knows perfectly well what happens to most people who get AIDS. Recently, his father explained, he had been asking about heaven, and someone had filled him in about wings and harps. "So Joey said to me, 'If they ain't got a McDonald's and a skateboard and a bicycle up there, I don't wanna go.' "

Infected children who, like Joey, remain mentally and developmentally normal are fortunate; one hallmark of AIDS in children is neurologic damage, which is seen in as many as 75 percent. Some suffer from a progressive encephalopathy. These children either stop developing or, in some cases, gain developmental milestones only to lose them, their brain growth is impaired, and they gradually become weak and apathetic. This syndrome implies advanced disease, and so far there is no therapy to reverse the neurologic damage, though some researchers have high hopes that AZT, an antiviral drug, might at least keep the virus from doing further damage to the central nervous system. Dr. Mark Mintz, the neurologist working with the Newark AIDS clinic, suggests that any treatment will have to take into account the possibility that the virus may "hide" in the nervous system, escaping the body's immune surveillance. Dr. Mintz does frequent neurologic exams on the children who come to the clinic, looking for evidence of degeneration, delay, weakness.

Neurologic involvement, like opportunistic infection, like frequent bacterial infection, defines a seropositive child as an infected child, a child with HIV disease. This is not just an academic distinction, and it is especially critical during the first year and a half of life. One peculiar aspect of pediatric AIDS is that as yet there is no reliable test for infection below the age of fifteen months. The test that is used measures antibodies in the blood; their presence reveals exposure to the virus. However, newborns often carry maternal antibodies, and a positive HIV antibody titer in the baby of an infected mother may tell you only that some maternal antibody has crossed the placenta; the virus may or may not have crossed as well. These maternal antibodies can persist until the child is fifteen months old, so a baby may repeatedly test positive, but ultimately may be negative. On the other hand, a baby may have been exposed to the virus but may fail to make antibodies effectively, so a negative test in an infant known to be at risk does not mean the baby is definitely uninfected. All this means that children of seropositive mothers come back to the clinic again and again, wait for test results again and again—but nothing definite can be said for fifteen months—unless the baby gets sick.

"What we tell the families," says Dr. Ellen Cooper, medical director of the AIDS program at Boston City Hospital, "is that we're left confused. It's not clear till fifteen months, unless the child becomes sick, so we tell them that we're happy as long as we're confused, and the longer we remain confused, the happier we are." Before fifteen months, after all, the question can only be resolved definitely in the direction of infection and illness. The Boston City Hospital clinic follows over eighty children, about half of whom are still in that limbo—maybe positive, maybe negative. The others are either old enough to have definitely tested positive, or else have ruled themselves in by qualifying for the clinical definition of AIDS.

An epidemic demands heroes; any great historical event demands heroes. It is all too easy to focus on the doctors and name them (in the great tradition of *Arrowsmith*) the heroes, nobly throwing themselves into the breach. And there is certainly some truth in that; in meeting with the doctors and the nurses and the social workers in several cities, all of whom have been drawn into caring for these children, I was repeatedly struck by the level of commitment, not just to their patients' health, but also to their quality of life. "I want these kids to have education," says Ms. Septimus, in the Bronx, "trips with their parents, camp in summer, good nutrition."

For doctors, there are also professional reputations to be made, grants to be gotten, research projects to be done. Most of all—and here I speak for myself as well—from the point of view of the doctors, this is all *interesting*. It's horribly sad, but much of medicine and medical training is built on the horribly sad. Working with an evolving epidemic, coping with a disease that was unknown fifteen years ago is challenging.

In adult AIDS, the patients are often the heroes, facing the destruction of their lives with grace and dignity. But in pediatric AIDS, the patients are simply children, and therefore they are as healthy and as active as they can be. This is always true in pediatrics; give children any chance at all—adequate nutrition, freedom from pain, a little respite from illness and deterioration—and they will promptly act like children. They will fill the hospital playroom with noise and joyfully smear their food into their hair. This is the great pleasure of pediatrics, but I'm not sure it's heroism.

If I had to nominate the particular heroes of this particular epidemic, I would choose the foster parents, who are bearing the unique burden of this disease, taking in children who they know may not have long to live, and caring for them, in sickness and in health. If not for the foster parents, many of these children would have nowhere to go, no reason to get better and leave the hospital. "I don't know how these people can do it, honestly," says Anita Septimus. "It's the grandmothers who are saving New Jersey," Dr. Oleske says.

Ashley is one year old now, and has been my patient for the last seven months. She was born prematurely, weighing less than four pounds, to a mother who used intravenous drugs, and was taken away from her mother and placed in foster care because of continuing issues of malnourishment and possible neglect. Her current foster mother, Ellen Brown, was called

about Ashley when the baby was three months old and hospitalized with a respiratory infection. Because of the biological
mother's history of drug use, the doctors had done an HIV
test, and when it came back positive, had informed Ashley's
original foster family that there was a possibility the child might
develop AIDS. Those foster parents decided they were not
comfortable keeping the baby, and the social service agency
embarked on the difficult task of finding a family that would
take her.

Ellen Brown and her husband are experienced foster parents who have cared for over a hundred children in their home
and adopted five; they are now trying to adopt Ashley as well.
The agency called them because they have taken in many children with special needs, the hardest children to place. They
had never taken care of a baby with possible AIDS, and their
family did not actually fit the agency guidelines, under which
such babies are not placed with families who already have
children under the age of two. Still, there was nowhere else
for Ashley. Mrs. Brown remembers that when the call came,
"My first reaction was, sure. I knew very little about AIDS—
I knew enough not to get hysterical, and the nurse came out
and talked about universal precautions, always wearing gloves
to change diapers, washing my hands a lot." She was not
worried that her other children might catch the virus; her
concerns ran in the other direction: "I said, are we exposing
this baby to more infections, having her in a home with a lot
of kids—I can't have my own children leave if they get sick,
but I can be more careful about letting them slobber all over
her."

Mrs. Brown calls to mind the somewhat obvious adjective,
motherly; a comfortable woman who handles a baby with su-
perlative confidence, she tends to punctuate her remarks about
Ashley with the phrase "God love her." When I talk to her on
the phone, she is always ready with Ashley's latest accomplish-
ment; from an obviously delayed and difficult start, Ashley has
made tremendous progress: she sits alone, she makes all kinds

of noises, and, most important of all, she is gaining weight.

There is still no way to be sure whether Ashley is or is not infected with HIV. She had to be hospitalized again this past winter for a blood infection (bacteremia) caused by a bacterium called *Streptococcus pneumoniae*. Immunologically normal children often get infected with this bacterium, and bacteremias are not uncommon, so this infection does not establish the diagnosis of AIDS. But most children, after all, get through life without pneumococcal bacteremia, and frequent bacterial infections, after all, are a hallmark of pediatric AIDS, so Ashley's illness is worrying. On the other hand, specific tests of her immune system have all come back normal. Ashley tested HIV positive at five months, and again at nine months; each time, Mrs. Brown was hopeful, waiting to be told that her foster child, who was making such excellent progress, had turned seronegative. And each time I hoped against hope as well, and will again when she comes for her one year appointment and tests.

Ashley is, you have to understand, an adorable baby. When she came to see me on Valentine's Day, dressed in a white dress with red trimming and a full pinafore, along with white stockings printed with red hearts, she looked like someone's greeting card fantasy of a valentine baby, and everyone in the clinic—doctors, nurses, social workers, secretaries— crowded into the room to hold her and coo over her. "She's a very easy baby to love," says Mrs. Brown. "She has a marvelous personality. You try so hard not to fall in love but there's just no way."

The older Brown children know that Ashley may have HIV, and their parents have discussed the disease with them. When the family made the decision to try to adopt, Mrs. Brown says, "I discussed with the older kids that we don't know what her life expectancy is, and they said, well, isn't it better she should have a family?" People outside the family, however, are not told about Ashley's diagnosis—"I don't think it's anybody's business. What makes me angry is dealing with professional people who are not educated; when Ashley was in the hospital, one nurse wore a mask, gloves, and a gown. I mean, really!"

I give Ashley special polio shots made from killed viruses; the regular oral polio vaccine contains live viruses, and may actually cause polio in someone whose immune system is not working well. I worry about whether or not she ought to be getting regular infusions of gamma globulin; can we afford to wait and see whether she gets another bacterial infection? Mostly, like her foster mother, I wish for the next HIV test to come back negative—but I don't really think it will. "She's so well, it's hard to realize," Ellen Brown tells me over the phone. "I have real good thoughts about her, but I think in the back of my mind, I'm realistic. I can't wait for you to see her, God love her."

Children with cystic fibrosis used to die, routinely, before the age of ten; now many live on into their thirties. Although a cure for AIDS remains out of reach, there is some reason to hope that with what we learn over the coming years, medicine may be able to prolong these children's lives, protect their nervous systems, improve their quality of life, offer them extra months and years of health and growth and development. But we have a lot to learn; because pediatric AIDS is so different, much of the understanding of adult AIDS, painfully acquired over the last decade, is only questionably relevant. And meanwhile, the numbers of infected children will keep growing.

In Newark I watched Dr. Mintz sort through a pile of pictures he has taken, big black-and-white photos of patients. The pictures are wonderful—children smiling, clowning, crying, completely comfortable with the camera. "She's dead. He's doing okay—a little encephalopathy, but a functional kid. This mother got it from a dirtball—a one-shot deal, just bad luck. This is the Christmas party, with Dr. Oleske as Santa Claus—it breaks your heart because one year they're here and the next . . ." He puts down his pictures and wonders aloud what he will ever find to do with them, since he wants to protect the confidentiality of his subjects. But one reason he goes on taking them is that he worries that the victims of this epidemic, the children of the underclass dying in the inner city, may simply disappear without a trace. "I want to record it, to prove it happened."

3

. . . .

Defense Mechanisms

Residency is a very vulnerable state. I don't think I have ever been so morbidly sensitive to criticism, so fragile, so completely lacking in objectivity. It was an interesting time and a very busy time, but I'm not sure it was a particularly healthy time.

I believed, rightly or wrongly, that whatever happened, it was essential not to show weakness in front of the higher-ups. It was okay to cry on my colleagues, because they cried on me; among us, it was an open secret that our egos were made of eggshells. But when those above you made inquiries, it was important to be strong. The whole time that the crazy person was after me, when I felt pursued and confused and completely exposed, I kept up a ridiculously tough front with my superiors: I just wish they'd stop all this nonsense, so I could do my job!

I tried hard to be tough about making decisions, about

taking control, about taking criticism when it came. And I tried hard to project an image not only of medical confidence, but also of personal and emotional steadiness. I did a very so-so job, I'm afraid, on both counts.

In my writing about medical education, I had taken trouble to assume the persona of the extremely sensitive young physician in training, and had at times disapproved of the callous ways that doctors less exquisitely caring than I talked about patients and disease. In my residency I found myself profoundly dependent on hospital humor to get through the day. Hospital humor is almost always black humor (what's the difference between the oncology ward and New York City? Well, on the oncology ward, the mets always win!—mets is medical slang for metastases, of course). It is hard to explain, hard to retell, and rarely funny out of context. But it offers an absolutely essential twist on the life-and-death realities of hospital life, on scientific explanations and professional posturings. It offers escape without leaving the premises.

Writing about what I was doing, laughing at what I was doing, high sensitivity and extraordinarily tacky jokes—they were ways out, or at least, ways around. They both offered a little of what a resident needs most—perspective.

THE WEAK AND THE STRONG

Residency is enough to drive you crazy. In order to make you into a compassionate, wise, competent doctor, they deprive you of sleep, keep you locked up in the hospital for days at a stretch, and subject you to pressures far beyond anything you have ever known. Between the self-centered performance anxiety of am-I-any-good-at-this and the relatively altruistic nagging worry of will-I-kill-someone-through-ignorance, an intern needs all her sense of self, her strength of character, to keep slogging along.

Well, when I was an intern, I worked with a resident who seemed to be going crazy. And I don't mean in the metaphorical sense. He said things that made no sense; he lapsed suddenly into strange conversations with himself, brought out bits of monologues that suggested he was not quite with us on this planet. Once, when a couple of us had been discussing patients with viral upper respiratory infections, he slammed his clipboard down on the table and said, fiercely, "Okay, so I'm a virgin! So what's so wrong with that?"

He took good care of his patients, but whenever his decisions were questioned, he became furious, abusive, and once almost violent. He suggested to other residents that certain nurses were involved in a conspiracy against him, and would refuse to do anything those nurses requested. He was, altogether, more than a little bit weird.

And so what did we do, the rest of the interns and residents working with him on that particular ward? Well, in retrospect, it seems to me that we spent an extraordinary amount of time and energy explaining away his peculiarities: "Lots of interns talk to themselves when they're tired," we would murmur to each other, or maybe, "God, when guys are insecure, they get so damn defensive." We described him to one another as "kind of bizarre," or "one of your kinkier residents," and always added, "but he takes really good care of his patients." Even the nurses, who judge residents fairly harshly, contented themselves with comments like "Threatening to hit a nurse is inappropriate behavior."

Well, the long and the short of it was, this guy was going nuts, and finally went definitively nuts (but that was in another hospital), raving on the wards, and just like in the movies, had to be taken away. And looking back, I would like to believe that it was just the extreme stress of residency that so altered my perspective and that of my colleagues that we considered his behavior only slightly outside the norm, and that we singularly failed him by ignoring his need for help and failed our patients by allowing him to go on working. But the truth is,

I think, that, resident or not, a doctor often does have to go completely off the rails before anyone is willing to admit that anything is really wrong.

There are horrific statistics quoted every now and then about doctors who drink, doctors on drugs. Once in a while, I hear a rumor about someone: you know that mysterious weekend last year when Dr. X was supposed to be on call, and no one could reach him, and finally Dr. Y, the head of the department, showed up and covered for him, no questions asked, no explanations given? You want to know the real story behind Dr. Z's divorce? Cocaine. Alcohol. There is, of course, a common scenario for medical scare stories: the surgeon whose hands are shaking, the anesthesiologist shooting up in the bathroom. To be honest, in my experience these rumors have been few and far between. But it's easy for me to imagine how ranks would close to protect such a doctor, or perhaps to protect that doctor's colleagues from seeing early warning signs.

But what about protecting the patients? Would I tell you if you were seeing a doctor I didn't trust, for one reason or another? Well, I might say something mild, like maybe, "Oh, he's very . . . traditional—maybe you'd like to see someone with a different style. . . ." And what would I do if I were signing out my patients for the night to a resident who seemed to have something wrong with her? I'd write down absolutely everything I could think of: if patient does this, do that. If patient does that, do the other thing. I'd tell the senior resident about anyone I thought was especially sick, not putting it in terms that reflected on my fellow resident, even though we would both know exactly what I was talking about, but saying only that I'm worried about this kid, you might want to check on her. Now, I don't mean that I'd actually stand by and watch someone hurt a patient; I'm only trying to be honest and admit that I've absorbed some pretty strict prohibitions about bad-mouthing other doctors, that I'm not willing to be alarmed by anything subtle. Or, to put it another way, you could work with me and have a problem, and it would be relatively easy to hide it, because I won't look for it unless it hit me over the head. And isn't that, in the end, because I don't want to find it?

I'm sure the same defenses function in other lines of work, but the peculiar ethics and ethos of medicine make the camouflage more extreme, the consequences more terrifying. For one thing, there is the stereotype of the godlike physician, above normal human emotions and vulnerabilities. Now, the general public may have given this image up for dead, but doctors have perhaps been slower to let it go. Many of us still like to imagine ourselves somehow immune to the frailties that are the stuff of our jobs—the illnesses of the body, the griefs of the spirit. It helps you keep yourself separate from all the pain you see: that could not happen to me.

I can remember getting on an elevator with another resident, both of us exhausted, in dirty hospital scrubs. "Oh, God," said my friend, "I am just so tired, I can't see straight." And a lady standing at the back of the elevator, the mother of a patient, I suppose, said sharply, "How do you think it makes me feel to hear a doctor say that?" We both apologized, and tried to stand up straight and look alert for the rest of the ride, and left the elevator feeling we had been guilty of an unprofessional lapse—and yet, he really was so tired he couldn't see straight. He'd been on call all night in the newborn intensive care unit and hadn't slept at all, and I knew for a fact that his marriage was in trouble, and that he wasn't getting much rest at home either. And, of course, the patient's mother didn't need to know any of that—but still, what's the lesson when you can't admit to being tired in your own workplace after they've kept you up all night?

I think that during our training many of us come to feel that we must protect our patients from seeing any evidence of human weakness, or they will lose their faith in our medical powers. My job is to reassure, to be always in control. And again, acknowledging a doctor's weakness—my own or someone else's—takes on powerful overtones of failure.

And what if I needed help, what if I felt myself slipping into madness, what if I knew I was taking chances? Could I possibly go to any of the people who supervise me? I know the official answer, the we-are-on-your-side-we-want-to-help answer, but in my heart I believe that if I show them any weakness, they will forever remember me only as weak.

And after all, I would say the same thing they do: *my job is to help.* That's why you go into medicine, that's what they train you to do. And in that training, they never teach you how to ask for help. And so, often, when a doctor needs help, but cannot break through the professional image to ask for it, that doctor's colleagues cannot allow themselves to see the problem, cannot offer help to someone who is proving, by example, that doctors, too, are vulnerable, weak, and human.

SICK JOKES

Because I write about medicine, I am not infrequently asked to reveal its dirty secrets. I have had a number of different editors suggest that I write about the terrible accidents and misjudgments I see, the patients who die from their doctors' errors and inexperience. People seem to assume that the material is there if only some doctor would be brave enough to tell the truth. Now, although I have certainly seen my share of mistakes (not to mention made my share of mistakes), they tend to be trivial and boring and not really worth lengthy narration—try and imagine making a story out of some highly technical, momentarily annoying, and ultimately insignificant screwup in your own workplace. I don't really feel that I am sitting on a Truth Which Dare Not Speak Its Name, at least not where mistakes and malpractice are concerned. It has, however, occurred to me that there is one area of medicine I take for granted cannot be offered to the scrutiny of the general public.

I am thinking about medical humor, about what makes residents laugh. This is not a virgin subject; there are plenty of novels and movies that have relied on the black humor of the hospital, on cruel jargon and the dark absurdities of illness and death. Still, I am not sure I have ever felt willing to acknowledge the kinds of things that make me laugh when I'm at work (yes, the sensitive and soulful me, not just the nameless callous mob).

First of all, residents laugh a lot. You might say, considering the hours we work and the things we see, that we belong in the category of people who have to laugh to keep from crying, and this may be true. But one way or the other, a hospital is not a sober, somber place from a resident's point of view. Obviously, we don't stand around the patients' beds chortling, but when we have our own time, sequestered on rounds or gathered around the cafeteria table, we do tend to indulge in what can only be described as sick humor.

I think that most consistently the things that make me laugh are stories at the expense of myself or my fellow residents, stories we tell on ourselves. Frequently the point is our own lack of experience, the terror we feel when a situation starts to get away from us. Consider, for example, my story about the time my patient's grandfather had a heart attack. Now, you should understand that one of the things about being a pediatrician is that you do not get a lot of experience in dealing with heart attacks; children do not come into the emergency room with chest pain very often and coronary artery disease is not high on your list of diagnoses when they do. I have prescribed a great many drugs over the past year and a half, but I am completely unversed in the various preparations people take for angina, high blood pressure; I studied those drugs in medical school, but that's about it. So there I was one day on the infants' ward, and a nurse came to tell me that the worried grandfather of one of my tiny patients was experiencing the worst chest pain of his life. I followed the anxious nurse (she too, after all, was a pediatric specialist) to the man's side; he was gray and sweating, his clenched fist held over his heart.

I thought back to the third year of medical school, my rotation in adult internal medicine. I thought back to the second year of medical school, my cardiovascular pathophysiology course. Finally I thought back to my first year of medical school, a conversation about how people thought we knew how to be doctors just because we had started medical school; anxiety about being called to help on the street or on an airplane, say if someone had a heart attack. I remembered someone saying, all you can do on an airplane is give some nitro if they have it, give oxygen, and then do CPR if the person needs it.

In my calmest, most doctorly voice, I asked the man's wife if he had any nitroglycerine; she produced the bottle and I gave him first one, then another pill, under his tongue. I asked the nurse to get the oxygen hooked up (we do not keep adult-sized oxygen masks next to cribs on the infant ward, but we managed). Meanwhile, the man's wife had begun pulling one bottle after another out of her purse, showing me the various medications that her husband took, and I would look at each one and try to remember what it was for—so he has high blood pressure, I would say casually, or so he's a diabetic, and she would nod. Aha, I would say, knowingly.

If I tell this story right, imitating myself, I can usually make residents smile at the idea of my outward cool as I stood there wondering what the hell else I was going to do. We all know exactly what it feels like to assume a posture of authority while praying that the situation will resolve itself immediately. We all do it from day one of internship.

Anyway, the next thing I did, since the man seemed to be stabilized, was get him hooked up to a cardiac monitor (wondering what I was going to do if anything funny showed up) and call the senior resident. In an elaborately casual tone, I said, "I just thought I should let you know, I have an obese sixty-seven-year-old grandfather of a patient here who is currently experiencing the worst chest pain of his life; he's gray and diaphoretic [sweaty] and I've given him a couple of sublingual nitros." "I'll be right there," said the senior; I later learned that he had been talking with a group of medical students and had left them standing and wondering when he took off at a run for my ward.

The man's chest pain was easing up, and eventually we put him in a wheelchair and a couple of doctors wheeled him to an adult emergency room in a connected hospital and he did just fine. But the point is not the medical care, the point is that I think this is a really funny story. It's a story about me feeling way over my head in a situation that would be old hat to any reasonably experienced internal medicine resident; it's a story about pretending to a confidence I do not feel; it's a story about the unexpected things the hospital can throw at you; it's a story which to me is fundamentally farce. Now, I grant you that if the man had died I would not find the story funny, and I grant you that if what I had done was panic and hide in a linen closet I would probably not be telling the story on myself. But I also admit that I don't think it's any less funny because the punch line is that when he got to the adult emergency room and they finished working him up, they thought he probably *had* had a small heart attack and wanted him to come into the hospital, but he refused, since the chest pain was gone, and came back to sit vigil at his grandson's bed; so every night when I signed out I had to warn the covering intern, the baby's stable but the grandfather is liable to code on you.

Or how about if some doctor who doesn't have a very good reputation among the residents admits a patient to the hospital for what we think are a lot of unnecessary tests, and we do them all, sticking needles into the poor girl, making her drink barium and get a barium enema, drawing out pints and pints of blood—if we start to laugh as the long list of test results is read out in a pedagogic deadpan, are we laughing at that girl's discomfort? Usually not, I think; usually we're laughing at ourselves, at other doctors, at the rituals and protocols of our profession. I worked with one resident who could reduce me to shrieks of laughter just by the way she said the word *interestingly*. She used it to give results of tests which had been completely predictable and done only for form's sake. "Interestingly, the thirteenth and fourteenth sets of blood cultures were also negative." Like that.

But no denying it, sometimes I am also laughing at my patients. Professional detachment is all very well, and the compassion we all strive for is all very well, but the fact is my patients make me angry, they make me happy, they make me frustrated, they make me cry—and they make me laugh. Sometimes with them, but sometimes at them—and that is the hardest thing to admit. If I were a teacher, I assume I could occasionally laugh at my students without guilt; if I sold shoes I would probably laugh at my customers all the time; but I see my patients in extremis, I see them frightened and in pain. I like to think that I am not in fact laughing at that pain, that I am allowing myself to laugh at the black humor which is their mortality and my own—but that is merely a highfalutin way of admitting that I laugh at them. I laugh in part to defend myself against their pain, in part to keep my distance, perhaps—but also in part because their pain is what I work with, it is the stuff of my workday, and you make your workplace humor, your in-jokes, out of the material at hand.

What else is the material at hand, what else makes me laugh? Well, when we find ourselves doing elaborate high-tech procedures just because we have the technology available. "Perri did a head CT for colic," for example. Or when something particularly absurd-sounding happens: "I got an emergency two A.M. admission for constipation." The wise sayings which explain how a teaching hospital works: when the GI service was consulted on a particular patient, they decided to endoscope him, a procedure none of the team caring for that patient had anticipated. The intern asked why, and the resident explained: "You go to Midas, you get a muffler," a phrase that became famous in the hospital, replacing the cruder aphorism that when all you have is a hammer, everything looks like a nail.

The hospital has a place for jokes, every bit as crude as their reputation—an April Fools' joke in an emergency room is to tell the intern when she walks in that there's a dying patient in room 3 and everyone else is busy so please go do CPR till someone is available to help. (The punch line to that joke, of course, is that the intern, still desperate to seem calm in a situation which engenders only panic, turns obediently to enter the assigned room, asking no questions, raising no objections—believe me, I know.) And then there are all the emergency room disaster scenario jokes: it seems there was a busload of pregnant teenagers on their way to diabetes camp, and the bus went off the road. . . .

What can I say? This is probably something that just does not translate. When I try to explain my hospital sense of humor, I make myself and those I work with sound both crude and callous; if I leave out the humor I am trying for a falsely noble and sensitive self-portrait. So in the end I am left with the failed comic's classic lame excuse—I guess you had to be there.

JOURNALS AND JOURNALISM

I have been sorting through the looseleaf notebook that contains my journal from the three years of residency. The first entry was written the night before internship started:

> And tomorrow she becomes an intern. The swing intern, thank God; I'm not on call till Friday night. When I will be responsible for ten beds on the A side of the

special care nursery, and, God help us all, ten beds on the A side of the newborn intensive care unit. We have now reached the state of terror which is truly and simply defined as what-if-I-kill-one. And despite all of the lovely first lines for magazine articles (My first patient weighed 960 grams. That's however many pounds for those of you who haven't yet gone metric. . . . They started me out in the NICU, of course. . . . "This is the most terrified you'll ever be," said my friend consolingly. . . . At our orientation, they told us how code calls were announced over the hospital loudspeaker. Especially at night, you drop what you're doing and go to the code. *Run* to the code. The new group of interns nodded. Then one of us asked, timidly, "And when we get there?" . . .), this is a state of terror which doesn't bear thinking about. I don't know anything about my patients. They have bronchopulmonary dysplasia, or twin-twin transfusions . . . I literally barely know what any of those things are. They have many tubes. I don't know what those are, either. They have, thank God, nurses, the legendary NICU nurses, who make doctors feel like they're just out of medical school. They don't anticipate any trouble with me. . . .

So there I was, the night before internship, already coming up with possible first lines for the article about my first night on call, already aware that it was a natural subject for an essay. Not just making my life into narrative as I went along, but anticipating some of the sensations to come. Talk about making yourself into a character!

It became, I think, my way of defending myself against the onslaughts of residency—as writing becomes, for many writers, including me, a sometime defense against all the onslaughts of life. And during residency I certainly needed all the defenses I could get.

The three-and-a-half-year-old boy I admitted my first night on the oncology service, the child I described in "Mirrors," was what we referred to as a "new leuk," just that very day diagnosed with leukemia, coming into the hospital to start chemotherapy. This was the child who hit too close to home for me, the child who was exactly the same age as my own son, the same size, at the same developmental stage.

And then I couldn't get an IV into him; his veins looked perfectly good, but I kept missing. After a couple of tries, I called the senior resident and asked him to come try, but he was having a busy night somewhere else, and let me know that by the second year of residency, a person should be able to start an IV. I felt hideously ashamed of myself, unable to meet the parents' eyes (the one who tortured their child), unable to face my fellow residents (the one who couldn't start a simple IV). Eventually another resident did come and start the IV, and the child fell asleep, and as a matter of fact he went on to do very well; he tolerated the chemotherapy without too much misery, and his disease went into remission.

But even that very first night, I found myself thinking about how my experience with this patient would be a good story to tell about the hospital, a way to explain the emotional defenses you build up as a doctor, the barriers between yourself and any "new leuk" who happens to come under your care, the reasons you come up with why the terrible things you see happening to other people will never happen to you—or to anyone you love.

Looking back now at this incident, I see in it not only a lesson in the personalization of vulnerability. It strikes me that this story combines in rather accurate measure the sweepingly tragic hospital storyline and the helplessly petty self-conscious concern of the junior doctor. There is the family, struck by what is surely the most horrible, most unexpected disaster they have ever faced, finding themselves in an alien, frightening environment, and then there is the young doctor feeling ashamed of herself because she couldn't get the IV started, agonizing over whether to call for help, over whom to call, over what that person will say. And looking at it all as subject material into the bargain, writing articles in her head that use the patient and the parents and her own emotional upheavals as illustrative anecdote to show the hospital to outsiders, to say, come see what this training is like, what I am doing to people, what they are doing to me. Come look how far I've come since this training began.

Residency is a time of transformation. By the time you start, you are already pretty familiar with the hospital as an environment, with its codes of behavior and its alphabet soup of abbreviations. You bring with you from medical school what you remember from the classroom and from your training time on the wards; this is referred to as your "fund of knowledge," to suggest that all contributions will be gratefully accepted.

Residency is supposed to take you and make you into a doctor. Expose you to everything important, everything you might need to know. Nudge you (or force you) into a position where you are making the decisions yourself, weighing what is important with the certainty of the practitioner, not the hopeful guesses of the student. The format of residency is meant to meet these needs. You work long hours, including nights, because you want as much experience as you can possibly get in a couple of years. You progress along to higher and higher levels of responsibility, always a little (or a lot) more than you feel ready for. And though there is supposed to be someone, always, for you to call when you need help, the essence of residency is that you are the one on the spot, in residence.

Writing about residency allows you to take notes on your own transformation, to preserve documentation of what you were like before and what you are becoming. It formalizes the storytelling which is always part of hospital life, always part of resident camaraderie (You'll never believe what happened to me last night. Wanna hear about a Transport from Hell? All right, wait till I tell you what the ER did this time). It also forces you to make decisions about how honest you are willing to be, and at what level your honesty operates; when I wrote the essay about the three-and-a-half-year-old with leukemia, I did not see any reason to compromise the pure sensitivity of my distress as I looked at that child and thought about my own son at home. So I didn't put in anything about how I was looking at him and turning him into anecdote, then and there, and I also didn't put in anything about how I stuck him again and again and couldn't get an IV started. It all depends on what story you want to tell.

The hard part about writing about residency is finding the time. Residency is designed to absorb you completely. It's training by total immersion. Despite what they claim, most senior doctors look at any outside interest as evidence that you aren't really serious about your training. I was extremely lucky in that after I finished my internship, the people in charge of my program decided to let me arrange a part-time schedule for the second two years, in which I got certain months off instead of doing electives. I used the time to write a novel. But even during the months I was working, the habit of journalism stayed strong, the need to come home and tell the story my way.

Writing about medical training changes medical training. By the time I started my internship, I was in the habit of looking around the hospital, searching for the next article. What would be the right size for a 1500-word column, what point about medicine does this incident illustrate? It produced, I fear, a certain ingenuousness. Maybe it also made me sharper, helped me understand what residency was doing to me. Maybe it even made me more sensitive to my patients, maybe I tried to understand what they were going through so I could describe it. It would be nice to think so. However, I worked with plenty of people who managed a high degree of awareness and sensitivity without needing to grind everything up into journalism.

Writing about medical training may have made me more conscious; it certainly made me more self-conscious. What I did, over the years, I think, was make myself into a character and create a situation where I was not quite able to experience my own life directly. No matter how serious the situation, no matter how engaged I was in what I was doing, there was often a little voice in the background transmuting the events into narrative, shadowing my actions and decisions with the whisper of what they would look like on paper. If I was crying in the bathroom because I had failed to get an IV in and a parent had screamed at me, then, even as I blew my nose, I could hear in my mind, "So I missed the IV four times in a row, and the baby screamed, and the nurse looked angry, and the baby's mother yelled at me to get out of the room. So I got out of the room with all the dignity I could manage, paged the senior resident to come try the IV, and then headed for the bathroom, where I promptly burst into tears. And as I tried to avoid the sight of my own contorted face in the mirror, I was conscious of a tiny ignoble hope that the senior resident would also fail, proving to the nurse and the mother that it hadn't been my fault, that the baby was just what we call 'an impossible stick.'" And then, as I washed my face with cold water and got ready to go back to my work, an internal editor would start wondering whether that last sentence could really be published, or whether it made me seem too dislikable, too ready to sacrifice a sick baby on the altar of my own self-esteem.

During residency, life was not gracious and I was not graceful. The peculiar twist was that though I was writing fairly honestly about this life I was leading, making myself into a character, but an insecure bumbling overstressed bitch of a character as often as not, there were other people interested in making me into a different kind of character. The publicity that attended my writing was usually flattering, and almost always ridiculous. The general theme was that someone who is a doctor and a writer and a mother is by definition a super-woman, by definition an object of hatred and envy to everyone who hears about her, especially other women. This is not an experience, as far as I know, that men who have written about their careers in medicine have gone through, whether or not they have children—this is presumably because it is assumed that having children for them is merely a hobby that consumes very little time. It is not an experience that Larry, the man I live with, has ever gone through—no one ever seemed astonished that he had a job, wrote books, and also had a child or two. No journalist ever wanted to know how he did it all.

And of course, when you protest that really, your life is a mess, your bathroom is dirty, your kid takes cold pizza in his lunch box, that just makes you even more of a paragon—she isn't only superwoman, she's also modest! Why, she's just folks!

And of course, that's true. The real reason all of this superwoman nonsense is nonsense is that all around are people leading complicated lives, managing careers and families, taking care of dependents of all ages, and still finding time for what matters most. Writing is a pleasure and an escape, an indulgence and a discipline, if you are someone who needs to write. I kept writing through residency not because I planned it that way but because, looking back, I never stopped. I must have needed to do it, wanted to do it, loved to do it, because heaven knows I stopped doing almost everything else (going to movies, answering my mail, reading the newspaper).

So I went through residency with a chorus shadowing me. There was the character I had created for myself, whose story I was continually writing, and there was also that dislikable superwoman created by other people. And then there was also her antithesis, the amiable slob persona that I always wanted to thrust forward when anyone started talking superwoman: look, she's overweight, she's grouchy, she doesn't think she's a very good doctor, and yes, her bathroom is filthy. And together, we made it through and became at least one full pediatrician.

A reporter came and interviewed me once, for what of course turned out to be one of those superwoman articles, and she kept asking me to come up with an anecdote from my life that would illustrate how I was a doctor and a mother and a writer. I offered that story about the new leukemic; she thought it was too complicated and anyway, didn't show me in a very flattering light. So I kept trying: well, there was the night I came home late from work (because I was being a Doctor!), and Benjamin wanted me to read to him (because I'm his Mother!), but I had an article due at a magazine (because I'm a Writer!) . . . so I cut the story short (and felt guilty) and went to write the article (and fell asleep at the keyboard) and had to get up early the next morning and felt depressed (because I was going to be on call). . . . The journalist kept telling me the stories weren't very interesting, which is actually a reasonably true observation about the nitty-gritty details of putting any given life together. She had obviously been hoping for some story about how I was walking down the street with my son telling him a very imaginative fairy tale (being a creative Writer-Mother) when suddenly across the street a child was mauled by a convenient wild beast, so I resuscitated the child with one hand, holding tight to my son with the other (the heroic Doctor-Mother), and was then inspired to write a very moving epic poem (the resourceful Writer-Doctor). And all I can say is that when I come up with such a story, I'll have no intention of passing it on to any journalist. I'll write it myself.

4

··

Back to the Beginning

In my program, we spent a big part of the second year taking care of newborns. We talked to parents who came to the labor and delivery floor when the women were in premature labor or when the fetuses were known to have congenital anomalies, congenital infections. We went to deliveries—either by plan, when the problems were known in advance, or by drop-every-thing-and-run emergency, when something went wrong at the last minute. And above all, we worked in the NICUs, taking care of the sick babies we brought back from the delivery rooms, but also taking care of sick babies born at other hospitals all around the state and transferred to us for intensive care.

I had suspected it as an intern, and I confirmed it as a junior resident: I don't really like the NICU. You either like it or you don't, and it depends on how you feel about intensive care, among other things. One of the residents I worked with, who had a sort of genius for super-high-tech medicine and for the care of the extremely sick, told me that being in an ICU always made her feel secure, because you were already *there*. She meant, she said, that in a regular nursery or on a ward, you were always worrying about sick kids—should you send them to the ICU, where maybe more could be done for them? But if you were in the ICU, the kids were already there, you had all the resources possible, you could do everything that could be done. The ICU never made *me* feel secure; it just reminded me of how little I felt I knew.

And in the NICU, you can't ever talk to your patients; you can't even usually play with them. You just do procedures, and more procedures, and you "tune" them—ICU slang for getting all the numbers balanced, all the systems working as well as possible.

In addition, as I grew more accustomed to the routine of the NICU, I was increasingly troubled by the ethical dilemmas which torment almost everyone who works in newborn medicine. To put it bluntly, we spent a great deal of our time and energy trying to save very tiny babies who were very unlikely to survive intact. Of course, we also helped lots of babies who did just fine, slightly older preemies who needed some help breathing till their lungs developed, babies born with infections who needed antibiotics and support, and so on. But some of the neonatologists I worked with seemed to be committed to the ideal that no baby should be too young to save, that no degree of brain damage should make you give up the fight. If anyone argued against routinely resuscitating babies on the very, very edge of viability, these doctors would point out that that edge had been moving steadily backward. Once, not long ago, twenty-seven weeks was too young to save; now it's twenty-four, maybe even twenty-three—and how will we learn to save those babies unless we save them, and practice?

The ethics of the NICU are not simple, and I have no simple answers. But I often found myself disagreeing with what I was doing, and this high-minded distress, combined with the

irritations of finicky detailed calculations and constant negotiation over every aspect of management, made it clear that I
wasn't cut out for the NICU.

From my journal, written postcall in the NICU:

> Sitting yet again in the intermediate room, wasting
> time, wasting time, not just on rounding but on extra-
> neous details. I am tired and grubby, pimpled and fat,
> argumentative and touchy . . . and I want to go home.

> I am becoming postcall irritable with my fellow, who
> is now worrying about whether two babies I admitted
> last night should get their twenty-four-hour labs at eigh-
> teen hours instead, because if they're septic, she wants to
> know it sooner rather than later, because even if they're
> very well, they might get very sick . . . but mostly it's just
> the feeling of the night, waiting for the twenty-three-
> weeker they said was coming. I can feel myself on the
> edge of being rude and letting her see open hostility/
> contempt—always a bad policy, especially with someone
> who's been real nice to me. . . . Long talk now with nurse
> about whether baby A's fluids should be based on birth
> weight or current weight (makes a difference of twelve
> ccs per kilogram per day in the hypothetical fluids the
> baby is getting). I'm so tired and spacey, I want to kill
> the nurse who yelled at me for wanting to LP [lumbar
> puncture] a baby with a temp of 102. She said: "All I'm
> saying is he was crying for two hours so he has a reason
> for a temperature, and I disagree with severely trauma-
> tizing him when we see this . . ." And off she flounces,
> how she flounces, and the tones she uses, and you want
> to say, You wouldn't talk to a dog like that, but instead
> you use sensitivity jargon and express concern for her
> concerns and you never say, fuck you, baby! Or OK, I'll
> just write it in the chart, no septic workup because the
> nurse was confident no infection existed. Boy, do I feel
> disgusting and disgusted.

On the other hand. On the other hand. I helped save a lot of babies, babies I could hope would go on and live normal lives. We used to joke that there are only a few things which can go wrong with a newborn, though when they go wrong, they go very wrong indeed. A newborn—premature or full term—can have an infection, can have respiratory distress, can have a malformed heart . . . and so on. Not all that many possibilities, not a long differential diagnosis, as we say.

Since I have no particular knack for intensive care, I had to fall back on being compulsive. Now, *compulsive*, as used by residents, is a relative term. The truly compulsive resident leaves no stone unturned, ever, no avenue unpursued. Never sleeps, never goes home. I was only a relatively compulsive resident, collecting data and scribbling it on my scut sheet— but going home as soon as possible. The NICU is a place which brings out the compulsive in you; all those sick babies with all those numbers to collect. We used to joke, in fact, that a really ace resident could present a NICU baby on rounds using only numbers, calling them out like football signals: "35—850—29—20/4—35 percent—8." Like that.

And everyone would know that meant: Hospital day thirty-five for this former 850-gram twenty-nine-week preemie now on vent settings of pressures 20/4, oxygen at 35 percent, and a rate of eight.

For one of my months in the NICU, I worked with two residents from absolutely opposite ends of the compulsiveness spectrum. One was a woman who wrote down everything there was to write down, with a different color ink for each category of data, and worried constantly about every possible bad outcome. The other was a man who was extremely laid-back, cheerfully picking up patient clipboards on rounds to look at numbers for the first time. He figured, he said, that the nurses would come get him if anything serious went wrong—and if anything serious went wrong, he did the right thing.

I was in the middle, both literally and figuratively. And I can still remember coming in one Saturday morning to take over from my more compulsive colleague. There were some really sick kids here, she told me, shaking her head, really sick kids. And no, she hadn't slept, she'd been going around and around the NICU all night, just checking on things. She provided me with a superbly detailed sign-out, offered to stay around if I needed any help. But in fact, it seemed to me that by ICU standards, the room was pretty quiet. Yes, there were sick babies, babies on ventilators, but everyone seemed stable, nothing was happening. I thanked her and sent her home.

I had a relatively quiet twenty-four hours. I stayed up that night till about two, gathering numbers and checking out babies, then went to bed and slept till seven, waking up occasionally to answer questions. At seven, I got up to gather one more round of data. At eight, the third resident arrived, and I told him about the kids, still basically the same group I had taken over the morning before. "Sounds quiet!" he said, his face lighting up. I nodded. He took a novel out of his backpack. "I'll be in the breast-feeding room," he said. "Don't tell the nurses where I am."

BEFORE THEY'RE BORN

Shakespeare, allowing Richard III to explain the origins of his villainy, had him announce that he had been "Deformed, unfinished, sent before my time/Into this breathing world, scarce half made up" (Act I, Scene 1). What could be worse than a birth defect, what tragedy greater than a baby born abnormal?

So you want to have a baby. And, naturally, you want to have a healthy baby, a perfect baby. You'll give up alcohol, and instead you'll drink your eight glasses of milk every day. You won't even take Tylenol. Maybe you'll finally go ahead and test your house for radon. Anything for a healthy baby.

As medicine marches forward, one of the benefits we seek is certainty: give me the diet that will keep me healthy, the special bran muffin that will lower my cholesterol. Do as many tests as you need, doctor, just make sure there's nothing wrong with me. And above all, promise me a healthy child. The astronomical rates at which obstetricians are sued by their patients reflect this; a good obstetrician is expected to deliver a perfect baby, and to foresee and circumvent any of the possible problems in pregnancy, labor, and delivery.

In medicine in general, and in obstetrics in particular, this search for certainty leads to many invasive procedures. Now the search for a perfect baby is leading us further and further back into pregnancy, as the possibilities for prenatal diagnosis multiply.

Prenatal diagnosis starts before there is a fetus to diagnose. If two people are thinking of having a child together, they should ideally give some thought to whether any genetic diseases run in their families, from the relatively common well-known disorders such as hemophilia and muscular dystrophy, to such rare disorders as ceramidase deficiency and glycogen storage disease. Any prospective parent whose family tree includes a number of childhood deaths, or a succession of children with congenital anomalies, should get genetic counseling sooner, rather than later.

Even if there isn't any such family history, those who come from certain populations may want to be tested to see if they carry specific genes—for example, those with African ancestry can be tested for the sickle-cell disease gene, while those with eastern European Jewish forebears can be tested for Tay-Sachs disease. Both of these disorders follow a Mendelian recessive pattern of inheritance: both parents must donate copies of the problem gene for the child to have the disease—in other words, both parents must be carriers.

Okay, so now you're pregnant. And sure, the obstetrician does the usual things to check up on the fetus—listens to the heartbeat, measures the uterus—but what about the new, high-tech ways of making sure the baby is going to be OK?

The only prenatal screen that is routinely recommended

for *every* pregnancy is an alpha-fetoprotein (AFP) level. This is a test done on a small sample of the mother's blood, measuring a protein that is produced by the fetus in increasing amounts throughout the pregnancy. If a woman's test reveals a level too low or too high for her particular stage of pregnancy, the doctor does an ultrasound, using sound waves to create a picture of the fetus. Most of the time, it turns out that the estimated gestational age was wrong; ultrasound allows very accurate dating of the pregnancy, and a high AFP level often turns out to mean a baby due sooner than anyone was expecting.

However, if the AFP is really too high, it raises the specter of congenital anomaly. AFP is elevated in spinal cord defects, where the spinal column never fuses properly, causing spina bifida. Other malformations that leave the internal organs exposed can also raise the AFP; gastroschisis, for example, in which the intestines are on the outside of the abdomen. Most such major defects will be seen on the ultrasound. But there are other less visible problems that are also associated with a rise in AFP—Turner's syndrome, for example, a fairly common chromosomal abnormality in which a fetus has only one sex chromosome (a single X, instead of XX or XY). Turner's cannot be diagnosed with ultrasound; you need an amniocentesis and a chromosome analysis—but that's already getting ahead of our story.

An AFP level that is too low brings up other possibilities. Low levels are associated with Down's syndrome, as well as with another, more serious syndrome, trisomy 18, in which, instead of the extra twenty-first chromosome seen in Down's, the fetus has an extra eighteenth chromosome; if carried to term, these babies have multiple birth defects in many organ systems and do not survive infancy. Again, these chromosomal syndromes can sometimes be diagnosed with ultrasound, but really require amniocentesis and genetic analysis.

Although the American College of Obstetricians and Gynecologists does not actually recommend ultrasound as a routine test in a normal, untroubled pregnancy, more and more doctors seem to be doing routine ultrasounds on more and more women. Some of this probably grows out of the parents' desire to be assured that all is well with the fetus; some grows out of the doctor's desire to guard against lawsuits by doing every test. Ultrasound may or may not be accompanied by amniocentesis, in which a sample of amniotic fluid is withdrawn by needle, and the fetal cells are cultured and their chromosomes analyzed. This test is now recommended for women over thirty-five, a somewhat arbitrary number. As women age, the frequency of Down's syndrome in their offspring increases, and thirty-five marks the age where this risk is thought to surpass the risk to the fetus from the procedure itself—there is a small incidence of miscarriage following amniocentesis. So now women over thirty-five tend to have amniocentesis done, and the vast majority of babies with Down's syndrome are born to younger mothers; this group has a comparatively low frequency of the defect, but a comparatively much higher birth rate, so the rare events add up.

Now, let me point out that we are already morally in deep weeds. All this prenatal diagnosis, after all, carries with it the implication that if an abnormality is found, the parents intend to do something about it, i.e., terminate the pregnancy. But the various abnormalities I have just listed constitute a wide spectrum. On the one end, a trisomy 18, or a trisomy 13, is a fetus that most parents would probably choose to abort. If carried to term, these babies are profoundly abnormal, severely retarded, and tend to die very soon. On the other hand, girls with Turner's syndrome have comparatively mild, unusual facial features, and grow up mentally normal. They suffer from certain medical problems—short stature and infertility, to name two of the most troubling—but they are by no means devastated children. Would most parents choose to terminate these pregnancies as well?

Or consider Down's syndrome, the reason for most of those over-thirty-five amnios. Many parents choose to abort fetuses with Down's—but I have also come across many who are indignant at the very idea, proud of their children's achievements. Such parents are quick to point out that our concept of what children with trisomy 21 can learn has changed radically over the past few decades, since these children have been kept at home instead of being placed in institutions, that their children are happy, loving beings. (In fact, doctors have also changed their tunes. In the past, surgeons often refused to operate on babies with Down's; the malformations of the gastrointestinal tract, the cardiac defects to which these children are prone, were often left uncorrected, and the babies allowed to die. Nowadays, after several very celebrated cases, infants with trisomy 21 receive a "full court press," including open-heart surgery, when necessary.)

All of this is not to say that parents who choose to abort an abnormal fetus are acting irresponsibly. I'm only trying to say that before we ask for information, we should decide what we are going to do with it when we get it. We are now able to ask more and more questions of the fetus, and we are able to ask them earlier and earlier. Amniocentesis cannot be done until the second trimester, but the relatively new technique of chorionic villus sampling (CVS) can analyze fetal chromosomes as early as the first trimester. Ultimately, and in the not too distant future, all this testing will be done on a small sample of maternal blood, taken from the mother as a routine blood test. Fetal cells, which have crossed over the placenta into the mother's bloodstream, will be selected out, and will provide all the necessary genetic material.

Although geneticists can now ask a multitude of questions, the vast majority are not routinely broached in your average pregnancy. A thirty-seven-year-old woman has an amnio, and the fetal cells are checked for major chromosomal abnormalities, such as trisomies. However, without specific indications, no one looks at this DNA to find any more subtle genetic diseases. If there is a family history of cystic fibrosis, say, or of some enzyme deficiency, then that test is done, but most genetic diseases are so rare that it would make no sense to screen the general population. The availability of these specific tests is a tremendous boon to families cursed with a deadly genetic disease. Consider, for example, Duchenne's muscular dystrophy, which is an X-linked disorder, a condition, like hemophilia, in which the mother is a carrier, with one normal X chromosome and one that carries the muscular dystrophy. If her son inherits that one, he develops a degenerative disease and slowly loses his muscular strength, ending up wheelchair-bound by twelve or thirteen, then losing the power of his respiratory muscles, and dying, usually of lung disease, often before the age of twenty. It used to be that what doctors offered parents who were watching one well-loved son deteriorate was this: next time you get pregnant, have an amniocentesis, and if the fetus is male, abort it. There was no specific prenatal screen to tell whether a male had inherited the normal X or the defective X from his mother, but a female, who would have inherited at least one normal gene from her father, could not possibly have the disease. Nowadays, at least, the difficult decision of whether or not to carry a pregnancy to term can be fully informed, because we can screen specifically for muscular dystrophy.

Geneticists would caution us not to think that we are buying certainty. Even if all the currently available genetic tests were done, they would not guarantee you a perfect baby. Although we can test for a number of syndromes that include mental retardation, these syndromes account for far fewer than half of children diagnosed with mental retardation—the great majority have causes we cannot possibly pick up prenatally. And congenital anomalies, developmental defects, occur more often than many people realize; by one recent estimate, one in every fifty babies has a defect of medical, cosmetic, or surgical significance. Most of these defects are not life-threatening, and even if we could detect them all prenatally, would we want to start terminating pregnancies for comparatively minor cardiac defects?

I believe that prospective parents are entitled to as much information as they feel they need, entitled to good genetic counseling, accurate testing, and medical support for their decisions. I also believe they are entitled to do whatever they want with this information. I just think that before we reach out eagerly for all the new knowledge our expanding technology can offer, we need to stop and think about how we are going to use this information, how much of it we need, how much of it we want. And we have to acknowledge that for all of the technology, the growth of a fetus and the birth of a baby remain processes that are not completely under our control. Perfect babies, in the end, are born, not made.

LABOR AND DELIVERY

The delivery room beeper is like a hot potato. I arrived on the first morning of my rotation, and someone almost threw it at me: Here you go, you're DR-1. DR-1—first call for the delivery room. The beeper was swaddled round with adhesive tape, covering the on/off button. This beeper is never turned off, just passed to the next resident. I clipped it onto the waistband of my scrubs, where it looked very nice, right next to my regular beeper. The DR-1 beeper goes off whenever they want a pediatrician to go the delivery room, that is, whenever it looks like a baby, about to be born, may be in some kind of trouble. Babies arrive (and get into trouble) at all hours of the day and night. The beeper sounds and you're off and running down the hall.

Full-term healthy babies don't need pediatricians in the delivery room. The nurses wipe them off, count fingers and toes, give them to the mother or the father. The pediatrician gets called when a premature baby is on its unstoppable way, or a baby suspected of having some serious congenital anomaly, or when the mother has a fever and the baby may be infected, or when the fetal heart monitor shows some kind of abnormal pattern. And most frequently, most routinely, the pediatrician gets called for meconium.

Meconium is the first bowel movement of the newborn infant, tarry sticky black stuff that is normally excreted soon after birth. But sometimes, no one knows exactly why, perhaps because the fetus is stressed, meconium is passed in utero. When a woman is in labor, the membranes around the sac of amniotic fluid rupture (or are ruptured by the doctors) and the fluid leaks out; it should be clear. If meconium is seen in the fluid, things get serious. The risk is that the baby may suck the meconium into its mouth and nose, and ultimately, aspirate it into the lungs. In the most serious cases, meconium aspiration syndrome leads to asphyxia, brain damage, and death. Fortunately, though meconium at delivery is not uncommon, serious meconium aspiration is rare. This, however, was not a tremendous comfort to me, when, half an hour after receiving my beeper, they summoned me: "Meconium in delivery room three!"

See, the idea about meconium is this: the baby doesn't take a first breath until after the umbilical cord is cut, so maybe if you suction the mouth and nose out before that breath is taken, the baby won't suck any meconium down into the trachea. And, if there is already meconium sitting in the trachea, maybe if you intubate the baby—put an endotracheal tube down and suction the airway—maybe then you can prevent the meconium from being sucked into the lungs. So when there's meconium in the amniotic fluid, the obstetrician will clean out the baby's mouth and nose as soon as the head emerges, often while the rest of the baby's body is still in the birth canal. Then, as quickly as possible, the baby is delivered, the cord is cut, and the baby is passed to the pediatrician, who is standing ready with her endotracheal tubes. You understand, theoretically seconds count here. Get that gunk out before the baby breathes or cries; get that tube into that tiny elusive hole (not into the esophagus, which is bigger and much easier to find); save that baby!

So I marched down to delivery room 3, and while the mother pushed, and the father and the nurses encouraged her, and the obstetrician got ready with the suction bulb, I nervously checked and rechecked my equipment, all sitting ready for me at the little warming table in the corner of the delivery room. This table is the domain of the pediatrician or the pediatric nurse. Until the cord is cut, the fetus "belongs" to the obstetrician; once the cord is cut and the infant put down on the warming table, it's, well, our baby. So I checked my oxygen and my full-term baby–sized oxygen mask, my suction machine, and my pocket full of endotracheal tubes, carried like amulets by the DR-1 resident. I knew that in the vast majority of cases where meconium is seen, the baby is just fine, and is breathing and screaming long before that tube gets into the trachea, and if the baby is breathing and screaming, many people think intubation is unnecessary because what's going to get into the lungs is already in the lungs, and it isn't enough to keep the baby from oxygenating properly. But naturally I was thinking, what if this baby has it bad, what if this baby's life depends on what I do in the next two minutes?

The head came out. I had no appreciation to spare for the miracle of birth. I was not even sympathetically contracting my own muscles when the nurses called, in those distinct cheerleader tones that everyone always uses on women in labor, "Push, push, push, push, push!" I was listening for one miracle and one miracle only: I wanted to hear that baby cry! The obstetrician stuck the nozzle of the bulb syringe into the baby's mouth, and I was glad to see that the baby grimaced, a sign of health (it's abnormal to just lie there limply while strangers stick things down your throat). I was also glad to see that the obstetrician did a thorough job with the bulb, sucked out lots of glop. Then with a little more push, push, push, push, out came the shoulders, the trunk, the legs; and the newborn squirmed, wet and slippery, in the doctor's hands. Yes, squirmed—I was already chanting softly to the nurse, in my relief, "Good baby!" That was not meant as encouragement; it was a delivery room assessment. There are the good babies and there are the bad babies, the ones who are limp and blue and don't grimace—or breathe.

The obstetrician was cutting the cord, and there it came, sure enough, loud angry crying, and with it the release of tension which always comes at that sound in a delivery room—yes, there really is a baby, yes the baby is alive. The parents gasped, the nurse said jubilantly, "It's a girl, look, you got a girl!," and I repeated, louder, "Good baby!" And then the good baby was deposited on my warming table; and the obstetrician went back to his work, and the nurse and I turned to ours.

When I was in medical school, doing my first month of pediatrics, a resident I worked with told me that she first knew she wanted to be a pediatrician when she was doing obstetrics. Whenever she went to a delivery, she said, she would always want to follow the baby, take care of the baby, not the mother. Though I have myself been in the position of the mother, though I identify with women in labor and now often do find myself pushing along with them till my muscles ache, as soon as there is a baby in the room, I lose any medical interest in the mother. Given a choice between an adult and a child, I prefer to take care of the child.

So there was this baby, red and screaming, and meconium stained. So the nurse held her head steady, and I went into her mouth with my laryngoscope—a little hand-held metal forklift with a light on it—lifting her tongue out of the way, looking for her vocal cords, the way into her trachea. And to my own surprise, I got the tube in, and we suctioned the tube and got nothing back. No meconium in the airway. I pulled out the tube. Good baby. So then we dried off the baby, rubbing off the vernix and blood and meconium, and we did a hasty finger and toe count, and I gave the baby Apgar scores at one minute and five minutes of life. The Apgar score (named after Virginia Apgar, who developed the system) is a standard method for assessing newborns; you give zero, one, or two points in each of five categories, and you get a score somewhere between zero and ten, where zero is essentially dead (no grimace, no heart rate, no respirations, completely limp, and blue from head to toe—not a good baby) and ten is perfect (good grimace, heart rate greater than a hundred beats a minute, regular respirations, moving actively, pink from head to toe). Actually, out of some kind of superstition, we almost never give a ten—only to pediatricians' children, we joke, mindful of our own paranoias, of the possibility that we would worry if a single point was taken off.

So this baby girl got Apgars of nine at one minute and nine at five minutes, losing one point each time for color— hands and feet were bluish, as they almost always are. I passed another little tube down into her stomach, and suctioned out the stomach contents, six cubic centimeters of meconium-tainted amniotic fluid which she had swallowed during labor. I didn't want her to spit any of that up and aspirate it later on. I put a little hat on her so she wouldn't lose too much heat from her head. I put a diaper on her to catch the next installment of meconium. Then I wrapped her tightly in a blanket, but my wrapping job didn't meet the nurse's high standards, and she redid it, explaining kindly to me that doctors never wrap babies properly. She also put erythromycin ointment in the baby's eyes to prevent infection that can be acquired during birth.

And then I took the little bundle over to the parents, and handed the baby to the father, who handed it to the mother, and I told them their baby had been just fine, and had ten fingers and ten toes, and they thanked me in tones so heartfelt you would have thought that it was all due to me. I congratulated them, and went back to the nursery to wait for my beeper to go off again.

Of course, the baby doesn't always come out screaming,

with an Apgar of nine. After a couple of days and nights as DR-1, I had seen my share of bad babies. Fortunately, almost all of them come around with some oxygen, some stimulation, maybe a little bag-and-mask ventilation. And you stand there with them, and you pray, please baby, breathe, cry, move, turn pink. Time will stop as you stand there, one of the other residents warned me, and it does. You'll think you can hear the brain cells dying, one of the other residents warned me, and I do. You'll be able to intubate and suck meconium in your sleep, everyone told me. When you carry the DR-1 beeper, you sleep when you can. So then at three o'clock in the morning, the beeper goes off, or someone knocks on my door: meconium in room 2. And I grab my talismanic pouch of endotracheal tubes, my box of emergency resuscitation drugs, repeating over and over to myself, if I have them I won't need them. And I put on my glasses, my surgical head cover, my shoe covers, my mask and my gloves, and all the while I go running down the hall to room 2, a picture of dashing glamorous medical efficiency. And since labor is beyond the control of doctors (despite years of trying), sometimes the baby is arriving just as I arrive, and other times I stand by my warming table and fuss with my equipment. And the nurses yell, "push push push," and the oxygen bubbles in the tube, and I mutter to myself, "please be a good baby, please be a good baby." And hold my tube ready. And it all feels a little bit surreal under the operating room lights, at three in the morning, my head covering slipping off my uncombed hair. And you know what's truly surreal? When someone asks how I like covering the delivery room, I hear myself saying the same thing other residents used to say to me: "It's scary, but it's really fun."

But please be a good baby. Please cry, please move, please turn pink. Be a good baby, please be a good baby.

TRANSPORTS
· · · · · · · · ·

The call comes early in the morning. A small community hospital sixty miles away, the newborn nursery calling. They have a brand-new baby who is having trouble breathing. You're the resident on transport call. You sling a stethoscope around your shoulders; you march out to the elevator. There are two emergency medical technicians (EMTs), pushing the Cavitron, a Star Wars contraption for transporting babies. An oversized metal object, shaped a little like a baby carriage, it has a built-in mechanical ventilator, a cardiopulmonary monitor, a heater, and, in the center, the small cylindrical niche where the baby actually rides. There is also a nurse; and you and she each carry a big metal box, the "tackle boxes" that are full of every conceivable drug and piece of equipment for tending to a sick baby. You ride down in the elevator with your troop, your equipment, off on your mission. Out to the ambulance door.

Many people get carsick in ambulances. As it happens, I do not, unless I look out the back window and see the road speeding away out from under the vehicle. I don't need the Dramamine that some residents and nurses dose themselves with—as long as I keep looking forward. It is considered bad form to arrive at the destination hospital, leap briskly from the ambulance, and throw up. As it happens, I like riding in ambulances. I take a juvenile delight in the screaming siren, in the cars getting out of the way, in the jolting around. This is all on the way to pick up the sick baby, of course; once you have a patient in the ambulance, you don't really have the extra mental energy to enjoy the siren or even to get carsick.

The two EMTs lift the Cavitron into the back of the ambulance and bolt it into place—there are many stories about these heavy machines coming loose and smashing around inside the ambulance. The nurse climbs in and takes the seat that faces backward—she's been on several hundred transports, and riding backward doesn't bother her at all. You climb in and take a seat on the padded bench that runs along the side of the ambulance, well positioned to stare into the empty Cavitron. You put on your seat belt. You notice, as you do every time you get into an ambulance, that there is no way to rest your back, only a too-high cushion set into the wall at the precise level to keep you from leaning back comfortably. The EMTs get into the front seats, turn around and ask how sick the baby is, how fast you want to go. "Pretty sick," you and the nurse say in unison.

They start the siren as you leave the hospital. The streets are pretty crowded, so even with the siren, you can't go very fast. You lean forward (you can't lean back) and look out the windshield, swaying a little from side to side. The ambulance gets to a main road and picks up speed, and you find yourself wondering whether people in the cars you are passing are looking at the ambulance with curiosity, with awe. You picture fascinated twelve-year-olds, dreaming of becoming doctors someday. You sit as tall and as proud as you can. Then you remember that you are a resident going to pick up a sick newborn, and you slump a little and begin your habitual prayer, please don't let the baby be too sick.

You know this baby is only three weeks premature, good-sized, not small enough to be a likely candidate for premature lung disease of the newborn. This is a disease caused by a deficiency in a substance called surfactant, which acts in the lungs to decrease surface tension, allowing the tiny air sacs to inflate. In other words, with surfactant, the lungs are pliable, the air sacs—or alveoli—are inflatable. Without surfactant, the lungs are stiff, the alveoli collapse, reluctant to open and let any air in. Rarely, full-term or near-term babies develop symptoms suggestive of these stiff immature lungs, and these babies, who should have plenty of surfactant, can be the sickest of all.

Your anxieties are interrupted by a sudden sharp turn of the ambulance, an extra blast on the siren; you almost fall off the bench, and a little drawer on the bottom of the Cavitron opens, spilling someone's hoard of sugarless gum into your lap. "Hey, guys," you call, "don't get us all killed."

Once, I was actually in an ambulance that had an accident—sideswiped a car and had to veer off the road. We all got thrown around a little, but no one was hurt, either in the ambulance or in the car. Somewhat shaken, we went on our way, picked up the baby, and came back to our home hospital, where lots of my colleagues topped my story of the accident by telling me about accidents they had heard of (the fabulous apocrypha of the medical world) with critically ill patients in the ambulance, with tubes and lines coming out left and right at the collision.

You get to the hospital, jump out, grab a tackle box. Stride in through the automatically opening doors, trying to look purposeful, ask an orderly where the newborn nursery is. Ride up in the elevator, trundle the Cavitron down the hall. "Hi, we're the transport team. Where's the sick baby?"

Actually, it's perfectly obvious where the sick baby is. The newborn nursery is a soothing room, decorated in salmon pink and aqua blue. Well-bundled infants are sleeping in little clear plastic bins labeled with pink cards or blue cards. And in the middle of the room is one baby lying on her back under a heating lamp, a Plexiglas oxygen hood shaped like a cake protector over her head. A nurse is attending to her. The other babies are wrapped; this one is naked. The other babies are small self-contained units; this one is attached to an IV and to the oxygen supply. And even from across the room, you can see that this one is working way too hard to breathe.

You wash your hands at the sink, put on the clean gown a nurse gives you. The local pediatrician who has been caring for the baby is telling you the story: thirty-seven-weeker (forty weeks is a full-term gestation), no problems during the pregnancy, normal labor and delivery, looked fine in the delivery room, Apgars 8 and 9. Then about four hours after birth, the baby was noted to be retracting (pulling with her stomach muscles) and breathing faster. Other signs of respiratory distress have appeared since then; the baby is now in 100 percent oxygen (as opposed to the 21 percent in room air, which was plenty for her before she got sick), and is still breathing fast, still retracting, and now her nostrils are flaring with every breath—another sign of distress.

The pediatrician has already drawn some blood to be cultured for bacteria, and started an IV. You ask him to go ahead and give the baby a dose of antibiotics; infection in newborns can cause all these symptoms, and can be devastating. You are by now examining the baby; the lungs sound wet and junky, but otherwise everything is normal. No heart murmurs to suggest a cardiac defect at the root of this baby's problems, no rashes, no malformations to make you worry about congenital syndromes. You take a tiny needle out of your tackle box and draw a sample of blood from the artery in the baby's wrist. Arterial blood gases are the best measure you have of how much oxygen the baby is getting, how much carbon dioxide she is blowing off, but the artery is tiny and elusive and the baby screams and squirms. You would like to be cool and efficient, of course, with all these people looking on; you are the expert who has come to help them out. You start to sweat. You get the blood, at last, and then your nurse decides to start an extra IV line for the trip back in the ambulance; two are better than one. She, of course, is an expert, and gets it in on the first try, even though the veins are even tinier than the arteries.

Nurses who work with newborns all the time develop unbelievable dexterity. I once saw a senior surgeon work for two hours trying to get an IV into a premature baby, dissecting out the veins with infinite care before inserting the needle. After he had failed completely, the nurses waited until he had left the room, then the most experienced one came over, and, in her own words, slipped an IV into an invisible scalp vein. I am not remarkably dextrous, even for a resident, and I have never gone on a transport without giving thanks that I don't have to start the IV.

The big question is whether this baby needs to be intubated before you leave. Can she safely be left in oxygen to breathe for herself, or does she need to be on a mechanical ventilator? You wait for your blood gas results, and are delighted to see that although the baby is working harder than she should have to, her numbers show that she is doing a superb job. The oxygen pressure in her blood is way over what it needs to be, and she is getting rid of her carbon dioxide beautifully. She can go on breathing for herself, and she doesn't need 100 percent oxygen either. This means you don't have to intubate her; you don't have to take on a crucial, difficult, and potentially dangerous procedure with all these people watching.

You go and talk to the baby's parents. Her name is Tiffany, you discover. You tell them a little about the main possibilities, the most likely reasons for their baby to be having so much trouble breathing. Surfactant. Pneumonia. You tell them that Tiffany is likely to get worse before she gets better; you tell them that there is a possibility she may need a ventilator. They look scared and confused, the mother only eight hours postpartum, lying in her hospital bed with the sound of the mother in the next bed trying to quiet *her* new baby, the father standing rather helplessly by the bed, not sure whether he should follow his daughter's ambulance into the city or stay here with his wife. You answer their questions as well as you can. You tell the father to wait and come in a couple of hours, give the nurses time to get Tiffany settled.

Finally, after warning them that it will look a little bit overwhelming, you wheel in the Cavitron, with little Tiffany ensconced under the clear plastic dome. Wires on her chest connect her to the monitor, fluorescent numbers tell you the heart rate and the respiratory rate, and another little gauge measures the oxygen content of her blood through a transcutaneous monitor taped onto her stomach. You open the dome; you insist that both parents reach in and touch Tiffany. They're afraid of disturbing her IV lines, her monitor leads; she looks like a high-tech Sleeping Beauty in this contraption. But at your urging, they both reach in and stroke her, feel the newborn softness of her skin. You know that this seeing and touching is important, that it will help them keep believing that they do indeed have a newborn baby, even after she is carried away to another hospital. You also have always in your mind the small but real possibility that she could die—maybe even before they see her again, and you want to be sure they touch her now.

Maybe even in the ambulance, I don't even allow myself to think. Ambulance time is a sort of limbo. If the baby gets suddenly sicker, I have to choose between telling the driver to head for home as quickly as possible, or telling him to pull over so I can do whatever I can. Depending on how far we are from home, how much sicker the baby is, how much time I think I have, I can go one way or the other. But what I really want to do is stabilize the baby well enough before we leave so that none of this is necessary. Again, the apocrypha are full of stories—babies intubated beside the road, chest compressions, heroic measures as the interstate traffic roars past. Not for me, thank you, if I have any choice in the matter.

You wheel Tiffany down the hall in the Cavitron. Nurses and patients lean over to look at her, make little comments of concern. The Cavitron, only very slightly heavier now, is lifted back into the ambulance. The nurse gets in; you get in. The siren is going in earnest now, the jolting is nonstop. You stare fixedly at the baby, at the monitors. Temperature, heart rate, respiratory rate, oxygen. Unfortunately, in a jolting ambulance, many of the monitors are unreadable. You do what you can. Tiffany, like almost any baby in a moving car, is sound asleep.

Ten minutes away from your home hospital, the oxygen monitor starts to drop, very slowly and very slightly. You and the nurse exchange glances. "Can't you go any faster?" you yell, forgetting all about accidents. You jostle the baby a little, check that all her wires are properly attached, try listening with your stethoscope, though it's hard to hear much. The monitor keeps dropping, just a little bit more. You are practically in the Cavitron yourself at this point, nose to nose with the baby. You are sweating.

The safest way to transport a sick newborn, so hospital wisdom goes, is when it is still inside its mother. The placenta will provide oxygen and nutrition, the mother will handle the temperature control—everything will be infinitely smoother and less clumsy than our high-tech approximations. So if you know something is going wrong, the baby is coming prematurely, the heart looks malformed on ultrasound, you send the mother to deliver at a hospital with a NICU. I am keenly aware that when I transport a sick newborn, I am taking that baby through a danger zone, moving a baby who ideally should not be moved, doing without perfect monitoring in a baby who may suddenly get much worse.

Fortunately for all concerned, you pull up at the ambulance door of your very own hospital. Out you get, down comes the Cavitron, and you start for the newborn intensive care unit, where there are other doctors and nurses, all the equipment you could want, help, advice. You barrel in, face the resident in charge, take a deep breath, announce, "I have a little something for you."

"It's just what I've always wanted," your colleague says.

ECMO
· · · · · · · · ·

Up in the nursery, they are losing the battle. In the newborn unit, there is a newborn baby—a little girl named Jessica— who is going to die. A normal pregnancy, a full-term baby, a labor which was going along fine, and then—meconium, thick sticky black fecal material which the baby excreted too soon.

In the delivery room at the small hospital where she was born, they got Jessica out as fast as they could, they suctioned out her airway, they gave her oxygen. Eight pounds, three ounces, lots of dark curly hair, her parents all ready with the name. For a little while it looked good—she seemed to be breathing—but then she breathed faster and faster, and a chest X ray showed both sides of her lungs had abnormal dense markings. Severe meconium aspiration. Her respiratory distress increased, and they put her on a mechanical ventilator and transported her to our neonatal intensive care unit.

So upstairs in the nursery, the resident and the nurse have been hanging over Jessica's bed. And now Jessica is receiving air that is 100 percent pure oxygen, blown into her lungs at very high pressure, many times a minute. In hospital parlance, this baby is maxed out on her vent settings. There's nowhere to go with her oxygen. Go higher on pressure, and they risk blowing a hole in her lungs. And yet she is getting worse.

The resident says to the nurse, "Goddamn it, she's PFC-ing on us. I think it's ECMO now, or else good-bye." In the hospital, even crisis and death are by acronym (maybe especially crisis and death).

PFC is not technically a verb. PFC stands for persistent fetal circulation (sometimes known as PPHTN for persistent pulmonary hypertension, if you really want to know). In the womb, Jessica did not need her lungs to get oxygen; she got her oxygen from the maternal blood pumped into the placenta. So the fetus didn't need to pump much blood to her own lungs at all, and the fetal circulation involved several shunts to bypass those lungs. And inside her developing lungs, there was very high pressure in the blood vessels, resisting blood flow, so the blood took the path of least resistance, flowing through the shunts. Normally, in the delivery room, within the first minutes after birth, all this starts to change. The blood vessels in the lungs relax, the blood begins to flow into those vessels, and as the baby breathes, she begins, for the first time, to oxygenate blood in her lungs and to breathe off carbon dioxide. Or at least, that is what happens when things go well.

Persistent fetal circulation is just what it sounds like. Sometimes, when a baby is severely stressed, as Jessica is by meconium aspiration, the blood pressure in the lungs stays high after birth, the blood continues to shunt, and what you have is a baby sitting in air, but sending no blood to her lungs to take advantage of that air. And it doesn't do you all that much good to have a tube in her trachea and a respirator blowing in 100 percent oxygen at high pressure sixty times a minute, because there isn't any blood in her lungs to take advantage of that, either. And that is what is happening to Jessica. It happens to babies under stress, but it happens idio-syncratically; it is not predictable. And it is often fatal.

Jessica's mother is still a patient in the small hospital where Jessica was born; she is only twelve hours postpartum. Jessica's father has left his wife's bedside and driven to Boston. He has been allowed into the NICU for a brief visit, and been warned that the baby is not getting better. Don't leave the hospital, the resident advised Jessica's father; we may need to talk to you about our options if she doesn't turn the corner soon.

I am sitting downstairs in the regular pediatric intensive care unit (the PICU, as opposed to the NICU), and every hour or so I call up to the nursery and talk to the resident about Jessica. Things are relatively quiet in the PICU, while in the NICU they are hairy as all hell; one dying baby makes the difference. A decision is being made: it is time to give up on "conventional ventilator management" for Jessica, and try instead a therapy so new, experimental, and hazardous that it is offered only to infants who have almost no chance of surviving without it. ECMO is just about as high-tech as you can get. From my point of view, I know that if Jessica comes to the PICU for ECMO to treat her PFC (at a certain point it stops being English) my evening and my night will be far more anxious, and things will quiet down notably in the NICU. But if she's going to come, I want her to come before it's too late, before she's been oxygen deprived past the point of no return.

ECMO is extracorporeal membrane oxygenation. And it basically means that the baby gets put on a heart-lung bypass machine for days, until her own lungs heal. Jessica is already on a ventilator, but her own heart is pumping the blood, her own lungs are supposed to be accomplishing the gas exchange (giving off the carbon dioxide, picking up the oxygen). Now we propose to take over all those functions—not for the matter of hours that heart operations can take, but for as much as a week. For a week, artificial pumps will force the blood through Jessica's eight-pound body, and a complex contraption called a membrane oxygenator will pull carbon dioxide out of her blood, exchanging it for oxygen.

Jessica's father is bewildered; he has barely had time to accept the tubes and machines surrounding his tiny, motionless daughter; and they are already telling him that all this glittering medical paraphernalia is useless, that Jessica attached to these machines will soon be dead. They are trying to explain a whole new approach they want to try, to save this baby he has been awaiting for nine months, but has had no time to care for yet.

At least, that is how I imagine him looking at it; this baby is his, and yet out of his hands. And maybe this is because I identify with him; the baby is about to be mine, in a certain sense, and yet she is also out of my hands. She will be attached to new apparatus, and though I understand the purpose of this apparatus, I would be as little able to build it or fix it or operate it as Jessica's father. I imagine him feeling like a nominal authority as he gives his consent for ECMO, because I feel almost like a ceremonial custodian myself, giving orders but completely dependent on others to see them carried out.

Putting a baby on ECMO is an emergency, always; by definition it is done only as a last resort. So when Jessica comes down to the PICU, the surgical team is already assembled. This corner of the PICU becomes an operating room, with sterile drapes over everything, with a scrub nurse and a circulating nurse and two surgeons, gowned and gloved and masked, all moving in their careful choreographed routines, while the rest of us hang back, outside the magic sterile circle. "Knife, please. And clamps, and suction."

Jessica is a newborn, and most of her blood vessels are quite small. For ECMO, we need to gain access to her circulation, to pump large volumes of blood in and out. Therefore, the surgeons are cutting into two major blood vessels in her neck, the right common carotid artery, which carries blood from the heart to the head, and the right internal jugular vein, which carries blood back down to the heart. The surgeons are quite literally working against time as they dissect down to these vessels, tie them off, cut them, and cannulate them with large tubes. They are working on a baby who cannot get enough oxygen; everyone knows that if we lose too much time, if we deprive her brain too much, if we take too long—then all the rest of this will be so much wasted effort.

When the surgeons are finished, Jessica's carotid artery now carries blood to her head from the membrane oxygenator, a large complex of metal and glass that stands beside her bed. And her jugular vein drains out into the same mechanical miracle. The wound is dressed, the surgical drapes are removed, the regular PICU personnel step back up to the bed. A little baby lies on her back, unmoving, anesthetized, her muscles paralyzed by a variety of drugs. She is connected to every monitor imaginable, and also to this machine, easily ten times her size, which is doing the job her tiny heart and lungs can't do. We are trying to keep her kidneys alive by giving them enough oxygen to keep her liver and her intestines and, of course, most especially her brain alive for a few more days. It's like a science fiction movie—we preserve the pieces, and then eventually (at the end of the space voyage) we reassemble them and have a functional baby.

Newborns, like almost all babies, like almost all children, will get better if you only give them the chance. If you can oxygenate their vital organs for a few days, their lungs will heal, recovering from PFC, from meconium, from overwhelming pneumonia, and from many of the other causes of the respiratory failure that still kills thousands of newborns every year.

I am, to tell you the truth, quite frightened of the ECMO setup. High tech is not my forte. I know what all the pieces of the hookup do—the pump, the oxygenator itself, the tanks of air and oxygen and carbon dioxide, the heat exchanger—and I know what questions to ask if I want to know how Jessica is doing. But I have no desire at all to touch a dial or move any tiny little piece of the machine. And that is why there are two specially trained respiratory therapists, twenty-four hours a day, on guard at Jessica's bedside. And of course, she also gets one-to-one nursing, and as much attention as she needs from me and all my superiors. But the respiratory therapists are the ones we have to rely on. They understand the machine. They know what to do if something goes wrong.

I spend a little time with Jessica's father. He doesn't want to hear any more high-tech details from me, and I suspect that the people who explained ECMO to him probably got a little carried away with the magnitude of the marvel they were offering, probably gave him too much information. In fact, he seems so bewildered that I am conscious of an illegal, disloyal, insensitive, out-of-line thought: maybe it would be better if we just told him we're doing what we have to do, trust us, we're the doctors. But all Jessica's father wants to know is, should he get his wife out of the hospital and bring her here, now, right away. And I tell him, if she can make the trip, bring her here tomorrow. Make sure she sees Jessica, while Jessica is still alive.

There are all kinds of risks to ECMO. There are the various risks of surgery, anesthesia. In order to avoid clotting in the blood, as it runs through the tubes of the machine, Jessica has to be kept on a drug called heparin, an anticoagulant. This means she is at high risk to bleed somewhere—notably into her head; her blood can't clot and stop the bleeding. And most frightening of all for me, as I stand next to the respiratory therapists, there is the risk of something going wrong with the machine. The entire volume of this baby's blood, after all, is flowing rapidly into and out of her body. What if the machine stops pumping in enough? She could be completely exsanguinated in a matter of minutes. What if the heat exchanger goes on the blink, and the blood goes in too warm or too cold? What if air gets into the system, and we send a big air bubble straight to her brain? She is completely dependent on this artificial heart and lung, and we in turn are completely dependent on the cluster of monitors and alarms that are supposed to warn us before any of these terrible things can happen. See, a baby on a normal respirator, even a very sick baby, is a baby I understand; if the tube came out, if the respirator malfunctioned, if the electricity suddenly failed, I would know what to do. I could replace the tube, I could breathe through the tube with an air bag—I mean, I individually know how to keep that baby alive for a little while. Not Jessica; she's flying in a spaceship I don't know how to fix.

The days go by. On day two, Jessica's mother arrives, and confides in me that she thought the baby had died and we just hadn't told her. I draw a diagram for her, trying to show her what ECMO is, and she nods and smiles, understanding I'm not sure how much, but believing that the more technology the better. I overhear her on the phone to a relative, proudly explaining that Jessica is on more machines than any other baby in the intensive care unit. Jessica's chart fills up with sheet after sheet of impossibly detailed records; every conceivable measurement is made at every possible moment. Her parents, with that amazing human ability to adjust to anything, are getting used to the PICU, in a worried kind of way. They now look right past the membrane oxygenator, the tubes, bright red with blood, leading in and out of Jessica's neck, and the monitors, and see their baby. They ask questions like, isn't she cold in here without anything on? The father claims to be able to see a resemblance to the mother's sister. Of course, that may be no compliment; Jessica is looking fat and puffy, edematous from fluid which has leaked out of her blood vessels into her tissues. But she is also beginning to send some blood to her lungs, and on day four we stop the ECMO for a short period, we turn the regular ventilator to certain regulation settings, and we watch to see what Jessica's heart and lungs can do. But an arterial blood sample sent for gas analysis shows that though she can take on a lot more oxygen than she could four days earlier, she doesn't do well enough to meet the criteria for coming off ECMO, and the machine is restarted. On day five, however, she has a terrific blood gas on 100 percent oxygen, and in fact we are able to turn the oxygen all the way down to 30 percent—and she's still getting enough into her blood. Her lungs have recovered, and she's ready to come off.

The right carotid artery and the right internal jugular vein cannot be reconnected; Jessica will have to live her life without those two blood vessels, which may be important later on, especially if as an adult she develops atherosclerotic disease. For now, there will be extensive tests of her neurologic status as she gets better; recent studies show that one year later, 75 percent of babies are normal neurologically. But she's alive. At the age of ten days, she is breathing all by herself, in room air. By now, of course, she's not in the PICU anymore; the bed is being saved for the next baby who needs ECMO. She's getting ready to go back to the little hospital where she was born, and spend a couple of days in their nursery—just so people can keep an eye on her.

I go up and see her parents, tell them how good I think she looks. They almost don't recognize me—I'm part of another existence. Jessica lies in her mother's lap, sucks on a bottle. Most of the edema is gone, and she wears a pink stretch sleeper, and what she looks like is a baby. Any old baby. And inside her body, her blood is circulating properly, like a well-behaved newborn's, going from her heart to her lungs, then back to her heart and off to oxygenate her organs. I lean over and tell her, "Baby, you are a medical miracle," and though she does not seem particularly impressed, she does offer up a burp, just to show everything is in good working order.

HYPOPLASTIC HEART
· · · · · · · · · ·

When he was born, he looked just terrific. He screamed vigorously, sucking down big mouthfuls of air, and clamped onto his mother's breast and nursed like a champion. He was a normal, full-term baby, plump and pink, with an impressive head of fine black hair. His proud parents had the name all ready: Joshua Brandon Robertson.

He was almost three days old when the first danger sign was noticed: a nurse in the nursery, getting ready to send him home, saw that his respiratory rate had increased; instead of breathing a normal twenty to thirty times a minute, he was taking eighty breaths a minute. A pediatrician was called in, examined him carefully, and thought she heard a heart murmur. She drew some blood tests, she ordered a chest X ray done, she gave him a dose of antibiotics—and then she called for a transport team to bring the baby to a big university hospital, thirty miles away.

I was on call the night Joshua came in. He was still breathing at eighty to a hundred, but otherwise he looked pretty good. He was awake and alert, his color was pretty pink, his blood pressure and heart rate were stable. There was a short list of big worries, reasons why the pediatrician at the other hospital had been so willing to send Joshua to us. He didn't seem to have any pneumonia; the chest X ray was clear, but he might have an infection, a bacterial sepsis in his blood. Such infections can be rapidly overwhelming in newborns. Or he might have something wrong with his lungs; occasionally a full-term baby acts like a premature infant, born with immature, too-stiff lungs. Or he might have something wrong with his heart; cardiac defects are among the most common major birth defects.

The evening proceeded. We did all manner of tests on Joshua, from an electrocardiogram to a spinal tap. We put him in 100 percent oxygen (room air is only 21 percent oxygen) to see how high the concentration of oxygen would go in his blood. He remained stable, but things were not looking good. As we say in the hospital, Joshua was beginning to look kind of cardiac. His electrocardiogram was abnormal, suggesting that the left side of his heart, the side that normally pumps oxygenated blood out to the body, was not properly developed. The oxygen concentration in his blood didn't go up as much as it should have in 100 percent oxygen, suggesting that the oxygenated blood was being mixed with deoxygenated blood before it was pumped out.

Finally we called in a cardiologist, who came pushing the echo (echocardiogram) machine, a sophisticated ultrasound device which allows excellent detailed imaging of the heart. The cardiologist sat by Joshua's crib, placed the ultrasound probe on his eight-pound patient, and started taking soundings. I drifted over to stand by the machine. Ultrasounds in general look like TV test patterns to me, so I asked him what he saw.

"I can tell you the diagnosis," he said, not sounding happy. "This kid is a hypoplast."

Hypoplastic left heart syndrome (HLHS) is an extremely serious malformation of the heart in which the left side of the heart is severely underdeveloped, and the right side has to pump blood to the lungs, and to the body as well. Up until quite recently, this malformation was simply accepted as fatal. But nowadays there is an operation—or, to be specific, two operations—that may correct the problem. But the operations are still relatively new, the mortality still relatively high.

Joshua's parents were due to arrive later on that evening; his mother had only just been discharged from the maternity ward, and they were driving up, full of anxiety, to hear what was going on with their healthy vigorous baby. The cardiologist told me that he, and the cardiac surgeons, would want to speak to the parents as soon as we had broken the news. They would want, of course, to ask the parents whether they wanted the surgery done—or not.

By the most comprehensive estimates now available, a baby with HLHS has about a two-thirds chance of surviving the first operation, a two-thirds chance of then surviving long enough to reach the second operation (usually done at two or three years of age) and again a two-thirds chance of living through that operation. Multiplying those probabilities gives such a child a 35 percent chance of surviving the whole process—two-thirds may sound like good odds, but remember that with each cut, you're taking two-thirds of a smaller group. In other words, those who finally survive are two-thirds of two-thirds of two-thirds of the original group, or about eight-twenty-sevenths. And nobody knows exactly what the issues are after that, since the first children to survive the surgery are still less than a decade old. They've been through a lot, and they may be at risk for problems later on, but the hope is that those children will go on to lead essentially normal lives.

I said to the other pediatrician, on call with me, "If this were your child?"

"If this were my child, I don't think I'd want the surgery," he said.

"Neither do I," I said.

Now, we might have been biased just because this is such a new procedure; even a couple of years ago, when we both formed our opinions, mortality rates were much higher, and there was some sense that the surgeons performed these operations largely to teach themselves the technique, expecting someday to be able to save these children. We might also have been biased because both of us had taken care of children sick and dying after cardiac surgery, both of us had seen families stressed and torn apart by the horrors of young children hospitalized again and again, spending hours and days in pain or else unconscious.

I think that I was mostly thinking that it is better to lose a newborn than to fight your way through and lose a two-year-old. In general, I have come to believe that the loss of a newborn baby, though tragic, is a loss that most people can bear when they have to. The baby is still largely a creature of hopes, dreams—the attachment is not the same as it is with an older child. You learn to love a baby by taking care of the baby, and I suppose I would not willingly risk the pain of caring, and then losing. Sometimes things happen that way, but I didn't think I would actually opt for such a prospect, not with those surgical odds.

Joshua's parents arrived, washed up at the sink, put on sterile gowns over their street clothes. They were young, and obviously completely bewildered by everything that had happened. His mother was holding the little striped sleeper she had planned to have him wear for his homecoming. I took them in and showed them their son, hooked up to monitors, IV solutions, temperature probes, but still recognizably their own baby. They wanted to know what we had learned, and they could already see, just by watching my face, the nurse's face, that the news was not good. The father, who had some experience with computers, wanted us to explain how all the monitors worked, maybe trying to put off the real explanation he could see was coming. So the nurse and I took them into a little family conference room and explained to them that their child had a serious cardiac malformation, that there were going to be decisions to make. I was the one who said to them, for the first time, "You have to understand, Joshua is very sick. He may get better, but Joshua may die. Children who have this problem do die." They were both visibly looking around for a bit of hope; the father kept saying, over and over, "This is the best place, right?"

The cardiologist and the cardiac surgeons came in and sat

down with the parents. The surgeons believe deeply in what they do. Infants with other cardiac malformations who would once have died are now routinely saved, repaired, their hearts reshaped and reconnected. For example, tetralogy of Fallot, a syndrome in which a hole exists between the two sides of the heart, along with other abnormalities, is always repaired; and even such a rare problem as transposition of the great vessels, in which the aorta and the pulmonary artery come off the wrong sides of the heart, is accepted as a surgical problem, a complication in need of surgery. HLHS is simply one of the last uncorrectable syndromes, one of the final most difficult surgical problems, and the surgeons feel they're on their way to fixing this one too. They believe in surgery, they believe in these operations, and this sincerity communicates itself to parents. They do not ignore the fact that surgery involves pain, but they accept the pain and discomfort as the price of medical aid. Any of those surgeons could have said honestly, if it were my baby, I would want the surgery.

But if it were my baby, I wouldn't. Part of it was mystical semireligious feeling; after months taking care of newborns, I had come to see the period right after birth as one of God's windows. Here was the chance, I thought, for parents (and doctors) to say, well, this child has been born too damaged to live. This baby does not have all the pieces it needs. This infant was not *meant* to survive (see, I told you it got mystical). No parent on earth can contemplate giving up that way on a child who is six months old or two years old. But a newborn, a baby who has never really gotten the chance to live—that baby, I have come to believe, you can relinquish, give back. You can grieve and mourn, but you can also heal and start again. But of course, I only have the right to speak for myself here. Other parents might find this cruel and inhuman; looking proudly down at children who had to struggle through medically impossible infancies, they may see only the triumph of the spirit, and judge me an emotional coward, a parent too lazy and wimpy to throw myself into a child's fight for life.

Joshua's parents agreed to the surgery. They heard the information like this: your child has a serious heart defect; it used to be considered fatal, but now there is a miraculous operation that maybe, just maybe, will keep your baby alive. No operation, and Joshua will die. Choose the operation, and maybe, just maybe, he'll live.

Over the next couple of days, though, Joshua's mother asked me repeatedly whether I thought they had made the right decision. She was disturbed, she found, on thinking it over, that the doctors had left this decision up to her, and she worried that they had done it only because the procedure was so dangerous and they didn't want the weight of responsibility. And of course, she was right; there are all kinds of treatments that we *tell* parents are necessary. Your baby needs antibiotics; your baby needs hydration; your baby just needs fever control. Your child has leukemia, and he needs chemotherapy; your child has appendicitis, and needs immediate surgery. The only reason that the decision in HLHS is left up to the parents is that the procedure is still regarded as new and experimental. So we left this decision to the parents, to people who were still stunned, unable to understand most of our jargon, unable to sort out all the information we offered. Still, there were no other people entitled to this decision; no knowledge or education or professional detachment could balance out the parents' qualification: they loved Joshua.

It's very hard, always, to counsel parents who have to make this kind of decision. And these decisions are becoming more and more frequent in medicine today, as the technology arrives to save sicker and smaller babies, as the medical capacity to extend life becomes more and more impressive. HLHS is the subject of honest disagreement among the doctors. There are those—the surgeons and the cardiologists especially—who look at Joshua and say, there is a chance this baby can be saved, so why not do everything? And then there are those—the other pediatrician and myself—who find ourselves arguing, at least internally, for an early, easy death. In modern medicine it often feels as if we have lost sight of the fact that death is not always the worst of all possible outcomes.

No one said any of this to Joshua's parents. What we all tried to do instead, what seemed the ethical and considerate thing to do, was to support Joshua's parents in the decision they had made. Though I whispered behind their backs with some of the other doctors, agreeing that we wouldn't make the same choice, though we grumbled about the overwhelming enthusiasm of the surgeons, which sweeps away parental doubts, in the end we showed these parents nothing but respect for their decision. Was I denying them the benefit of my hospital experience, or simply holding back my prejudices, allowing their own religious beliefs, their ethical standards, their particular degree of attachment to their newborn son, to assume the importance they deserve? I don't know. There have certainly been times when I have taken aggressive care of children who I thought should be allowed to die. Parents have the right to make those decisions. If asked point-blank, what would you do if this were your kid, I try to answer honestly, but otherwise I do not introduce the subject. And I waver between the feeling that this is the moral woman's matter of principle and the feeling that it is the lazy woman's way out.

Joshua lies on his little table, under the warm lights. He is not a moral dilemma, he is a baby. He was born to his parents, and his life is, for the moment, theirs. All the technology of the hospital, all the skill of the surgeons, these are only devices to help Joshua survive and grow up—under the care of his parents, who day by day will make millions of decisions, large and small, decisions that will make Joshua into whatever he finally becomes—if he lives so long.

5

······································

The Feminization of Medicine

In the middle of my junior residency year, *The New York Times Magazine* invited me to write an article about women doctors. Their question, they said, was will women change medicine—or will medicine change women? The working title for this article, while I was writing it, was "The Feminization of Medicine."

I interviewed doctors about career patterns, about mentors and role models, about training issues, about families and children. One question I always asked, of course, was this: do you think women doctors do anything different? And one theme that emerged in the answers was that yes, many of the people I interviewed thought that overall there were some differences between the way women practice medicine and the way men do it. So I wrote that into the article with some trepidation—I was, after all, quoting women doctors on women doctors. I had done no scientific survey. But it was interesting, I thought, that within this group there seemed to be a sense of special pride.

The editor called me up and told me that the article would be on the cover of *The New York Times Magazine*, and the title would be "Why Women Are Better Doctors." After some negotiation, this was changed to read "Are Women Better Doctors?" Even so, it generated an enormous amount of angry mail, mostly from doctors, both male and female, most of whom had apparently read only the title. And several years later, when I spoke to a student group at Harvard Medical School, one young man told me that when he had read that article in college he had felt as if someone were saying to him, you won't be a very good doctor, you won't be the best.

I can't help it, I think this is all pretty funny. What it reminds me of most, to tell you the truth, is when I was back in medical school, and went to a meeting with the director of admissions. I was there representing the medical student women's association, along with the people in charge of the black students' group, the Asian association, the Native American group, and the Gay Students' Association. The director of admissions told us that he was very concerned that all our groups were sending out letters to students when they were accepted into the medical school, welcoming them, offering advice, students to contact. He was concerned, he said, because no one was writing to the straight white men, and it didn't seem fair. There was a pause, and then someone said, in a mystified tone, "And still they keep coming!"

It seems to me that newspapers and magazines are still very much in the business of making women feel bad about having jobs. If you ask me, the whole "having it all" fuss is mostly just an excuse to warn you that if you have a job your personal life will suffer, your children will be deprived.

I find this in my journal from when I was working on this article:

I picked up a magazine and found someone running on about the joys of staying home and someone else running on about how she gets no respect because she has no child. I mean, can you have it both ways? Either the moms are getting all the respect, since no childless woman is considered truly fulfilled, or else the career gals are getting all the respect, because only money and career count in this soulless society, or else everyone just likes to whine. Everyone just likes to whine. I like the amazed surprise of women who discover that having a baby while working full-time means either leaving the baby to go to work or else not working, and I like the amazed surprise of women who discover that staying home full-time leaves them without an exciting job to go to. But what more worthwhile job could I be doing? they ask. Well, they could be helping those in need, or writing nonwhiny columns, or repairing broken machinery. Or else staying home, if that is more fun. Who cares? I can see I'm not going to get very far in the dilemma-of-the-professional-woman market.

Every article about a successful woman dwells on the tragedies and failures of her private life, while articles about successful men jump blithely over marriages that came to nothing, children left by the wayside. Certainly, no one ever writes about men in a way that suggests that because they have remained uncoupled everything else they have achieved is worthless. No one suggests that because they did not spend enough time with their babies, their accomplishments are ashes in their mouths. I was glad to contribute an article that weighed in on the other side. And someday when men are a minority in medicine, no doubt there will be an enterprising journalist who will examine the phenomenon of the male doctor, and wonder whether men bring any special strengths to the profession.

ARE WOMEN BETTER DOCTORS?

There was a conundrum which used to turn up now and then, when I was in high school, designed to test your level of consciousness: a father and son go fishing, and on the way home, they're in a car accident. The father is killed instantly, the boy is rushed to the hospital, where the surgeon takes one look at him and screams, "Oh, my God, it's my son!" What is the relationship between the surgeon and the child?

Well, obviously, the surgeon is the child's mother. Surely no one had to think twice about that? Well, fifteen years ago, lots of people would ponder that puzzle, making up complex stepfather/grandfather linkages, trying to explain how a child could have no father, but still have a parent who was a doctor.

In 1969, 9.2 percent of the first-year medical students in America were women; in 1987 it was 36.5 percent. In 1970, women accounted for 7.6 percent of all the physicians in America and 10.7 percent of the residents. In 1985, 14.6 percent of all physicians and 26.2 percent of all residents were female. Perhaps the most important and most interesting question that confronts female MDs as they become more and more a fact of life in the medical profession is this: are women actually changing medicine, are they somehow different as doctors— or does the long and rigorous medical training produce doctors who are simply doctors, male or female?

I did not go to medical school during the pioneering age. When I started, in 1982, 53 of the 165 students in their first year at Harvard Medical School were women. Moreover, I chose to go into pediatrics, a field that has the highest percentage of female residents of any medical specialty—50 percent nationwide. I have never had the experience of being the only woman in the lecture hall, the only female resident in the hospital. Occasionally, I have been the only woman on a particular medical team, but often I have been on all-female teams.

During my own medical training, so far at least, I have not had reason to feel like a scholarship student from an alien tribe. When I set out to write about women in medicine, I wanted to bypass the tone of patronizing surprise that so often attends women doing untraditional jobs ("She uses a scalpel! She has curly blond hair and a white coat all covered with blood!"). I also wanted to leave behind some of the classic topics that apply various kinds of prurience to the situation of the female doctor. So what's it like when you have to do a physical exam on a man? So how do women doctors get along with nurses? And so on. With women going into medicine in large numbers, it's time to look more specifically at what kinds of doctors we are choosing to be, both in terms of specialty and in terms of style.

According to data compiled by the American Association of Medical Colleges, men and women applying to medical school have similar acceptance rates—of all applicants to medical school for the year starting in September 1986, 60.5 percent of the men were accepted into at least one school, and 59.6 percent of the women. After medical school, you choose your field of medicine. Here, men and women differ, according to statistics compiled for 1986. Fifty percent of all pediatric residents were women, but only 11.8 percent of all surgical residents were female, and in vascular surgery it was only 1.4 percent (that added up to one woman in the country). Women are still heavily concentrated in psychiatry (40 percent of the psychiatric residents in the U.S. in 1986 were female), and also make up large proportions of the residents in dermatology (43.9 percent), preventive medicine (36.2 percent), pathology (37.5 percent), and obstetrics and gynecology (45.1 percent). The "frontier" for women in medicine, then, is really not in medical school, but in some of the medical specialties, in which they are almost as rare as they ever were. The traditionally acceptable areas for women doctors (pediatrics, psychiatry) are still attracting large numbers of women. Speaking as a pediatrician, I know that one reason I like my field is because of all the women, both at my own level and up ahead of me, already established. But how does my experience then compare to someone else's training in surgery?

It seems to be pretty well agreed that back when there were fewer women in medicine, medical school and residency were often fraught with unpleasantness and loneliness; many women have written about the sexual innuendoes, the what's-a-nice-girl-like-you comments, the exclusion, the sense of being singled out and put on the spot—all the petty persecutions that added up to anger and alienation. On the other hand, while the more recent medical school graduates I interviewed could remember incidents, individual rotten professors, bad moments, none felt she had been the victim of any real discrimination in medical school. However, in those specialties where a woman is still a rarity, all those old problems may still confront the resident or the young doctor trying to get started in practice. Furthermore, there are very few women in the upper echelons of academic medicine: in 1987, two medical schools had female deans (out of 127); seventy-eight academic departments (out of approximately two thousand) had female chairs.

In examining the position of women in medicine, I talked to many women doctors. Some are colleagues of mine, teachers of mine, friends of friends in the vast and complex Boston teaching hospital system. But Boston is hardly a typical place to learn or practice medicine. Affectionately and not so affectionately referred to as "Mecca," Boston is the most heavily academic city for medicine in the U.S., probably in the world. (A cartoon used to hang on the wall of the residents' room in the intensive care unit of the hospital where I work: a scientist is scrawling complex equations on a blackboard, respectfully watched by a group of fellow scientists. In balloons we see the thoughts of his audience; each one is thinking "What is he doing?" And the scribbler himself is thinking, "What the hell am I doing?" In big letters on the top of this cartoon, someone had printed, MECCA.) The female experience in medicine in

Boston can never be considered typical. Some people will swear that women have it easy in Boston because medicine here is dynamic, young, on the cutting edge; and others will insist that nowhere is the old boy network stronger than in the Boston hospitals.

I told a friend—a fellow resident—that I was writing about women doctors. "What are you going to say?" she wanted to know. "Are you going to say they're better? Are you going to come right out and say it?" Now, if I read an article saying that men make better doctors than women for certain reasons, I would probably be offended, even hurt. The best I might hope for would be to laugh it off as so much antediluvian their-egos-are-threatened prejudice. Now, I have known superb, brilliant, sensitive male doctors, residents my own age, teachers and attending physicians. Lots of them. The doctor who delivered my son, the pediatrician who takes care of him are men—and yet, I feel I am protesting too much, that these statements have a some-of-my-best-friends air about them. Okay, then, some of my best friends are male doctors.

When I interviewed women doctors, I came always to a point where I asked, are women doctors different? And with only a couple of exceptions, I got versions of the same response from the doctors I interviewed, young or old, avowedly feminist or not. First you get that disclaimer, the one I just offered; I've known some wonderful male doctors, I've known some awful female doctors, generalizations are impossible. And then, hesitantly, even apologetically, or else frankly and with a smile, comes the generalization. Yes, women are different as doctors: they're better.

Kansas City announces proudly in the courtesy magazine found in fancy hotel rooms: "When Procter & Gamble wants to know if people like its toothpaste, it turns to Kansas City. Market researchers call Kansas City a 'typically American' market. The label fits: Kansas Citians thrive on family, hard work, and tradition." In Kansas City, I interviewed a wide range of female doctors—residents, women just out of residency starting up private practices, academic physicians, specialists, older women, and recent graduates. I was surprised by how tight the network of women physicians was. I was immediately referred from doctor to doctor; in specialties where there were fewer women, their names were mentioned again and again by their colleagues. I was able to interview female physicians who stood on both sides of two classic relationships: a mentor and her student protégée, a doctor and her patient—who was also a doctor.

Linda Dorzab started medical school at the University of Missouri, Kansas City, when she was thirty-three years old. She had spent eleven years as a teacher, working with emotionally disturbed children. In June 1987, she finished her internal medicine residency, and is now beginning a private practice as an internist, affiliated with Menorah Medical Center. For the first month or so there were few patients, maybe only one a day, but by February it was up as high as nine a day, mostly new patients coming for their first appointments with her. Dr. Dorzab is proud to make a visitor welcome in her newly arranged office; an ebullient, friendly, informal woman, completely delighted to be starting up a new solo private practice. Ever since she started medical school, she says, she has dreamed of an office where she could make her patients comfortable, where there would be an atmosphere that would make her look forward to coming to work in the morning. Her office is a welcoming, plant-filled place, with gleaming mahogany furniture, including both a large desk and a small table designed for less threatening, more comfortable doctor-patient conversations. I, in the middle of my residency, find myself asking how she figured out the details of starting a practice—what supplies to order, how to find patients. Dr. Dorzab laughs, remembering how she sat down and made a list—"Cotton pads, tongue depressors—I ordered too many syringes and needles. And my proudest possession is my sigmoidoscope" (a device inserted up through the patient's rectum to give the doctor a good look at the lining of the colon). Given her background in working with disturbed children, Dr. Dorzab had originally considered going into psychiatry, "but they gave me a stethoscope and it was all so interesting. You can't get more interesting than medicine." She was older than most of the other students, and had a comparatively weak science background, but the art of medicine, she thinks, came more easily to her than to some of the younger students. Still, she had trouble performing on rounds, the high-pressure on-the-spot situations which can often be the traditional hazing occasions for medical students. "I still have the same personality as when I was a teacher, I tend to show my vulnerability—which is okay with my patients. But with colleagues the smile dims, I can turn on a more businesslike manner."

I asked her about role models, mentors, teachers from medical school who meant a lot to her. She names two women, saying of both of them that "they maintained femininity and class, and always looked confident." One of those women was Dr. Marjorie Sirridge, who is a dean at Dr. Dorzab's alma mater, UMKC. Marjorie Sirridge graduated from medical school in 1944. There were very few women in her class, but she never felt what she considers overt discrimination. To be sure, her academic advisers told her she'd never get to medical school—but that only made her more determined to go. "I was first in my class from grade one through high school—that gives confidence." Sure enough, she graduated from medical school first in that class too. But during residency she got pregnant and was informed that "pregnant residents were not acceptable." She dropped out of medicine for several years, then found her way back in by working for no pay and no training credit, went into private practice as a hematologist, pursued research on her own, and eventually found her way to academic medicine. Dr. Sirridge's office is decorated with pictures of her children and a poster of Marie Curie. Her white hair is bound up in a knot. She is extremely cordial, but she speaks with the authority of someone who is accustomed to giving out her opinions publicly. It is clear that she feels protective about the medical students she watches over, and that she is proud of Dr. Dorzab, who is striking out on her own, off into solo practice.

Dr. Sirridge worries that female medical students do not seem to take leadership roles as readily as their male colleagues. On the other hand, she thinks women do much better when it comes to human relationships. "For the women, relationships with patients are very important, a very positive thing. Many men also have this quality, but men in positions of power in medical education and government by and large do not."

The craving for female role models, female mentors, is very strong in medicine. You learn science in medical school —biochemistry, physiology, pathology; you learn these subjects in traditional classroom settings. Then you serve a kind of apprenticeship in the hospital for the second two years of medical school, consolidating the science you learned in the lecture hall, learning hospital logic and medical routine, and also learning how to be a doctor. How will you explain to a patient that he has to undergo a painful diagnostic procedure, how will you tell parents their child is dying, how will you help someone overcome bad habits that are crippling his health, how will you take command when someone is critically ill? Some medical schools are trying, more and more, to teach these skills, or at least to get students thinking and talking about them, instead of just piecing their styles together as they go along. But basically, since there is no single consensus on the best manner of doctoring, you pick up your style by trying to emulate the doctors you admire. And if you're female, it can be very instructive (and very inspiring) to watch women doctors, to learn your style from them. Many of the techniques used traditionally by male doctors tend not to work for women; and many female doctors have found themselves evolving new ways of interacting with patients, with nurses, with fellow doctors. So it isn't just vague inspiration that we're talking about here, it's who you're thinking of as you get ready to walk into that room and tell those parents about their baby dying. Who do you know who could do that as well as it could be done, offer comfort to the parents, inspire trust that their baby's last moments will be made as comfortable and easy as possible—how do you acknowledge their grief, the failure of medicine to help, even take part in their grief, and yet retain the authority you need as the doctor? And how much authority *do* you need as a doctor, anyway? Medicine is full of these situations, and you model yourself on the people who seem to handle them best.

Nevada Mitchell, MD, practices internal medicine. Her subspecialty is geriatrics. She was born in Kansas City, went to college at Vassar, then came back to KC, got married, started teaching—she had thought about medical school, but didn't feel she had what it would take to go. But reading in the Vassar alumnae magazine about classmates who had gone to medical school, she decided she wanted to try for it, and five years later she was in medical school. Dr. Mitchell has no doubt at all about the difference between male and female doctors. "There's a world of difference. The women I come into contact with are less aggressive, more likely to have one-on-one-type relationships with patients than men, less likely to go for high volume of patients—but also less likely to be out here in private practice." Dr. Mitchell returned several times to the issue of being "out here," explaining that many women take jobs with HMOs, which offer regular salaries and limited working hours. "You need a certain aggressiveness to choose private practice," she said, with some satisfaction.

Dr. Mitchell feels that older patients are often more receptive to women doctors, since they are looking for more than medical therapy. Her original decision to go into geriatrics was related to watching her younger colleagues in medical school trying to deal with the many elderly patients, and feeling those patients were often neglected or taken for granted. Her medical practice now includes many older patients, but she also does general internal medicine. With a smile, she ticked off the various groups on her fingers: older people are fine, younger and middle-aged women usually have no problem with a female doctor, younger men are initially hesitant, feel self-conscious about the complete physical examination.

Dr. Mitchell cannot think of a female doctor she wanted to be like. "I didn't have that many examples. I developed my own style and image." She did, however, tell me that I ought to talk to the doctor who had operated on her when she needed some gynecological surgery. She felt that when she had discussed the medical issues with a male doctor, he had placed less of a priority on maintaining the option of future pregnancy. Dr. Mitchell, who is thirty-nine and has a sixteen-year-old daughter, wanted to keep her options open, and felt that a female doctor, Marilyn Richardson, had been more willing to take this seriously.

Ironically, Dr. Richardson herself thinks that's nonsense. An obstetrician-gynecologist specializing in reproductive endocrinology, she was a pianist for years before she went to medical school. She is highly professional, authoritative, and decided in her opinions. Patients who come looking for a female gynecologist, she says, are "erroneous—it's a patient's misconception that has evolved with consumer awareness, an erroneous belief that women doctors are more compassionate, more understanding. Well, I don't have menstrual cramps, I didn't have severe pain in labor. Women who come asking for a female doctor are looking for a buddy, and they're not going to find that in me."

I repeat to her what Dr. Mitchell said, and she laughs and says with affection, "Nevada Mitchell played the violin in my first piano recital." And then continues to deny that being female has anything to do with her mode of doctoring. "It was a male mentor who taught me sensitivity toward the preservation of fertility." Her style, she says, is a composite of this mentor and of her father, also in OB-GYN—and of techniques of doctoring she has developed for herself.

I mention to Dr. Richardson that one of the places I always felt a very sharp difference between male and female doctors was in the operating room. I ask whether she believes this is also erroneous. No, she agrees, the way that women run an OR is different. "Women manage more efficiently if they can strike a balance of authoritativeness and humaneness. Men are often arbitrary, demanding, and disrespectful, and the level of efficiency suffers. Women don't usually command quite as fiercely, will *ask* for an instrument . . . you get camaraderie with the other staff members."

Dr. Susan Love agrees. One of the first two female surgical residents at a major Boston teaching hospital, Dr. Love finished her training in 1980. She went into private practice in general surgery, though she initially had trouble getting a position on the staff of the hospital where she had just been chief surgical resident. In her practice, she found she was seeing many patients with breast disease, who preferred to go to a woman doctor, and she eventually decided to specialize in this field. She now has a partner, another woman surgeon, and they have as many patients as they can handle. Dr. Love feels strongly that she had to suppress many of her basic values in order to get through her surgical residency: "Most women have problems—unless they can block out their previous socialization. Surgeons don't really like having women, don't make it comfortable for them. Things that women like, talking to patients, aren't important, it's how many operations you've done, how many hours you've been up, how many notches on your belt. If you get through your five or six years of training, you can regain your values, but it's a real if. Most men never get them back."

Dr. Love runs an operating room, she says, by "treating the nurses like intelligent people, talking to them, teaching them. I'm not the big ruler." Are men always so different?

"Surgery is a lot of ritual and a little science. The boys need high mass, incense, and altar boys, they need more boosting up. The women are much lower church." A concrete example of something she does differently, something no one taught her: before the patient is put to sleep, she makes it a practice to hold the patient's hand. "I'm usually the only person in the room they really know, and it's the scariest time. The boys scrub, come in when the patient's asleep. I got razzed for it, but they're used to it now."

Unlike Dr. Richardson, Dr. Love does think that women doctors behave differently with their patients. "I spend more time in empathy, talking, explaining, teaching, and it's a much more equal power relationship." And then there's not taking people for granted—she tells the story of a recent patient, an eighty-four-year-old woman with breast cancer who was asked by a male surgeon, "Are you vain?" Embarrassed, the woman said she wasn't. The surgeon advised her, in that case, to have a mastectomy, rather than a more limited procedure—"But then her niece pointed out, but you bought a new bra to come to the doctor, but you combed your hair over your hearing aid." The doctor had simply assumed that an elderly woman would have no particular desire to keep her breast, no vanity left to speak of. Dr. Love's anecdotes are often sharp—she describes a male surgeon who explained that a particular implant used in breast reconstruction felt just like a normal breast; he meant, of course, that to someone touching the breast, the texture was close to natural, not that the woman actually had normal feeling in the implant.

I heard over and over that women are better at talking to people, better at listening. Dr. Carol Lindsley, a rheumatologist at the University of Kansas, says the female medical students are "more sensitive to patient and family needs, more patient, pay more attention to detail." Dr. Marilyn Rymer, a Kansas City neurologist, says that many of her female patients come looking for a woman doctor, some because they feel they can talk to a woman more easily, others because "they find that women listen better, are more empathic, care about explaining things, dealing with the family." Dr. Dorzab agrees: "My patients say women listen better, are better at acknowledging when something is bothering the patient." On the other hand, Dr. Debbie Stanford, a resident in internal medicine at the University of Alabama in Birmingham, feels that there is no difference at all between the male and female interns she supervises: "Capabilities, compassion, endurance—no difference." And Dr. Michelle Harrison, who wrote *A Woman in Residence* in 1982 about her experiences doing an OB-GYN residency, comments, "I think women sometimes *feel* different because they are not totally accepted; as outsiders, we experience ourselves as different, but are we all that different in how we see patients? I don't see any major revolution."

Then there is the question of how women get along with their coworkers—with other doctors and with nurses. The assumption has traditionally been that nurses resent female doctors, respond to them with a why-should-I-take-orders-from-*her* attitude, and then there are prurient little remarks about how women doctors resent nurses because of all the romantic attention the nurses supposedly receive from the male doctors.

Women doctors, of course, are often mistaken for nurses; many patients assume that a woman with a stethoscope is by definition a nurse. Some doctors mind this, others take it in stride. "You have to have a sense of humor," said Dr. Lois J. McKinley, an internist in Kansas City. "I took care of one patient for weeks, and when he was getting ready to leave, he was still saying, 'Oh, nurse, would you prop up my pillows.' Nursing people are good people; being mistaken for a nurse is not the worst thing that could happen." Dr. Mitchell agrees: "If I walk into a room and someone asks me for a bedpan, I just go ahead and put 'em on it!" She is laughing. "But when they call my office and assume I'm the nurse and ask, Dr. Mitchell, when will he be in, I tell them, 'He will never be in!' "

It is generally agreed, among women doctors, that we have to be more polite and more careful with nurses than our male colleagues; a fairer way of putting this would probably be to say that nurses have had to take a lot of rudeness and bad behavior from doctors over the years, and that while they make some of the traditional female allowances for traditional male patterns, they are unwilling to accept these same behaviors from women. Or, to quote Dr. Richardson again, "When you make a big mess in the operating room, there's something different in your mind when you walk out and leave it for another woman to clean up." I have found in my own training that nurses generally expect me to clean up after myself (i.e., to gather up all the little alcohol pads and pieces of gauze left on the bed after I draw blood from a baby), to do a fair amount of my own secretarial work, and not to take too high-and-mighty a tone. What would be taken as normal behavior in a male (especially a male surgeon; they have the most traditional doctor-nurse power structure) is considered aggressive and obnoxious in a female. Dr. Lore Nelson, who will be chief resident in pediatrics at the University of Kansas next year, complained, half seriously, "A male surgeon can walk in to do some procedure and everything will be all ready, but if I go to draw blood, nothing's set up for me and I have to go ask a nurse, 'Can you please help me. . . .' " Dr. Sirridge agrees: "The women aren't successful at doing the things men do without criticism—it's easier if they ask politely."

This does not seem to be a bad thing—the traditional doctor-nurse relationship, like the traditional male-female relationship that it parodied (the man as authority figure, making decisions, issuing edicts, bearing ultimate responsibility on his broad shoulders; the woman as caretaker, tending to immediate needs and cleaning up messes, but without any real power) left a lot to be desired. Surely a good doctor is part caretaker;

surely a good nurse's observations should be part of any decisions being made. I suspect that the more polite, more politic
behavior that is demanded of female doctors may be closer to
good manners and good medicine than the supposed norm—
the license that we sometimes envy our male colleagues.

"Cleaning up messes," a number of doctors told me, is
something women do well. "Women are better at dealing with
the nitty-gritty," says Dr. Sirridge, because they have been
taught to clean up, "to do the dishes at home. They tolerate
tedious nitty-gritty-type things better." Medicine is full of
messes, both palpable (the patient is dirty, the patient is vomiting, the patient is having bloody stools) and impalpable (the
patient is ready to be discharged but has no home to go to,
the child is medically healthy but will not eat). Some doctors
do hold themselves aloof from these messes, seeing their role
as something exclusively medical and dignified ("I didn't go
to medical school to learn to clean up vomit"). And women
do tend to be better at dealing with messes; it is more often
what they have been raised to do, less likely to compromise
their dignity, less likely to jar their image of themselves.

Medical training and medical practice are stressful for
everyone, male and female. Women often face additional pressures; the issue of combining family and career comes up constantly when you try to write about women in medicine. Why
are there discrepancies in status? For example, one study looked
at medical school faculty (those with MDs only, excluding
those with PhDs or other degrees) given their first appointments in 1976. By 1987, 17 percent of the men were tenured,
but only 12 percent of the women. Twelve percent of the men
had attained the rank of full professor, but only 3 percent of
the women. And 15 percent of the men were not on a tenure
track at all, as compared with 22 percent of the women. So
either women are meeting prejudice and resistance as they try
to make their way in the world of academic medicine and
research, or else, as is often suggested, they are diluting their

ambition, going more slowly on their climb, usually in order to give time to family. Dr. Harrison, now a family physician and psychiatrist, feels that there are different standards for men and women. "Personality factors enter into the promotion of women, while arrogant and obnoxious men are promoted without that being an issue." But she also thinks that women "have tremendous problems around leadership, issues of power. We aren't raised with the skills to even make it up to the glass ceiling." And finally, she adds, "there's the problem of how to combine a family with a medical career, which tends to relegate women to salaried positions with less possibility for advancement."

I had my baby in the second year of medical school; it was not an extremely common thing to do, but neither was it unheard of. Certainly, I didn't feel any pressure to drop out, to take time off, to get my belly out of sight. I didn't feel it would be held against me, or against women in medicine, for me to have a baby along the way, and for that I suppose my medical school and the changing times deserve a lot of credit. Dr. Sirridge got pregnant during her internal medicine residency in the nineteen forties and had to drop out—"Pregnant residents were not acceptable." In my residency program there are several pregnant residents; the program is not particularly designed to accommodate them, but it seems to have been stretching. On the other hand, that's pediatrics again, a field with lots of women, a field where even the biggest guns have to be committed to the idea that babies are important.

Residents work nights and come home rarely and in poor condition. Many programs don't have much coverage available in case of sickness; there's a macho ideology that gives points for working when you're sick. So taking days off to stay home with a sick child is really against the rules, and ends up loading more work on your already overloaded fellow residents, which in turn creates animosity toward people with children. Nevada Mitchell's daughter was three years old when her mother started medical school, seven when she started residency. A single mother, she chose her residency program because she could live in the same building as her brother and sister-in-law, requested Friday night call because she didn't have to get up and bring her daughter to school the next day. When her daughter got sick and she decided to stay home, the attending physician commented, "interns don't stay home unless they're hospitalized or dead." Dr. Mitchell stayed home for that one day only, then sent her daughter, who had mononucleosis, off to stay with relatives. "One Halloween we spent in the CT scanner," Dr. Mitchell recalls. "I brought her candy and her trick-or-treat bag."

Most annoying of all, perhaps, for parents, is that being a doctor makes you in a certain sense unreliable. Emergencies come up, unexpected calls come in, and you're home hours later than you promised; you can't keep the promise you made about a family outing. "She knows she can't depend on me to be where I say I'm going to be at any particular time or be home when I say I'm going to be. She has to catch me when I'm there." When Dr. Mitchell opened her practice, her daughter would come by the office after school and they would go home together. Her daughter, who is now sixteen, wants to be a veterinarian.

These difficulties are not, of course, unique to the women. Males also have to cope with the hours, with not being there when their children need them, with promises made and broken. They are somewhat more likely to have spouses who delay their own careers. Still, I have heard complaints about male colleagues of mine who are too eager to leave the hospital and get home to their families; some men may even be much less self-conscious about this precisely because they bear no if-I-make-a-fuss-about-my-kid-they'll-think-women-shouldn't-be-doctors burden. No one, after all, is likely to say that fatherhood and medicine don't mix. The fact is, though, that certain intensities of career are essentially incompatible with any kind of parenthood. You don't have very much to do with your child if your ideal is to spend every waking moment in the hospital, whether you are the father or the mother. The influx of women into medicine, we can hope, will help us design medical careers for both men and women that will enable doctors to follow some of their own recommendations (reduce stress, eat a healthy diet, keep regular hours, spend time with your family—we pediatricians, for example, are always telling parents how important it is that they pay lots of attention to their children). Dr. Nelson is married to another doctor, who is doing his residency in internal medicine. She had a baby in her second year of residency, and felt that her fellow residents were very helpful and supportive. She and her husband had been in the habit of taking call on the same nights, so they would be home on the same nights; since the baby, they take call on alternate nights. Her husband, she thinks, has had much more trouble with his colleagues than she did: "The times he had to stay home when the baby was sick the men he worked with said, your wife should stay home."

After residency, many doctors continue to work long hours, to cover night call. One way to keep your hours regular is to work for an HMO. Another solution for doctors who want protected time for their families is a part-time practice. Anne Regier, MD, and Perry Ginder, MD, are rheumatologists in practice together in Kansas City. Each works three days a week and they split night coverage. Dr. Regier is married to an orthopedic surgeon. "We do a lot of juggling," she says. "I'll bring the kids to the hospital and drop them off with you so you can do your consult—or who will round first on the weekend."

Women are a presence in American medicine today in such numbers that in many fields they are no longer curiosities. Not being a curiosity gives you a certain amount of freedom; you don't have to be better than the men, you don't have to pretend that you actually are a man in disguise. But questions remain. Will women move ahead into positions of leadership? Are there subtle prejudices that will allow us the MD degrees, but then shunt us into the less prestigious career paths within medicine? Will the remaining all-male fields ever integrate? Janet Bickel, senior staff associate and director for women's studies at the AAMC, wonders whether we will in fact end up with a medical establishment in which certain jobs (less well paid, less well regarded) will be filled largely by women. And to what extent does this depend on the choices made by the women themselves? It is very difficult to make predictions; the makeup of the medical profession has changed so rapidly from this point of view that there is really no way to say what will happen next.

Many women doctors believe that women do medicine differently, that there are advantages to the way they approach their patients. Almost no doctor I talked to believes that women have simply been transformed by their medical education into cookie-cutter doctors with all the mannerisms and techniques of the male prototype. If this is in fact true, and not just a convenient prejudice on our part (and one I still blush to acknowledge in print), then the effect of women on the medical profession may be larger and more far-reaching than we have yet imagined.

Recently I told my four-year-old son that he was due for a checkup with his pediatrician. He looked distinctly nervous (rumors about shots had obviously been making their way around the day-care center), and asked me anxiously, "Is she a nice doctor?" I thought about the doctors my son knows— me, my close friends, mostly female. I picked my words carefully; it was clearly one of those critical moments when all of a mother's wisdom and tact is required. "Benjamin," I said, "I have to tell you something. Boys can be doctors too, if they want to. If they go to school and learn how, boys can be very good doctors, really."

6

....

Moving On

As I mentioned, I got many, many letters about the are-women-better-doctors article. Along with letters from furious doctors, there were many letters from nondoctors, all of them testifying in great medical detail about the joys of women doctors, about doctors who hold your hand or offer you a drink of water when you're hot and tired or take the time to play with your child and make her smile before taking her away to surgery. No one, for whatever reason, wrote to eulogize male doctors.

Again, this has no sociologic or scientific significance whatsoever. But I do want to quote my very favorite letter, which seemed to me to wrap the whole thing up nicely. It came from Arlene Spark, who wrote:

To the Editor:

Unlike Perri Klass's son, Benjamin, who knew mainly lady physicians, my neighbor's son Paul and my daughter Danielle had both male and female pediatricians. Yet, when these four-year-olds played doctor, Danielle assumed the role of compliant nurse to Paul's order-barking doctor.

"There are male nurses and female doctors," Paul's mother offered one day, wanting to apprise them of all their options.

"Okay," Danielle answered, "then I'll be a male nurse."

It would be nice to think that interviewing all sorts of interesting female doctors and giving some thought to the whole issue of mentors and admirable women helped me pull myself together emotionally. It would be nice to think that I have gradually become more grown-up and less self-obsessed —as you can imagine, I did not particularly enjoy going through my journal from my junior residency. What a self-absorbed self-critical self-justifying soggy mess I was! But I got through the year, and went back to the NICU yet again, and worried yet again about whether I was perceived as authoritative enough:

I feel ashamed of myself for caring, but tomorrow at 11 the attending wants to meet with me and give me feedback (that irresistible image of regurgitation) and I know it will prey and prey on me—I wish I could just get it over with today and decompensate tonight. The thing which bothered me so much last night was an incident where nurses called for help and I ran over to find little Gonzalez choking, with someone bagging her and others doing this and that, and I listened to her—she wasn't moving any air—and told them to suction her, and ultimately they got up an enormous mucous plug and she was fine, but in the interim they had paged the fellow ("Where's Bob?" some of them kept asking) and I felt like, well here again, I knew what to do well enough, I could have handled it alone, they have no confidence in me.

Well, after all the angst, I feel I should in all fairness report that the feedback session was truly nothing but positive. I was told I have really grown, I was doing a very good job, everyone has confidence in me. I am using my unique personality, talent, and wit, for niceness instead of evil. And ironically, that whole incident with Gonzalez was cited to me as an example of how competent I am, Bob telling me how much more willing he was to leave me on my own than he had been at the beginning—me making the right decisions, doing the right thing.

I was glad to stop being a junior resident. It's humiliating to be thirty years old and still desperate to hear that you're okay, you're not as bad as you think. Internship had been everything it was supposed to be, the hardest year, the most frightening year—but it had also been a year during which I felt the freedom of the beginner, a freedom to be insecure, to need help, to move slowly. Somehow I had much more trouble taking those next few steps, believing in the knowledge and the skills acquired in the hospital, and convincing other people to believe in them as well.

FLIP-FLOPS
· · · · · · · · ·

I was in a little clothing store not far from my home when I heard a horrible noise out in the street—a crash of metal on metal followed by screams, automobile screeches, and general clamor. Without thinking, I ran out of the store and headed across the street; I had reached the island in the middle before it consciously occurred to me, *you're running to help because you're a doctor, you need to take charge*. Inevitably, I was wearing a tee shirt, ratty pants, and flip-flops; and I was particularly conscious of the flip-flops as I arrived at the crowd and pushed my way through. A motorcyclist had smashed into a pickup truck and been thrown far into the air; he lay now on the pavement with broken bones protruding through the skin of his wrists. I knelt down next to him and was relieved to see he was breathing, talking—he did not need cardiopulmonary resuscitation. What he was saying was this: "For God's sake, take my helmet off!" He gestured ineffectually with his wounded hands.

Helpful voices from the crowd immediately broke in: "He wants his helmet off, he said to take his helmet off." Someone else suggested that he be carried into the nearest shop, someone else that he shouldn't be moved.

I raised my voice. "I'm a doctor," I said, not sounding terribly convincing to myself. "I'm a doctor," I repeated. "The helmet stays on." I was shooing away a helpful bystander who was already working on the strap.

I had to say it maybe fifty times before the ambulance arrived. I didn't want to explain in detail, with this man already terrified and in pain, that a severe neck injury could be made worse if we moved his head, pulled off the helmet. I was also keeping an eye on his heart rate, on his breathing, on his general condition. And over and over I kept saying, "I'm a doctor. Please don't touch him. Please leave the helmet alone."

Do you know what I was wishing? Well, first and foremost that I wasn't wearing those flip-flops; they seemed to me to undercut my authority completely. But what I really wished was that I was six foot four, male, and an ex–football player, someone who could just bellow, "Stand back, everyone, I'm in charge here!" And, in my fantasy, everyone would immediately stand back, relieved to have someone in control.

Well, I did the right things. The ambulance arrived, and the EMTs splinted his broken bones and stabilized his neck, took him off to the hospital where X rays would show whether there was in fact an injury to his spinal cord. And I walked away feeling dissatisfied with myself, because I know perfectly well that you don't have to be an ex–running back to claim authority—when that authority is rightfully yours. You ought to be able to do it by force of character, manner, and self-confidence. But it isn't always easy.

Part of medical training is a rapid increase in authority; over a couple of years, you go from being a medical student —a novice in the hospital with no real power—to being an intern, a junior resident, a senior resident. You find yourself teaching medical students, supervising interns—you find yourself taking on, quite literally, responsibility for life-and-death decisions. And you have to come to terms with this authority. You have to accept it, learn to feel entitled to your own power. You have to develop a style for making decisions, giving orders, a style that works effectively with other doctors, with nurses, and with patients.

I've had a lot of trouble accepting my own authority over the past couple of years. It seems to me, in general, that women struggle with this whole question more than men do. Maybe men feel more entitled to power—or more unwilling to admit it if they are insecure. Also, there are time-honored styles of male authority in the hospital, and it often seems that men giving orders get immediate results—even if they aren't football players. But women may have to earn their authority, and it's just harder, in general, for women to use those commanding military tones that have traditionally gotten results for male doctors ("Scalpel!"). At the same time, women may not be easily forgiven for sounding brusque, or for taking control too assertively. We have to find our own way, develop our own special manner—and you can only do that if you feel entitled to your authority, if you are really ready to claim it.

In my training program, we have practice emergencies, situations where a group of doctors and nurses "resuscitate" a plastic dummy (the dummies come in baby, child, and adult sizes). At the beginning of my second year of residency, they told me it was my turn to run the resuscitation, give the orders. I said, quite honestly, that I wasn't ready, that I had no idea how to run a resuscitation. I knew how to follow orders—how to do chest compressions, give the "patient" oxygen, or start the IV, but I couldn't run the damn thing. "That's the point," said the supervising doctor, gently. "You need to hear yourself say it. You'll hear your voice saying, 'Why don't we give him some—some—some—*epinephrine!*' And there you'll be." Epinephrine, or adrenaline, is one of the drugs we give most commonly in resuscitations, since it acts as a cardiac stimulant. I had never ordered it before in such a situation. That night, I practiced saying it to my bathroom mirror. First I practiced Taking Control. "I'm in charge here, I'm running this resuscitation," I said firmly to the mirror. "Let's give him some epinephrine."

The next morning, at the resuscitation, a gang of interns and nurses looked at me expectantly, clustered around the plastic dummy. I heard my own voice, an octave higher than it had been when I talked to the mirror. "Why don't we give some—some—some—epinephrine!" I squeaked, and they did.

The authority of the "crash," the sudden life-and-death emergency, is the authority residents tend to fear most—a child will be found not breathing, and I'll be the only one there. Someone who was doing just fine will start to die before my eyes. But as residency moved along, I found that that authority did in fact come to me when I needed it. When I had to give those orders I gave them, though my voice still has a lamentable tendency to squeak. I find that I no longer automatically look around for a doctor when a sudden emergency occurs; it seems to have gotten through to me that I *am* a doctor. But there are other kinds of authority that may not loom quite so large, but which are even harder to assume, even harder to own. I remember once when a baby was brought to the emergency room essentially dead on arrival, a victim of sudden infant death syndrome, or crib death. We tried for half an hour to resuscitate that baby, not willing to admit that the small, perfect, still-warm body could really be beyond our help. But he was, and the senior doctor asked me to go out and tell the parents. And so I sat down with them and tried to explain, tried to give them answers they could believe, about a disease that nobody understands. I had to tell them, no, this did not happen because your apartment is too warm, no, it did not happen because you gave the baby a different brand of formula today—*it was not your fault*. I needed a particular mix of confidence, authority, and sympathy for that family, and I hope I found it.

As I have slowly claimed my authority as a doctor, I have worried that I may carry over some of those mannerisms into my life outside the hospital. I have learned to behave, in certain situations, as if I am the one with the final say, the one with the power. This does not go over particularly well on the home front. I have learned, when the going gets rough, to cut through the argument and give orders, make my choices, and accept the consequences. This is not a recommended technique for resolving arguments with one's significant other. The cliché of the surgeon's wife, who is constantly reminding her husband that he is no longer in the operating room, is relevant. Women cannot get away with this kind of behavior at home, by and large, and sometimes I think that the fear of sounding like I am trying to give orders has actually made me more wishy-washy in my personal life.

In a way, the most difficult authority for me to accept has been the responsibility in situations where I cannot help. A couple of months ago I was working in the newborn intensive care unit, it was the middle of the night, and a baby was getting sicker and sicker. I was working with the baby's nurse; together we did everything that could be done, increasing the help that the baby got from her respirator, adding one drug after another. It was becoming very clear that the baby was going to die, and I wondered whether I should wake up a more senior doctor and ask him to come help out. But the more I thought about it, the more I realized that there was nothing else he could do; I would be calling him in only so that he could be there to preside over our medical helplessness. The baby could not be saved. So I didn't call him. I just stayed there, with the nurse, doing what could be done. And toward morning, as I bent over the baby, I heard the nurse say, "You know, it's at moments like these that I'm really glad that I'm the nurse and you're the doctor." So I looked over my shoulder to see what doctor she was talking to—but there was no one else there. She was talking to me.

III

. . . .

END

Indeed, we were rather proud of our doctor at Cranford, as a doctor. We often wished, when we heard of Queen Adelaide or the Duke of Wellington being ill, that they would send for Mr. Hoggins; but, on consideration, we were rather glad they did not, for if we were ailing, what should we do if Mr. Hoggins had been appointed physician-in-ordinary to the Royal Family? As a surgeon we were proud of him; but as a man—or rather, I should say, as a gentleman—we could only shake our heads over his name and himself, and wished that he had read Lord Chesterfield's Letters in the days when his manners were susceptible of improvement.

Elizabeth Gaskell
Cranford

enior residents run things. They run the ward teams, run the ICU, run the emergency room. They tell the interns what to do, back up the junior residents if necessary. They are spared most of the burdensome time-filling detail work of the hospital, the daily notes and the discharge summaries.

One sign of my own slightly improved mental health, I suppose, is that in my journal, as time goes on, I began to mention patients, to tell other people's stories and not just obsess about my own. Could it be that I had finally noticed that all around me were real tragedies and real pain, as opposed to the languishings of a resident who thinks someone may say something less than enthusiastic about her on an evaluation?

I saved my sign-out sheet from the school-age ward, the list of patients I prepared for the senior who came on after me. The three-year-old who was admitted with meningitis, his spinal fluid grew out a bacteria called *Neisseria meningitidis*, because of its predilection for this particular site of infection. The next day his seven-year-old brother came into the hospital. The sign-out on the brother:

> Spent a night in ICU but never had any cardiovascular instability, now feels better, on penicillin. Spinal fluid growing meningococcus. He looks great.

The nine-year-old with a malformed brain, seizures, and severe mental retardation with cerebral palsy:

> Has occasional fevers, with urine culture negative (has been her source in the past), basically at her baseline but will be here through the weekend for respite care; twenty-four-hour nursing at home should be in place by next week. NB: she is DNR by parents' request.

Healthy children hit by devastating infections, like a three-year-old boy who had been having fevers of unknown origin (FUO, by hospital jargon), got admitted to be worked up for uncommon infections and other causes, and then developed life-threatening blood abnormalities. Children with multiple congenital anomalies who had never really been well, like a seven-year-old with cardiac disease, spina bifida, and chronic vomiting, in the hospital because the vomiting had gotten worse again and he had gotten dehydrated again. And children with chronic diseases, a six-year-old with cystic fibrosis, here for her first cleanout.

These are the various subpopulations of children's hospital wards—and also, of course, there are the children with mild illnesses, with asthma that is usually not too bad but got out of hand this time, for example. And the children with social problems, sitting on the ward because they have no safe homes to go to.

And most of them—almost all of them—end up doing pretty well, because this is pediatrics.

I spoke earlier about the sense that medical training is parasitic, that we learn off the sufferings of patients. I have been a double parasite, not only learning off patients, but also writing about them, turning the agonies of sick children into articles, using them to point little morals either about my own development as a doctor or about the dilemmas of modern medicine. As I continue to practice medicine, and to write about the practice of medicine, I find myself more and more confused about the different ways I touch patients' lives, enter their stories.

In this last section are pieces in which I try to return to most of the main concerns of this book. The first is a piece about the NICU, once again, this time addressing more directly the issue that hovered around my head all those weeks in the NICU, that hovers around everyone all the time in this remarkable field.

During my last nights covering the delivery room, I found myself called to deliveries where babies were expected to be borderline, maybe too small to save, maybe just big enough. I was experienced enough now to be part of these matter-of-course decisions. I became very uncomfortable, as many people do, about the ethics of aggressive medical care for very tiny preemies. And then there was one terrible night when I found myself wishing that I could save a baby so tiny and so immature that no neonatologist, no matter how overenthusiastic, would ever have agreed.

A diary entry, written on the back of a scut sheet, in bits and pieces over the course of a night on delivery room duty:

Now 6:00, back from the delivery room where a twenty-four-week baby boy was delivered footling breech [breech presentation with the baby's feet coming out first] and we decided not to intervene—we being the fellow, the attending, and me. The extraction, as they say, was hellishly difficult, baby came out all bruised and not breathing. So we held back, all very gentle and very sad. I baptized it (him) and when I said I'm sorry to the parents, they both, automatically, said that's okay. Now I am knee-deep in death certificates, waiting for a call from the medical examiner. The labor and delivery nurse told me at length what a dog show it had been (also the OB's pronouncement, looking down at the little body) and how they had made it a teaching case to show the residents— vaginal extraction of a footling breech.

The labor suite is a strange place—we keep getting called down to talk to the mothers who are going to have preemies, or the mothers with bad prenatal diagnoses— and all around are the triumphant mothers coming back with pink, crying babies, sometimes their third or fourth—

Most heartbreaking of the night, even more than the twenty-four-weeker, was the forty-one-year-old woman who had lost her first eight babies, miscarried them all at about twenty weeks, and now here she was at twenty-three weeks and developing chorioamnionitis [an infection of the fetal membranes and amniotic fluid]. A tremendously sweet lady, lying there in bed and crying, "All the other times I lost those babies, they said if only I could have carried them a couple of weeks longer—and this time I did, and you say you still can't do anything? Isn't there any chance?" So what could I do—I hung crepe [resident slang for painting a bleak picture, warning patients about a probable bad outcome]. And seemed to imagine, so very close, this same face resplendent, the arms holding that final miracle baby who would truly be as wonderful as she might have imagined.

Now I am sitting here in L & D, waiting to talk to a mother about to deliver a trisomy 13—sad but not too scary—of course I'm going to make the fellow go with me to the twenty-three-week delivery so if anything can be done, it will be. This is no time for nonintervention. Dialogue after I talked with that mother, me and the nurse:

"Maybe she'll have the most mature twenty-three-weeker on record."

"Anything's possible."

"Nah, the most mature twenty-three-weeker on record is gonna be born to some fifteen-year-old with no prenatal care who's really twenty-six weeks pregnant . . ."

"And already has another kid."

Next morning on rounds, having successfully given away the DR beeper. I went to bed at two last night, and at three they woke me for the twenty-three-weeker in labor room 13—woke up and went running down with box, and shortly thereafter a tiny (480-gram) fetus arrives, and I'm giving it oxygen, and I was extremely glad to see the fellow arrive—we stood there with the nurse, watching the big bruises our stethoscopes were leaving on her chest. Her eyes were fused, her skin was gelatinous . . . so we stood over her, three doctors and a nurse, and the fellow slowly said, in spite of the mother's history, he still didn't want to intervene, and we agreed—and we agreed. Though I swear, part of me was for trying—it just seemed so unfair (as the mother of the trisomy 13 baby kept saying). We gave the baby to her mother, baptized her (third baptism of the night), we took Polaroids—but the saddest was listening to the mother talking to her, "Princess, my little princess, love . . ."

These discussions of who to save and when to act and who should decide all took on an increasingly personal resonance as I went through my senior residency. I was pregnant again, with a baby due in July. And I was precisely twenty-four weeks pregnant the day we had the fight in senior rounds.

Senior rounds happened every weekday morning, after work rounds on the wards and in the units. Leaving the interns and the juniors to get on with their work, the seniors would congregate, together with the chief resident and the directors of the program and some of the senior faculty, and we would discuss interesting patients, trace back over cases that had gone wrong, thrash out political problems. And one morning, when I was twenty-four weeks pregnant, we began to argue about something that had happened in the NICU the night before, an aggressive resuscitation of a twenty-four-week baby led by the neonatology fellow, when the baby's parents had requested that nothing heroic be done. Who makes these decisions, after all? Does the baby belong to the parents absolutely, or are we, the pediatricians, meant to function as the baby's advocates, even if that means going against the parents' wishes?

The classic moral dilemma was restated: abortion is legal into the second trimester; does that mean that a woman carrying a twenty-three-and-a-half-week fetus with known anomalies, say, has every right to abort it, but if she goes into labor on the way to the abortion and gets brought into labor and delivery, she loses her say—the doctors go to the delivery and if the baby looks vigorous, they resuscitate?

A famous NICU resuscitation story was brought up: the fellow let one tiny twin die, then decided to go ahead with the other, full court press, and the baby did great, no problems at all—so you know what the fellow said? "Maybe I should have resuscitated the other one." Basically, I realized, everyone else at the table seemed to feel that this decision could not be left to the parents. How could they live with the pain of knowing they had decided to deny care to their own baby, let their baby die? How could they understand the subtleties of why one twenty-four-weeker looks great while another just doesn't seem to have what it takes? How could we even contemplate delivering different medical care to two babies with the same medical problem, just because one set of parents said we don't want a damaged child, while the other said they'd take anything as long as they could have a baby?

I got furious. I wrapped my arms around my belly, thinking of the fetus inside, still a secret from my colleagues. What was in my belly was *mine*. And no one better think about taking away any of my rights. I found myself making speeches about how parents make life-and-death decisions about their children again and again, and they also make all the smaller decisions that add up to determining quality of life and kind of life. And why not take into account how a given set of parents feels about the possibility of a severely impaired child, before committing enormous sums of money and hours of effort to create that severely impaired child? And why not take into account whether the parents were young or plainly fertile—when women had miscarriages, back in the days when there were miscarriages instead of just very premature births, people used to try to comfort them by saying, you're young, you'll have other children.

One of the other residents asked me point-blank: If a baby is very premature, but is strong and vigorous, the doctor can't be expected to stand by and let the baby die, right? You have to explain all this to the parents, you let them know you're going to be constantly evaluating, you'll let them know what you think, you'll advise them on their baby's chances . . .

And that way, I said miserably, you end up intubating them all, they all get brought back to the NICU, they all get painful procedures without anesthesia—and then, if they aren't holding their own and the neonatologist in charge isn't too crazy, they might eventually be allowed to die. And I rubbed my belly and promised the baby inside, you come out tonight, you die in my arms. No neonatologists will get anywhere near you.

TOO SMALL
· · · · · · · · ·

A call comes from labor and delivery: there's a woman who just came in, in labor, twenty-eight weeks pregnant. They'll treat her with tocolytics—medications that can arrest the progress of labor. But in the meantime, a pediatrician needs to talk to her. So, accompanied by a NICU nurse, I wander down to L & D and meet the mother and father to be. I verify the dates: just how sure are they that this pregnancy is twenty-eight weeks old? Everyone in neonatology has seen babies emerge a month older or younger than expected. The parents have already heard from the obstetricians that another ultrasound and an amniocentesis will be done, and I go over the reasons once more: the major cause of death and disease in premature babies is lung disease, also called respiratory distress syndrome, also called hyaline membrane disease, caused by a lack of surfactant. When a sample of amniotic fluid is removed by amniocentesis, it is possible to analyze the fluid and find out how much surfactant the fetus is likely to make. If the tests show immature lungs, the mother is treated with a short course of corticosteroid therapy, which sometimes speeds up maturation.

By now, I am well launched into my "preemie spiel." I developed my own over the course of several months in the NICU; I offer the information I imagine I would want myself in this situation, the predictions that will certainly come true, a few of the bad possibilities, a little reassurance. . . .

I tell them, for example, what will happen in the delivery room if their baby is born prematurely. There will be a pediatrician and a NICU nurse standing by, who will take the baby immediately to a table over on the side of the room, look at the baby carefully, and try to assess degree of prematurity, give the baby oxygen—and if the baby doesn't breathe, put down a tube into the baby's airway. I do not mention the possibility of a full-blown delivery room resuscitation, with chest compressions and an emergency IV line inserted through the baby's umbilical cord stump.

Then the baby will come back to the NICU with us, I tell them, and you'll be able to come visit as soon as you get out of the delivery room. I talk for a while about the twenty-four-hour visiting privileges of parents, about how they should call at any moment to talk to the nurse, about how involved we want them to be. But then I have to go over what they may see when they come to visit their baby: a completely sedated infant with IV lines in the umbilicus, in the arm, maybe in the head, a tube in the nose, a baby hooked up to a respirator. The baby may need help breathing because the lungs are immature. The baby will not be able to eat immediately because the gastrointestinal tract is immature, and will have to be fed bit by bit, probably through a tube. And the baby will be very vulnerable to infection because the immune system is immature, I finish, and will probably need to be on antibiotics.

Here are some of the things I don't mention as a matter of course, talking to the parents of a twenty-eight-weeker: I don't mention the possibility of head bleeds, though very premature babies are at high risk for blood vessel rupture in their heads. Some of these bleeds are mild, some severe (with resulting brain injury). I don't mention the dangers of mechanical ventilation of tiny babies—you have to use high pressure to blow those air sacs open, and if the pressure gets too high, an alveolus can spring a leak, necessitating a tube in the chest to suction out air and allow the lung to expand. I don't mention the possibility of necrotizing enterocolitis, a frequently fatal syndrome in which overwhelming bacterial infection kills all or part of the intestine. None of these complications is rare; they are all everyday terrors of the NICU. But this, it seems to me, is more than anyone really needs to know, right now, waiting to see whether the labor can be stopped, waiting to see how the baby will do. One thing at a time.

Through all this, the mother is lying down, a fetal heart

monitor strapped around her belly, an IV in her arm, and periodically a nurse comes in to check the monitor. The contractions have been getting less frequent, and everyone has been hoping that the tocolytics will do the trick after all, and the pregnancy will proceed; the fetus will stay where it belongs. But then the mother notices that she is passing some fluid, and it turns out that the amniotic sac is leaking, which puts the fetus at a higher risk for infection and makes a premature delivery more likely.

A twenty-eight-week baby is probably going to weigh somewhere around a kilogram, 2.2 pounds. Its head will look too big for its body, its hand will be the size of a quarter. According to recent statistics from the institution where I work, such a baby has about a 90 percent chance of survival —at that particular hospital. Such statistics vary from institution to institution, and the capacity to keep tiny preemies alive at all exists only at major medical centers, tertiary care hospitals. Women in premature labor are transported to such hospitals, if time allows, before their babies are born; otherwise the babies are transported immediately after birth—if they survive the delivery room. Even at the best hospitals, many of these very small babies do not survive undamaged; but still, most of us would agree that with odds like that, a twenty-eight-week baby deserves all the heroic medical attention we can provide. And that's how I present it to the parents: a long haul, beset with problems, two steps forward, one step back, one day at a time, but worth the effort.

But what about a twenty-six-week baby? Three years ago, in 1986, when I first worked in the NICU, we told parents of twenty-six-weekers that the baby might well be too small to save. We told parents of twenty-four-weekers that the baby would definitely be too small to save. Last month I went repeatedly to talk to women who were in labor at twenty-three weeks. The baby will probably be too small to save, I would say. We'll be there in the delivery room, we'll assess the baby and see how mature it looks, but if it's really twenty-three weeks, there won't be anything we can do.

A twenty-three-week baby might weigh around five hundred grams, just over a pound. Those same statistics, from my hospital, give no chance of survival to a baby who starts out weighing less than five hundred grams, and a 9 percent chance to a baby who weighs between five and six hundred grams. The survival percentages are based on weight, but you don't weigh the baby in the delivery room. That initial, critical assessment is based on other things. A twenty-three-weeker looks like a fetus. The skin is still gelatinous, an inadequate barrier against the harsh world outside the womb. A stethoscope, however gently placed, leaves a large bruise on the tiny chest. The eyes are fused shut. This is a baby beyond the outer border of viability, a baby whose body is too immature to survive our medical ministrations. And between twenty-three weeks and twenty-eight weeks the chances of survival rise steadily from 9 percent to 90 percent; this is why exact dating is so crucial before a premature delivery.

As for all things in the hospital, however cosmic, however tragic, there is a routine for such births and the deaths that follow them. We look at the baby in the delivery room. We exchange glances—usually at least two doctors and one nurse. If anyone is unsure about the maturity of the baby, if anyone thinks that there is reason to hope for survival, then we go through the medical rituals of resuscitation. If, however, we all agree that this is a baby we cannot save, then we wrap that baby in a blanket and bring it to the parents. We tell them, you have a lovely little boy or girl, but the baby is just too small to live. We tell them, the baby is perfect (if the baby is indeed perfect). We ask them if they want to stay with the baby, and usually they say yes. We arrange baptism, we encourage them to name the baby, and we get the labor and delivery Polaroid camera and take pictures. We all know that at the end of this, they will be left with a birth certificate, some

Polaroid pictures, and the memories we are helping to create.
We try to serve as a lifetime's worth of people: the psychiatrist
on the spot, and often the chaplain as well, the physicians, the
nurses, and also the admiring friends and relatives who will
never have the chance to admire this baby. The message is
supposed to be, you *did* have a baby. The baby died, but there
was a baby.

But what about that baby who actually is on the borderline? That twenty-four- or twenty-five-week baby who has a
chance of survival somewhere over 50 percent, but probably
a much lower chance of surviving intact? There's a very high
risk of head bleeds, a very high risk of devastating infections,
and a very high risk of oxygen deprivation as we try to support
those extremely immature lungs. There's the risk that the baby
will be dependent on the ventilator for a prolonged period of
time, which in itself can damage the lungs and lead to chronic
disease—a three-month-old baby with the lungs of a seventy-
year-old chain smoker, the radiologist may comment, looking
at a chest X ray. And the process of keeping this tiny baby
alive will involve needle after needle, tube after tube. The very
premature baby does not live a very comfortable life, and even
doctors who believe in what they are doing sometimes feel like
torturers. Up until quite recently, there was some controversy
over whether preemies had nervous systems that were too immature to feel pain; surgery on such babies was often done
without painkillers. It is now accepted that the babies can and
do feel pain—and the NICU can be a painful place. We still
don't give the babies any painkillers when we put tubes in—
the risks are too high, the situation too critical. The parents
may find five different tubes going into their five-hundred-
gram offspring—an arterial line in the belly button, a regular
IV in the hand, an endotracheal tube in the lungs, a nasogastric
tube in the nose, and a chest tube, naturally enough, in the
chest.

So we try to offer these parents some degree of choice,

to get a sense of how aggressive they would want us to be. How old are the parents? Do they have other children? Have they had fertility problems? How desperately do they want this child? But in fact, the right of the parents to express this opinion seems to be further and further compromised. The drive is to save more babies, younger babies, smaller babies. Neonatology has progressed quite literally by leaps and bounds over the last couple of decades, and the most severely premature babies are the frontier. Before the sixties, it was not possible to keep newborns on mechanical ventilators—in 1960, the President's premature baby died of respiratory distress syndrome, a thirty-four-weeker who weighed more than two kilograms. True, most twenty-four-weekers don't make it, goes the argument, but a few years ago that was what they said about twenty-six-weekers. We'll save more and more of them, we'll learn to take better care of them. And it gets harder and harder to say no, to pull back, to acknowledge that a baby wrapped in a blanket and given to its parents to die quietly is not the worst of all possible outcomes.

I like saving babies. I have been to deliveries where the baby was obviously too small to survive, but was much wanted, where the parents were eager to have even a severely damaged baby, as long as they could have a baby. I have stood there with my colleagues and wished for the baby to give us a sign, to cry or kick or somehow prove us wrong, signal us to go ahead with our bag of tricks. And of course, it's very hard to know what I would want if I were in the situation faced by those women in premature labor to whom I deliver my preemie spiel. Still, this is something I've thought about a lot, and what I think is, if I were in labor very prematurely, if the labor weren't stopping, I would want to be at some small community hospital somewhere far away where they might understand that a twenty-four-week preemie was just too small to save. There might well be no one in the hospital who would even try to take care of such a tiny infant. Why, they might even just call it a miscarriage. And I hear comments like that from other doctors and nurses in the NICU, even as they labor, day and night, over the tiniest patients anyone has ever cared for. I'd drive off into the woods, people say, and have my baby there. There has to be such a thing as just too small.

DR. ZAY
. . . .

Doctor Zay by Elizabeth Stuart Phelps is a novel that was originally published in 1882, and has recently been reissued by an academic press.* It is the story of Waldo Yorke, a young Bostonian of excellent family, who is injured on a trip to Maine, and when he comes back to consciousness finds that his doctor, who has saved his life and will now supervise his protracted recovery, is, of all things, a woman. It is quite a shock.

> "Is that the doctor's hand I feel upon my head at this moment?"
> "Be quiet, Mr. Yorke,—it is."
> "But this is a woman's hand!" . . .
> "It is a strong hand, Mr. Yorke. It does not tremble. . . . It is not afraid. It has handled serious injuries before. Yours is not the first."
> "What shall I do?" cried the sick man, with piteous bluntness.

Throughout the novel, Dr. Zay's profession allows the author to arrange a complete reversal of the traditional nineteenth-century literary romance—for a romance it is: Waldo soon falls desperately in love with his physician. But he is a wealthy young man who does nothing in particular, a peacock and idler; and she is a brilliant young woman with a mission

* Originally published in Boston by Houghton Mifflin in 1882, reprinted in 1987 by The Feminist Press at The City University of New York.

—exactly the opposite, say, of the pair in George Eliot's *Middlemarch*, Lydgate, the brilliant and ambitious young doctor, and his wife, the fair and trivial Rosamond, whose shallow nature and petty social ambitions blight her husband's scientific dreams. Also, Waldo is an invalid for most of the book, restricted by his weakness to sitting passively by and watching Dr. Zay as she hurries through her overcrowded days, saving children's lives, even restoring life to an apparently drowned man, coming home in the evening to sit down with new energy to her medical books—and always called away yet once more on a medical errand. Waldo is left in the traditional position of the weak, admiring, but ultimately useless female.

It's an interesting book; it would be an almost completely conventional romance if the sexes were in fact reversed, and it's oddly disconcerting to read nineteenth-century prose about nineteenth-century characters who are behaving in such unexpected ways. It is also very interesting for the picture it gives of medicine, of a doctor who is meant to be bringing the very latest in medical science (rigorously scientific homeopathy) to a poor rural area. Many of Dr. Zay's emotions are instantly familiar; the overwhelming drama of an everyday acquaintance with life and death, for example, which seems so strange and out of focus to those who are not physicians.

At one point, Waldo finds the doctor in the grip of strong emotion and offers help.

> "You cannot help me," she said, gently enough. "Nobody can. I have lost a patient."
>
> Yorke was on the point of crying, "Is that all?" but saved himself in time, and only said,—
>
> "Who is it?"
>
> "The little Bailey baby. It was doing so well—out of danger. The mother took it over to a neighbor's. You cannot conceive the ignorance and recklessness that we have to manage. She took the child out, like an express bundle, rolled in her shawl. Coming home, it got wet in

that shower. I had ceased to visit there every day; they did not send at once,—I suppose every doctor makes these excuses for himself; what would become of us, if we couldn't?—but when I got there, I could not do anything. . . . It was a dear little thing," she said softly, "and fond of me. I had always taken care of it, ever since it was born. It was just beginning to talk. . . . It is terrible that a child should die—terrible! It ought never to happen. There is no excuse for it. I can never be reconciled to it!"

I suspect there is no way for a pediatrician to read those lines and consign them to a different century. They speak of motivations and anxieties and angers that go with the job of trying to heal, with the experience of failing. Technology moves fast, and journal articles more than ten years old are often regarded with suspicion. It is therefore always instructive to hear a voice from much longer ago to remind me that the profession is not reinvented along with its tools. And of course I found it especially compelling to hear a woman's voice—a woman novelist speaking with the voice of a woman doctor.

However, the most eerily familiar speech in *Doctor Zay* was not any of her speeches about her patients. For me, the real shock came at the end of the novel, in the climactic scene in which Waldo Yorke, his health recovered, his life inspired with new direction and energy (he will no longer be idle and useless), returns to claim his love. At first she denies any feeling for him, then admits that she loves him in return, but she still refuses to marry him. And then comes this speech:

"You see, Mr. Yorke, you have been so unfortunate as to become interested in a new kind of woman. The trouble is that a happy marriage with such a woman demands a new type of man. By and by you would chafe under this transitional position. You would come home, some evening, when I should not be there (but I should

feel worse not to be there than you would to miss me).
You would need me when I was called somewhere ur-
gently. You would reflect, and react, and waver, and then
it would seem to you that you were neglected, that you
were wronged. You would think of the other men, whose
wives were always punctual at dinner in long dresses, and
could play to them evenings, and accept invitations, and
always be on hand, like the kitten. I should not blame
you. Some of the loveliest women in the world are like
that. I should like somebody myself to come home to, to
be always there to purr about me. . . . With you it is more:
it is an inherited instinct. Generations of your fathers have
bred it in you. You would not know how to cultivate
happiness with a woman who had diverged from her hereditary type."

Well, there it is—1882 and there it is. More than a
hundred years later and that speech does not seem at all out
of date. I am doing a residency; evenings, I am not there. I
envy families whose schedules allow for normal domestic life.
Obviously this would all be easier if one had a partner devoted
only to smoothing the way, caring for hearth and home, and
obviously that is still a more common option for male physicians than for female. Actually, I don't mean to complain; life
is not so hard right now and it's certainly very interesting. I'm
just struck by hearing those words spoken more than a century
ago. A new type of woman, she said; that makes us quite old
hat by now. A new type of man, she said—some would claim
we're still waiting. On the other hand, there are a lot of us
working on the whole dilemma. So, though I don't intend to
tell you how Dr. Zay's story is resolved (it is against my moral
principles to give away book endings), I will close with Dr.
Zay's cautionary words: "This is not like simple happiness,
such as comes to other people. It is a problem that we have
undertaken,—so hard, so long!"

HONEY, YOU SHOULDN'T BE WORKING NIGHTS IN YOUR CONDITION
· · · · · · · · ·

The last week of my residency was the first week of the year for the new interns. I was the senior resident on the school-age children's ward, and I greeted four interns, all bright, competent, and understandably nervous. I welcomed them, gave them the requisite orientation speech and pep talk. "Hi," I said, "I'm your senior resident. We're going to have fun. Let me show you where the graham crackers are. Let me show you how to call a code. Together, we're going to try not to kill anyone." They all smiled, humoring me. "Well," I said, shifting my bulk, "the astute diagnosticians among you will have noticed that I am well into my eighth month of pregnancy. I'm going to try very hard not to go into labor prematurely and leave you unsupervised."

Maybe they were actually scared of losing me, or maybe they were just being nice, but those four interns took superb care of me, all week long. They reproached me whenever they found me on my feet, insisted that I spend as much time as possible sitting down in the conference room, holding court. One morning the first code of the new medical year was announced over the public address system, and we all went clomping down the stairs and through the halls to help out. When we arrived, there were already too many doctors on the scene, and the patient, who had only fainted, was fully recovered. As one of the attendings left the room, she took a good look at me, panting and pregnant, and ordered my interns to keep me in line. "The last thing we need at a code is a doctor giving birth," she said.

Pediatrics is probably a pretty good place for a pregnant resident—or at any rate, it ought to be. Even the most august and pompous pediatricians, after all, ought to be able to acknowledge that children are worth having, that it's worth taking steps to see that they get off to a healthy start, that the women who bear the children deserve respect and accommodation. I know that pregnant women have encountered hostility and inflexibility in many residency situations, but I was lucky. For the most part, pregnancy was an interesting real-life twist on residency, that somewhat surreal period during which we all pretend that we do not have to recognize the limitations and exigencies imposed by our bodies. Stay up all night and work the next day? Forget to eat for twelve hours? Forget to pee for even longer? Why not? Well, pregnancy lets you know why not, in no uncertain terms; it reminds you that while the traditions of residency may be venerable, they cannot compare with the laws of nature.

During the first trimester, I had a certain amount of nausea. It was worst in the morning, classically enough. During my second month, I worked as night float, coming on at night to help out the interns. I worked every night from midnight to 8 A.M., and my physiological clock went completely haywire. Morning sickness began to hit me at around 10 P.M., improved in the very early morning—and then grew worse again around 8 A.M. I felt quite sorry for myself as I dragged around the hospital, sleepy and sick to my stomach. This was no job for a pregnant woman, I thought, but I stuck it out, very impressed with my own stoicism. Then my term as night float ended, and another resident took over the job. After he'd been doing it for a week, I noticed that he looked more or less the way I remembered feeling in the morning—tired, disoriented, and faintly ill. So I asked him, and sure enough, he was having all the same symptoms: his body clock was off, he felt nauseous much of the time, and he never seemed to catch up on his sleep. And, as it turned out, he was not pregnant.

I had more or less decided not to tell my colleagues about the pregnancy until it became obvious; I had my first child when I was in medical school, and I remember that everyone was very kind and very interested; there is little biological privacy in an environment in which people are so accustomed to discussing the details of body function. I felt that once other doctors and nurses knew I was pregnant, they would want all the intimate details. Now, if I were thin and glamorous, and given to tight clothing, the pregnancy would have become obvious fairly early on, I suppose. But in fact, I got to the sixth month before people started noticing.

I tried to be subtle about the big-time Tums habit I had developed. It turned out that the hospital gift shop sold Tums, and I had almost constant heartburn, so I stopped by every day or so and stocked up. Tums in the back pocket of my scrubs, jammed in along with the code card and the microscope slide with someone's sputum on it, carefully wrapped in a paper towel, which you mean to hand over to someone and carry around all day and finally break. It turned out that many doctors have secret antacid addictions; when a colleague saw me indulging, the response was usually "May I have a couple of those?" Everyone in the hospital, I finally figured out, is always having a stressful heartburn kind of day, and if you're always taking antacids, people just figure you're stressed, not pregnant.

Finally, though, people at work began noticing my condition. Not doctors. Not even nurses, though they noticed before the doctors did. No, the people who knew soonest were the patients' mothers. I would come down into the emergency room to pick up a new admission, march into the room to introduce myself authoritatively ("Hi, I'm Dr. Klass, the senior resident, the doctor in charge tonight—"), and the patient's mother would look me over and say something like, "Honey, you shouldn't be working nights in your condition!" And as my pregnancy became more and more obvious, the mothers began pointing it out to their children. "You know what that lady has in her belly?" No one ever carried the reproductive physiology lesson any further, though I was prepared to have it happen any day: "You know how that baby got into that lady's belly?"

In fact, being emphatically pregnant did change the way that parents treated me. Not surprisingly, pregnancy reduced formality. I was not just "the doctor," or even "the lady doctor," because my belly put me immediately into the category of mommy, or at least incipient mommy. Many of the mothers would ask if it was my first pregnancy, and then they would want to know my older child's age and what he thought about the new baby coming.

People were also remarkably considerate, even to the point of embarrassing me. A mother who had spent hours in the emergency room with a sick child would insist on getting up and giving me her chair. "Honey, you shouldn't be on your feet so far along," she would say.

I tried to be careful, of course. But there's a limit to how careful you can be. I was scrupulous about X rays: No, I can't be the one to take this patient up to radiology and hold her for the spinal films. No, I won't be the one to stand by and monitor his vital signs during the head CT. It came up three times during the pregnancy, I think, and all three times my colleagues were extremely obliging.

And I tried to be careful about infections. After three years of contracting every viral illness that swept through the pediatric population, I was probably immune to most pathogens. What I hadn't picked up at the hospital, Benjamin had probably brought home from the day-care center. Pregnant, I became more compulsive about washing my hands, more scrupulous about wearing a mask when I went in to see a child who might have meningitis. During three years of pediatrics, you take a certain number of courses of an antibiotic called rifampin, given when you're exposed to someone who turns out to be infected with *Neisseria meningitidis*. And I've had two weeks of erythromycin because I had been breathed on by a child who turned out to have whooping cough—and I didn't want to repeat any of these experiences during the pregnancy, if I could help it. I also worried about mysterious rashes; I've had chicken pox, and I'm immune to German measles, but I didn't know whether I was immune to regular measles or not, since I'm too young to have had measles as a child, but too old to be sure I got effectively vaccinated. In fact, while I was pregnant, we did have a measles exposure in the hospital, and a number of residents had to be vaccinated. Measles vaccine is not recommended for pregnant women, and I was glad I had not examined this particular child.

I worried about cytomegalovirus, a virus which is excreted in the urine of infected children, a bug which is usually asymptomatic in adults but can cause serious birth defects in the fetus. I was careful about handling wet diapers. I tried to be meticulous about wearing gloves to draw blood and start IVs. Worrying about infections, I suppose, was for the most part reasonable, since I could take some sensible steps to protect myself and my baby. Unfortunately, I also had to worry about each and every anomaly I saw in the NICU, from thanatophoric dwarfism to severe heterotaxy. In the middle of the night, in the on-call room, I would find new syndromes to worry about, new one-in-a-million possibilities that seemed at that hour to be not only possible but probable. In the end, I dealt with these worries as doctors have always had to deal with them: firm denial. No, these terrible things will not go wrong with my baby (as in, no, I will not get the diseases my patients get).

For all my worrying, I was a terrible patient. Fortunately, my obstetrician was realistic about residency; she had dealt with pregnant residents and physicians before. She didn't pretend that I was going to eat a proper pregnancy diet or keep reasonable hours or stay off my feet. Instead she concentrated on essentials: when you're on call, she kept reminding me, drink frequently and pee frequently. Sit down on rounds and put your feet up. Make them come to you.

Sometimes I thought wistfully about the perfect pregnancy I could have had if I had not been a resident; the relaxed mug of warm milk before bed instead of the gobbled ice cream sandwich from the vending machine at 2 A.M. But who am I kidding, anyway? I hate to drink milk, warm or cold, and I'll never have nine months to devote to a perfect pregnancy. Yes, somewhere out there is that perfect pregnancy, with tasty,

wholesome meals prepared from fresh ingredients (not cafeteria french fries in the middle of the night)—herbal tea, regular exercise, the pregnancy doctors recommend.

I did my weak best. I swore off alcohol (residents don't
have much time for drinking). No tobacco (I don't smoke,
anyway). But no one can get through residency without caffeine, and I didn't give up tea, or frequent sodas, from the
other vending machines.

Maybe it was all the caffeine that made the time go so
fast—but I think it was residency itself. The last weeks of the
pregnancy, when my residency had ended and I was home,
waiting out the baby, the time crawled by, day by distended
heavy-footed day. Over and over, I took out a little plastic
gauge, the so-called wheel of fortune that obstetricians use to
calculate due dates, and I recalculated my own, counted the
days left to go, tried to argue myself into believing that the
baby would come a few days early, rather than a few days late.
I didn't have time for any of that when I was dragging myself
out of bed every morning to rush in and run rounds, with my
feet obediently propped up on a chair, and with one hand on
my stomach to feel the baby move.

There were many strange moments. I found myself leaning
over my belly to do CPR on a baby, thinking confused
thoughts about the beginning and the end of life, while some
other part of my brain calculated medication doses and called
out orders.

And that, I suppose, just goes to show that medicine is a
job that repeatedly brings you up against the extremities of
life, against the ridiculous and the tragic, the delightful and
the disgusting, the unbearable and the triumphant. And pregnancy, of course, exposes you to all those same elements from
a different angle; you become vulnerable to the complexities
of your own body and to the embarrassing awkwardness of
pregnancy, from varicose veins to stress incontinence. You
become very protective toward your passenger, taking precautions to keep the baby safe even when you never take them

for your own sake. You begin to be bound up, both your hopes and your terrors, in the primal connection you make to your child. And at the same time, you go on taking care of patients—of children, all with parents bound to them by that same connection.

I finished my residency. I did not go into premature labor. I tried drinking warm milk. I hated it. I got a lot of sleep. I loved that. And then I had a baby. And because babies are resilient, she managed to be beautiful, despite all the irregular hours and the improper diet, the stress, the extra time on my feet, the days I forgot to pee. She was just beautiful.

And I'll tell her someday, when she's old enough to understand, about the months she and I spent together on the wards. I'll tell her that even though it was a stressful job, I always took excellent care of my own health, and followed every possible precaution to prevent infection. I'll tell her about the excellent prenatal diet I followed, and the exercises I did in the on-call room. I'll tell her how I cut out caffeine completely. I'll tell her how my obstetrician told me I was a perfect patient. And she, presumably, after years of experience as my child, watching me in action, will take all that the same way I took my middle-of-the-night french fries: with many big grains of salt.

CHECKING OUT

When it comes to physical exertion, I want you to understand that I am a firm believer in doing things the easy way. If there is a beginners' trail and an advanced experts', my choice is clear—and frankly, my idea of a good vacation involves no trails at all. No one has ever marveled at my powers of endurance. So when I tell you that when I had my children, both times, I left the hospital four hours after the birth, you will not be deceived into thinking that I did this because I have the soul of a timeless peasant woman (the squat-in-the-field-and-have-the-baby-then-get-back-to-work type) in the body of a perfectly toned athlete (the my-marathon-time-is-better-since-I-had-my-baby type).

Nope. I just had to get out of the hospital. I hated being a patient. I despised it. It made my skin crawl. I couldn't relax. I couldn't start to feel better. I could barely unclench my teeth.

Now, I spend most of my working life in hospitals. They are not alien to me, and have not been alien for years. I know their secret codes, I interpret the alphabet soup of medical jargon without thinking twice, and I automatically register the difference between a routine announcement over the public address system and an alarm call that will send people rushing to a resuscitation. I am accustomed to eating in the hospital, gossiping in the hospital, even sleeping in the hospital. So it should really be a more comfortable place for me than it is for most people, a place habit has made less threatening.

But I can't help it: I cannot tolerate the hospital when I am the patient, instead of the doctor. I rebel, pointlessly and persistently, against everything I am told to do. When I was in labor and the nurse said, "Try lying on your side," I wanted to get up and walk. When she said I might try taking a walk, I said I wanted to nap. *Don't order me around! Who's in charge here, anyway?* It wasn't that I thought I knew more than my doctor, or even more than my nurse; I just had some permanent chip on my shoulder, some truculent assumption that I was being pushed around for the sake of meaningless hospital routine. And this was with a hospital I liked, doctors I thought were wonderful.

Probably, the hospital is intrinsically a frightening place, even to doctors. It is full of people, after all, who remind us that bodies are vulnerable, subject to all kinds of insults, all kinds of processes that can quickly get out of control. In order for doctors to function, to inhabit our hospitals day after day, while still inhabiting our own vulnerable bodies, some of us cling to the illusion of *being in charge*. Yes, this is a hospital and bad things are happening to some of the poor souls in it, but I am a different sort of being altogether: I am the one in charge. I don't really like to think of myself as dependent on that kind of reasoning, but how else can I explain my inability to relax and let myself be taken care of?

Doctors make terrible patients, according to hospital folklore. When I was a pediatric resident, I always dreaded the news that some new patient's parent was a doctor. I can still remember one six-year-old boy, admitted with an asthma attack (asthma is by far the most common diagnosis on a pediatric ward), not very sick—his father, an internist, announced to everyone who walked into the room that he was a close personal friend of Doctor So-and-So, the famous immunologist, and also an acquaintance of Doctor Such-and-Such, the pulmonary pathologist, and they would both be stopping by tomorrow, to advise on his son's care. He also (and this we residents found hard to forgive) quizzed us all on how much training we'd had, and then refused to deal with the intern at all, directed a few condescending remarks to the senior resident, and asked to speak directly with the senior supervising physician, please. And all this for a child with a mild case of a common disease who was doing fine.

Was he merely being an entitled yuppie, jerking us around to relieve his own tension, because his son was sick? Or was he honestly scared, as anyone is when a child is hospitalized, but attempting to exercise some wildly inappropriate doctorly *control*: if only the best specialists see my child, then my child will be taken care of in the best possible way. I may not be his doctor, but I will call all the shots.

Doctors like to call the shots. All through our training, we're patted on the back, encouraged to take control, make decisions, give orders. We tend to diagnose ourselves, treat ourselves—my medicine chest is full of half-empty bottles of antibiotics that I prescribed for myself at one time or another, took for a few days, then forgot. Why prescribe them for myself? Well, I don't have a regular doctor, of course. I don't like going to the doctor. And anyway, there's nothing wrong with me.

Doctors make terrible patients. I have seen a sick internist, in the hospital with pneumonia, insist on changing his medications because he was convinced he would suffer an extremely rare side effect of the drug he was taking. Why was he so sure he would get this one-in-a-hundred-thousand complication? Because he knew it was associated with the drug.

A little knowledge can be a dangerous thing, and a lot of knowledge can be even worse. A doctor, sick, can imagine all sorts of horrible complications, dimly remembered from back in medical school, or from some worst-case patient cared for years and years ago. When I was in labor with my second child, I thought about all the deliveries I had been to over the past three years, all the babies I had watched being born. But since the pediatrician gets called only when there is a problem with the baby, the images that came to mind were of babies with congenital anomalies, babies born asphyxiated, babies born with serious infections. And there I was, making the same noises all those women had made, going through the same process. I reminded myself of all the hundreds of normal deliveries I had missed, while I was running to the occasional emergency, but it didn't help. I had to keep finding ways to show I was not one of those women in labor, one of those *patients*.

It may seem petty, but I wouldn't wear a hospital gown; I brought a long pink tee shirt to the hospital and wore it all through the labor. And I wouldn't eat the hospital food; with my first baby, I was in labor for twenty-four hours, during which time I ate nothing at all. When the baby was finally born, I was ravenous, and I still remember my sense of outrage at the hospital tray that was produced (desiccated chicken, reconstituted mashed potatoes). I wanted *real* food, not the stuff that patients eat. And, more significantly, I wouldn't let my babies go to the newborn nursery; I insisted on having them weighed and examined right there in the birthing room.

Now, I work in nurseries; I know that nothing bad goes on. I know no one is mean to the babies, or mixes up the babies —but not *my* babies. No way. I didn't let them out of my sight.

And as soon as I got home, both times (no, I didn't bound gracefully up the steps; I shuffled along, leaning on a helping arm or two), I started to feel better, I started to enjoy my new baby. Exhausted, in pain, overwhelmed, I could finally relax and let my guard down, safe in my own house.

What all this means, I think, is first of all that deny it as we may, being a doctor is partly about power. Doctors have power in the hospital, and though we don't actually have power over disease (unfortunately), we do have power over the system that deals with disease. We give the orders, we decide how hard to push. We bend the rules. Hell, we make the rules. And this power is an important part of my adaptation to spending much of my time in a strange, frightening, and even hostile environment. And put me in that environment, stripped of my power, and I can't breathe properly.

And then, again, because I am a doctor, because I work with doctors, I know that doctors are human. I know hospitals are fallible. I know that mistakes get made. It is probably easier, when you are putting your health into another person's care, to imagine that that person does not make mistakes, that that person is a thousand times more conscientious than you are. I know this isn't necessarily true. I know that people screw up, that drug doses get miscalculated or get misread or get given to the wrong patient—not often, but every now and then. I know that diagnoses get missed, X rays misread. And I know all this not with the theoretical frisson which comes from reading scare stories in the newspaper, but with the in-my-bones shameful certainty of having made all these mistakes myself at one time or another.

So what does this mean? Because I'm a doctor, I'm not willing to see myself as a patient, i.e., as human, heir to human vulnerabilities and ailments. I need to preserve my illusion that

I am somehow safe from all the dangers I see around me. And yet, because I'm a doctor, I know that the doctors and the nurses are fallible, i.e., human, and therefore I am not willing to entrust myself to them.

When I was pregnant with my second child, any number of women told me that I would enjoy my hospital stay, a time when other people would be taking care of me, when I would have no responsibilities, a brief hiatus before going home to the job of a new baby and an older sibling. It's like a vacation, several of them said, specifically. What can I say: to me, a vacation is when I *don't* go to the hospital.

STORYTELLING

I'm always writing endings. Every person is a story, every patient is a story. When I admit a new patient to the hospital, I start writing the endings in my head. Every patient is a story of one kind or another. In the emergency room, they walk in off the street and present themselves: my kid is throwing up, my kid turned blue, my kid has transcarbamylase deficiency and he's getting a hyperammonemic crisis. We pop them into the little box examining rooms of the emergency department, each child waiting behind an equivalent uninformative door, and you have a whole anthology—serious, scary, quick, and comic—another installment in the saga, the opening chapter of a Russian novel. And if every patient is a story, then what am I, with my clipboard in my hand, my stethoscope around my neck? Am I the reader, am I the translator, maybe, or am I part of the narrative voice?

I'm always writing endings. And then the baby got well, and they all lived happily ever after. And then the baby's brain turned slowly to mush, until he couldn't even swallow his own saliva, and so he drowned in it. And then the parents found out that if they ever had any more children, there would be a

25 percent chance of the same thing's happening again. And then the baby got well, and they all lived happily ever after. And she stopped wheezing. And his mysterious fevers went away. And it wasn't AIDS after all. And she never had another seizure. And then he got better, and went home from the hospital, but somehow he was never quite the same again, and when he was five years old, he still couldn't really talk.

The happy endings I try to tell the parents: the antibiotics will take care of the infection. Nowadays, over 95 percent of children with leukemia achieve complete remission. In my head, I check over the other plot twists, worry myself over what I'm not treating, not preventing. I cling, superstitiously, to the belief that bad things are less likely to occur if I have named them first, called them out of the darkness under the bed where they crouch, examined their evil, planned what to do if they should menace my patient. So endlessly, in my head, I write the bad endings: he got one dose of antibiotics and he was infected with meningococcus, so after a few hours all the bacteria died and released poisons into his bloodstream, and his blood pressure dropped, and he went into shock.

Every patient is a story, every family is a story, every illness is a story. Some I know, some I just walk through, or brush against. Before I go to sleep in my on-call room, I call the page operator, give her the number of the phone at my bedside, ask her to call me, rather than page me, if anyone needs me —because this way she'll ask anyone who pages me whether it's worth waking me up, and also because I would rather be woken up by a phone than by a beeper. I fall asleep immediately, with the useful reflexes of the hospital, but I don't sleep deeply, another hospital reaction; a nervous light sleep, waiting to be broken. After a couple of hours, the phone rings, and the operator says to me, politely, "There's an urgent on five."

Now, an urgent (or a code, or a stat page) is a common enough thing in an adult hospital; all those people with heart disease and lung disease. But in a pediatric hospital, it's rela-

tively rare, and always frightening. So I am out of bed, grabbing stethoscope and code card, my little printed list of
emergency drug dosages, putting on my glasses and my shoes,
running down the hall in my rumpled scrubs. Clatter down
the steps to the fifth floor, ask the nurses where, which room.
Go running into the room to find (to my immense relief, maybe
my very slight disappointment) that there are three doctors
and five nurses there already, that the little girl on the bed is
almost hidden from my view by the amassed medical aid. She
has a mask on her face and someone is bagging her, squeezing
rhythmically on the black balloon, pushing oxygen in. And it's
getting in; she's nice and pink. The monitor shows a heart rate
of 160, no chest compressions necessary. The senior doctor
standing by the bed turns and says to me (and to the fifteen
other doctors crowding into the room behind me), "I think
we have things under control here. Thanks for coming."

As I leave the room I see a nurse escorting a woman in a
nightgown, close to hysteria, back to the head nurse's office;
the little girl's mother, who must not be allowed to stay in the
corridor and piece together random bits of information from
what she may chance to hear. Someone will come and report
to her as soon as the doctors know what they're going to do
with her daughter. A group of other assorted parents and older
patients also wait in the corridor, their sleep disturbed, wondering, has there been a death? Another nurse is trying to get
them all to go back to bed. I, of course, need no persuading;
I am back in my bed within minutes.

And that is all I know, or will ever know, about that child,
whose bed I stood beside when she was somewhere not far
from death. I don't know her name or her diagnosis—and the
second tag, in the hospital, can matter almost more than the
first. I don't know whether her mother has ever been through
anything like this before, whether she and the doctors have
been half expecting, half dreading such a scene, or whether it
came as a complete shock. I don't know whether this is a story
of chronic disease, of a family life shaped by visits to the hos-

pital, medications, and diagnostic procedures—a saga of endurance and courage, a family trying to stand up to one blow after another. Or is this illness, whatever it is, an acute dramatic interruption, a sudden and unexpected plot twist in what was a normal childhood—by hospital standards, an idyll, a pastorale.

And then there are the children I take care of for days, weeks, months, come to know in ways not necessarily open to their parents; quite literally, the details of their ins and outs. Can she usually suck well enough to take a bottle? Has he ever had blood in his stool before? What does his serum sodium usually run? What do her seizures usually look like? The doctor is like some obsessive novelist who insists on composing full minutely detailed biographies of each character, biographies that will never enter into the text of the novel, but will inform the actions of those characters, the phrases of their creator; the doctor tracks the innumerable bits of information, sorts them, checks them, looks for something that will help move the story along.

Some I know, some I don't. In the hospital, you intersect strangers right at their most dramatic moments, you charge into the room just in time for the denouement. Or else you hang on grimly and see it through, scene by scene.

When we actually tell the stories in the hospital, we observe a particular narrative formalism, both in language and in structure. Here is a tragedy for you: This was a previously healthy three-month-old white female, formerly the seven-pound-three-ounce product of an uncomplicated full-term gestation to a twenty-five-year-old gravida one, para zero to one mother, normal labor and delivery, no problems in the nursery. The baby has been feeding on Similac and growing well and immunizations are up to date. Last night the mother noted some upper respiratory infection symptoms, chiefly mild rhinorrhea, but no cough or fever, and the baby was feeding well. This morning the baby did not wake as usual for a 6 A.M.

feeding; the mother went to wake her at eight and found her blue, cold, and stiff in her crib. CPR was given both by parents and by EMTs but no pulse was ever established. No significant family history, including no history of SIDS, apnea, or neonatal or early childhood deaths. And so on. So this three-month-old baby was found dead in bed.

But that is really how I talk in the hospital, how we all talk. It's how the story is told. And actually, if I had to write that down, it would depart even further from normal narrative; it would probably look something like this: 3 mo wf, former 7'3" product nl FT P/L/D to 25 yo G1P0-1 mother, doing well, IUTD. Last noc noted URI sx, esp. rhinorrhea, s̄ fever. And so on.

You tell the story this way for convenience, to provide the answers to the questions you know will be asked, and to sort the information neatly into the slots in which other doctors will know to look. You force the craziness, the randomness of life and death into a certain formalism, and reassure yourself that at least you can impose an order. You can pick apart the story and rearrange it so that at least it makes sense as a medical narrative.

Does it buy me a little distance, as I sit with the parents of the three-month-old, trying to explain crib death, which no one understands anyway, in language they will find acceptable? Probably it does; my language is not theirs. My story would not match their story, the story they will tell their relatives. My story is providing answers to a specific set of questions, falling neatly into an informational form that assures answers to the questions that determine the structure. And so I am guaranteed a certain satisfaction, a certain narrative success. The baby's parents may be searching for a way to make this into a story they can tell—perhaps the hospital chaplain will help, or perhaps the bits of medical jargon that they get from me will be what they need. They have never had such a need before. But me, I need to tell these stories all the time, and I carefully do not tell them in any language I would use for the

other kind of stories in my life, the stories of what happens to
me, to the people I love.

The formalism has other uses, too. It allows me to pretend
to a control over events that really I am only chasing, always
a few steps behind. All the conventions of hospital language
connive to suggest this control; for example, the doctor writes
the orders in the order book. This military language might
suggest that the patients are under our orders; in fact, the ones
who obey the orders are the nurses, dutifully initialing them
and recording them and carrying them out. But the nurses,
like the doctors, are part of the hospital-imposed regime. The
patients—and their internal organs and their diseases—do as
they please.

I have other stories to tell. I can sit down and write True
Tales of the Hospital in normal language, stories to be read
by normal people, not doctors. Or I can sit down and write
fiction. I can escape. If I write True Tales, then the temptation
is always there: change the ending, make the bad doctor wrong
and the good doctor right, make the test come out the way
you predicted it would. But then they are not True, and so
the uncontrollable spiraling chaos of illness intrudes there too,
and regretfully, I have to let the baby die, if indeed the baby
died, or let myself stand, helpless, ignorant, and not heroic,
by the child's bed.

But not in fiction. In fiction, finally, I am in control. The
proverbial writing student says to the proverbial writing
teacher, "But that's the way it really happened," and the proverbial writing teacher responds, "So what?" If it doesn't work
as fiction, you can't use it in fiction. So when I turn away from
the amoral workings of hospital stories, from the good who
die young and the undeserving who flourish, I can allow myself
the luxury of rewarding and punishing as I see fit. I can kill
for the sake of pathos, or, greatest luxury of all, I can tell a
story without a dying child in it, think for a while about a
world in which there are other exigencies than fevers, labored

breathing, and all the rest. Fiction, however tragic, however powerful, is sanctuary. In the hospital, even as I tell the formal stories, even as I write the alternate endings, I can sense that I am in no one's sane imagination. The hospital is an eventful place, full of melodrama and disaster, but nothing happens for any recognizable narrative reason. No rules hold good; no nineteenth-century moral imagination is at work, no twentieth-century authorial aesthetic. This is presumably true of life in general, but the hospital is so busy, so full of stories, so ready for the climax, the high drama, the catharsis, that the lack of an intelligible underlying narrative structure is always with me there. And so I retreat into the somewhat stilted but utilitarian formalism of the doctors, as if these conventions of narrative would replace the gaps in the structure of events.

Writing is an escape. To write, I sit down with myself; I turn inward to see what voices are there. Instead of the tremendous availability I feel all day in the hospital, connected by beeper, phone, overhead page, electronic mail, carrying out my business in a windowed room so the nurses can see where I am if they need me, when I write I sit down alone. No one else to pull at me or ask questions, interrupt one story with another, beg or demand, judge or plead. A resident in a hospital is constantly turned outward, constantly trying to meet a multitude of needs. Writing is healing myself, a little bit, reminding myself that there is in fact another way to turn, at times.

And so, perhaps, writing is a defense. I am defending myself against the entropy of the hospital, the entropy of disease and degeneration, which is the enemy in the hospital, but also, inexorably, the ultimate victor. It is the entropy of reality, only made more intense; writing, the creation of my artificial universe, is my attempt to assert an order. Not the life-and-death self-defense of the hospital jargon, the doctorly sentence structures and conventions I use at work, but a more considered, solid, long-term defense, an attempt to build something that will resist, at least a little, that entropy.

The final entropy, the final, usually unspoken lesson of

the hospital, is mortality: this child is dead, you will die, I will die, everyone we love will die. The forms and formalisms of doctors are in part designed to help us avoid this knowledge, which is brought home to us so sharply every day. Very few people can bear reality at this level, this repeated reminder that yes, if you didn't get any oxygen for a while then you too would be stiff and blue, cold and dead, that your own precious body (your child's body!) would look and feel like this dead baby's. And the doctor tries for separation, hiding behind language not to be applied to me, to my child. And offers cold comfort to the parents of the dead baby: maybe if we do an autopsy, maybe if your child's death helps us understand, then maybe we can help other children. Offers it as a very slight immortality, since such scientific immortality is part of the hospital ethos, part of the meaning we can try to find in all the deaths, in all the pain and misery and waste.

But writing is also a defense against mortality, an attempt to do something that will stay behind. Our bodies are not permanent; the hospital makes it impossible to escape that knowledge at its crudest and most basic. So to write is to escape once again, escape the hospital, escape the entropy, escape the demands, and escape even myself and my own limits. And then, from this vantage point, I find myself reaching out, reaching back, thinking more and more of those patients, of their stories, of the endings I write over and over in my head, and of the endings that really happen in the hospital.

ABOUT THE AUTHOR

PERRI KLASS is a pediatrician in Boston. She is the author of two novels, *Other Women's Children* and *Recombinations*, and a collection of short stories, *I Am Having an Adventure*. She first came to public prominence when her nonfiction reports about going to medical school were published in *The New York Times*, and later as a book, *A Not Entirely Benign Procedure*. She was graduated from Harvard Medical School in 1986 and lives in Cambridge, Massachusetts, with Larry Wolff, a writer and history professor, and their two children.